PLANNING GUIDE FOR

Developing

Number

Concepts

Kathy Richardson

Dale Seymour Publications®
Parsippany, New Jersey

Managing Editors: Alan MacDonell, Catherine Anderson
Developmental Editors: Harriet Slonim, Beverly Cory

Production/Manufacturing Director: Janet Yearian
Production/Manufacturing Coordinator: Joan Lee
Design Director: Phyllis Aycock
Design Manager: Jeff Kelly
Text Design: Don Taka
Cover Design: Lynda Banks
Cover Illustration: Christine Benjamin
Text Illustrations: Linda Starr
Composition: Claire Flaherty

DALE SEYMOUR PUBLICATIONS®

This book is published by Dale Seymour Publications®, an imprint of Addison Wesley Longman, Inc.

Dale Seymour Publications®
299 Jefferson Road
Parsippany, NJ 07054

Customer Service: (800) 872-1100

ISBN 0-7690-0061-4
DS21857

1 2 3 4 5 6 7 8 9 10–ML–03 02 01 00 99

Over the years many teachers have asked me for help in planning a year-long math program based on my first book, *Developing Number Concepts Using Unifix® Cubes*. For a long time, I thought it would be impossible to write a single guide that could serve teachers who work in so many different settings with children who have so many different needs. I hesitated to share my plan because I believe that teachers should look at their children and address their particular needs as those needs unfold throughout the school year. However, as I spoke with my colleagues from all over the country who are using my book to teach mathematics, I found that they move through the year in similar ways— much as I do in my own classroom. When I saw that a planning pattern naturally emerges when teachers watch their children and work with them over the course of a year, I knew that other teachers using this approach would find this information helpful.

This guide is not intended to do your planning for you, but is designed to help you do your own planning; only you fully understand your children's abilities and the circumstances under which you teach. I do not want these suggested plans to limit or frustrate you. Rather, I hope they will give you the support you need so that you will be eager to try this approach and will be persistent enough to work through any problems that may arise. Most of all, I hope this guide will free you to present a math program that makes sense to you and to your children.

KR

Richardson, Kathy and Leslie Salkeld. "Transforming the Mathematics Curriculum," in *Reaching Potential: Transforming Early Childhood Curriculum and Assessment,* Vol. 2, Sue Bredekamp and Theresa Rosegrant, Editors. National Association for the Education of Young Children, ©1995, page 24.

Richardson, Kathy (1997). *Math Time: The Learning Environment.* Norman, OK: Educational Enrichment.

Richardson, Kathy (1998). *Thinking with Numbers.* Norman, OK: Educational Enrichment.

Richardson, Kathy (1999). *Understanding Geometry.* Bellingham, WA: Lummi Bay Publishing Company.

Contents

T his planning guide accompanies the three-book series entitled *Developing Number Concepts*. Each of the books presents cohesive and organized sets of experiences designed to help children develop particular mathematical ideas and concepts. *Book One* includes beginning counting, pattern, and the concepts of more and less. *Book Two* focuses on beginning addition and subtraction. *Book Three* covers place value and beginning multiplication and division. By making full use of the activities in the *Developing Number Concepts* series, you will see the power of this approach to teaching math, and you will find these books to be much more than resources from which you can occasionally pick and choose activities.

■ Included in this planning guide are year-long plans for teaching kindergarten through third grade as well as notes to the teacher of multi-age classes. This guide is not designed to tell you exactly what to teach one day at a time. Rather, it is intended to help you present sets of related activities, each for a period of four to eight weeks. Focusing on a particular concept for several weeks helps children to fully develop their understanding of that concept and to gain competence and facility with the mathematics they are learning. (This also means that the time you spend planning will serve you for several weeks and so, in the long run, will be time well spent.)

■ To be successful in mathematics, children need to be actively involved. They need to make sense of their work. The activities they work with must challenge the children and cause them to think. We must remember, though, that children also need time and meaningful practice in order to become good at what they are learning. If we provide the right kind of practice, children will internalize the concepts, and the mathematics they learn in their early years can serve as a foundation for what they will learn in years to come.

■ This planning guide is designed to make sure that all children are given the time they need to work with particular concepts and to experience these concepts in ways that will help them make connections and see relationships. The underlying structure of the "math-time" routine, as described in this guide, gives teachers a practical, reasonable way to respond to children individually as the children work to make sense of the math they are doing.

What concepts should we be teaching?

In the past, mathematics for children was limited to the study of arithmetic. This was generally presented to children in ways that interfered with their ability to know and understand important mathematical ideas. In 1989, the National Council of Teachers of Mathematics developed curriculum standards that acknowledged the changing needs of an increasingly technological and quantative world and broadened our view of what kind of mathematics can and should be presented to children. In the document *Curriculum and Evaluation Standards for School Mathematics,* published in 1989 and in the revised document, *Principles and Standards for School Mathematics* (under revision in 1999 and to be published in 2000), both content and process standards are identified as important for students to learn.

The first set of standards deals with the *content* of mathematics:

> **Number and Operation**
>
> **Patterns, Functions and Algebra**
>
> **Geometry and spatial Sense**
>
> **Measurement**
>
> **Data Analysis, Statistics and Probability**

The remaining standards look at the nature of mathematical thinking and focus on the *process* of doing mathematics:

> **Problem Solving**
>
> **Reasoning and Proof**
>
> **Communication**
>
> **Connections**
>
> **Representations**

The "process" standards remind us that mathematics is a discipline that is used in the real world to help us solve problems and understand information. They influence *how* mathematics is taught rather than *what* mathematics is taught. In the book *Reaching Potentials: Transforming Early Childhood Curriculum and Assessment, Volume 2,* * I describe the process *Standards* in the following way.

---

* "Transforming the Mathematics Curriculum" by Kathy Richardson and Leslie Salkeld in *Reaching Potentials: "Transforming Early Childhood Curriculum and Assessment, Vol. 2,* Sue Bredekamp and Teresa Rosegrant, Editors, National Association for the Education of Young Children, ©1995, p. 24.

Children need to experience mathematics as problem solving: *investigating, seeing what happens if..., and using mathematics to find out things for themselves that they don't already know. Rather than trying to figure out what the teacher wants them to do, children need to understand that mathematics is about* reasoning: *making conjectures about why something is the way it is and then checking out those conjectures; thinking for oneself rather than trying to figure out what the teacher wants. Rather than being a task done quietly by a child at her desk, mathematics is about* communication: *clarifying her thinking by talking to her friends, by listening to what they have to say, by finding ways to write down her experiences and her thinking with words, with diagrams and pictures, and with mathematical symbols. Rather than being a set of isolated skills and procedures to be practiced and drilled until they are mastered, mathematics is about* connections: *seeing the relationships between mathematical ideas, seeing mathematics everywhere one looks.*

The "content" *Standards* point out that mathematics is more than arithmetic and that the study of mathematics should include a broad spectrum of mathematical ideas. NCTM's *Standards* have influenced the development of district-level curriculum guides throughout the country. Most primary teachers are now expected to present mathematical experiences that include topics such as geometry and statistics. In addition, teachers are urged to provide more problem-solving experiences than before, to connect math to the real world, to find ways to integrate math into other subject areas, and to make sure that children are writing about the math they are doing.

If we viewed all the *Standards* as separate and discrete topics to be taught, it would be easy to feel overwhelmed. This might cause us to rush through a variety of activities in an attempt to provide all the required experiences for our children. However, when planning for a year of mathematics, it is important to remember that not all concepts listed in a curriculum guide require equal amounts of time and emphasis. We must be clear about what our students are going to be expected to do in the future so that we are sure to give them the experiences necessary to provide them with a proper foundation. If we try to do too much, we run the risk of not covering any one concept in depth—resulting in our children not learning anything well. We must carefully decide what it is that will best benefit our children in the long run.

When we consider which concepts will provide the foundation for children's future work in mathematics, we see that both number and pattern concepts are central and, therefore, should be at the heart of the primary curriculum. The majority of time spent doing math should be used to develop these concepts in depth. Other mathematical ideas naturally lend themselves to the work with number. Measurement, for example, provides a strong context for developing number concepts and relationships. Data collection and graphing activities, which can be woven into the math program throughout the year, also support the development of number relationships. When children play games that involve number cubes and notice that they roll some numbers more often than others, they begin to become aware of the idea of probability. Other major areas of emphasis, such as geometry and sorting, can be interspersed throughout the year for periods of two to three weeks at a time.

The activities in the *Developing Number Concepts* series provide you with all the activities you need to support children's development of number and pattern concepts. Measurement, sorting, graphing, probability, and geometry are integrated into many of the activities, but additional experiences with these concepts should also be provided. The Concept Development Charts in this guide indicate which of these concepts should be studied at each grade level and show how the concepts integrate into the basic work with number and pattern.

Children also need mathematical experiences that are not a part of their ongoing work with concept development. I refer to such experiences as "mathematical events." You might present a mathematical event because you think that it will interest the children and because you think that they will enjoy the challenge. Children's literature can often be a source for these tasks. These events can be interspersed throughout the year for a day or two at a time. For example, on any given day, you may choose to replace the regular math-time routine by reading a story to the children and then presenting them with a problem related to the story.

There are a few other mathematical skills that children have traditionally been introduced to in the primary grades but which are not core, or basic, at these grade levels. For example, children are expected to learn to tell time, to use rulers, to read a calendar, and to read and write the date. But these topics involve complex mathematical ideas that are beyond the young child's ability to fully understand. Thus, children learn about time and the calendar as social conventions, rather than as foundational skills. At a certain point in time, money becomes a means of helping children understand number concepts. However, children need to understand equivalence before their work with money makes sense to them. Instead of spending large blocks of time focusing on these ideas, you can help children become familiar with time, the calendar, rulers, and money through real-life experiences and through the shorter mini-lessons that are a part of this program.

How do we determine the appropriate pacing and set realistic expectations for the children?

Because children's ability to do well in mathematics will profoundly impact their future, what we do to prepare children in these early years is critical. It is important that we give children experiences that will help them become confident and skilled as they work with mathematics. If we are going to plan appropriate experiences for our students, we must be aware of the complexities of seemingly simple mathematical ideas. We must recognize how young children develop an understanding of these mathematical concepts and we must observe our children closely to determine what they do, and do not, know and understand. When planning a math program, we must look further than just preparing children for their next year in school. We must make sure that what we do each day will serve children as they move on through school and beyond.

This guide describes when to focus on particular concepts at each grade, from kindergarten through grade three. The decisions to focus on certain concepts at particular times have been made very deliberately—based on what we know about how children learn. The suggested sequence and timing has been validated by the years of experience of many teachers who have carefully assessed their students' developing understanding and have reached a consensus on the pacing recommended here.

Many teachers have expressed concerns about being asked to have their young students meet expectations that do not take into account the natural stages of development that influence children's abilities to understand certain mathematical ideas. Children sometimes learn to repeat words and follow procedures even though they do not understand what they are saying or doing. This leads some adults to assume that children understand more than they really do. When teachers feel pressured to have children do more than they can do with understanding, they rely on showing children procedures and leading them through tasks that they cannot do on their own. It is futile to have children work with ideas and procedures that do not make sense to them. Such procedures are then easily forgotten by the children and become virtually useless as tools for solving problems. Learning these procedures takes time away from the important work that should be done and may leave children with dead-end skills rather than foundational understandings.

Sometimes children's lack of fluency with numbers and lack of understanding of these basic concepts show up later—in upper elementary and in middle school. This results in teachers often having to spend time reviewing topics that the children failed to learn in the primary grades. We see then that children are not served when we set goals they can meet only if they learn the content by rote. They are not served if they learn to get answers but don't learn to see relationships between quantities. They are not served if they never have time to become good at what they are doing.

If we want the time we spend with children to lead to a deeper understanding of foundational skills, then it is important that we look at what the children really know and understand. We need to respect the real work of the young child. We do not want children doing work that only looks challenging but that is, in reality, meaningless to them. It takes time for children to develop competence and understanding. Children must be given the time they need to build the foundation for understanding the concepts that they will be expected to work with in the future.

When deciding when and how to present mathematical ideas in this guide, I paid particular attention to making sure that children are asked to work with those ideas that enhance their understanding of mathematics and help them experience mathematics as a sense-making process.

How do I make sure that I am expecting enough of my children and challenging them all?

When we help children build a strong foundation that will serve them in the future, we are raising standards and expectations—not lowering them. The activities in the *Developing Number Concepts* series are designed to meet a range of needs so that no child works at a level that is either too easy or too difficult to be of value. Every chapter in each book in the series has a section entitled "Meeting the Range of Needs" which will help you see how to use the activities to fulfill your children's various needs.

What is meant by "meaningful" practice?

Children develop their understanding of math concepts not through rote memorization but through a process of internalization. Once a child has internalized a concept, he or she will not forget it. It becomes a part of the way the child sees the world. We want to provide the kind of practice that helps children internalize the concepts they are working with. To internalize a concept, children need multiple experiences over time using related activities that confirm, challenge, and extend their thinking. No single activity is of particular importance in and of itself. Rather, it is through repeated experiences with various related activities that children begin to make generalizations and to know number relationships.

Children can get meaningful practice through the activities in *Developing Number Concepts*, which are intended to be experienced by children over and over again. If we were to continually present children with new and different activities, then we would find that they would be focusing more on how to do the activities than on what they are learning from them. However, when children work repeatedly with familiar activities that provide the appropriate amount of challenge, they become increasingly engaged in the tasks over time and thus become able to get the full benefit from them.

How do we fit everything in?

Each concept introduced to children must be developed throughout the year. Some concepts will be emphasized more than others during any particular planning period. Once introduced, however, they should never be dropped completely. To make sure that the math program is balanced and that all the major concepts are developed throughout the school year, I divided the year into three blocks of time. I then made sure that each concept is worked with in some way during each block of time. For example, pattern is introduced to kindergarten children through whole-group experiences at the beginning of the year. In the middle of the year, the children may spend quite a bit of time working at pattern stations. Near the end of the year, the familiar pattern stations with new challenges can be made available to them once again. Although pattern should not be children's primary focus at all times, natural opportunities for them to notice patterns and/or to work with them will also arise throughout the year.

First-grade children need to spend long blocks of time in which addition and subtraction is the major focus. This work can be interrupted occasionally with a week or more of geometry or sorting activities. The children should then return to their focus on addition and subtraction to ensure that they develop a deep understanding of these basic operations and the number relationships with which they are working.

Second-grade children need to spend much of the year working with place-value concepts. Place value can be introduced sometime during the first three months of the year. Children can then spend several weeks working at place-value stations through which they learn to *organize* quantities into tens and ones. Later in the year, the familiar stations can be brought out again with the focus changing to *comparing* quantities. Pattern and measurement concepts are naturally integrated into the place-value activities. Blocks of time devoted to sorting and geometry can be interspersed throughout the year.

Meeting the Needs of Your Children

Rather than using the year-long plans, you may choose to use selected activities to meet your children's particular needs. The Meeting the Needs of Your Children charts identify the particular concepts and skills presented in each chapter of each book in the series and cite the specific activities that help develop the the concepts and skills. These charts can be found beginning on page 205 of this guide. (They also appear in the introduction to each of *Books One, Two,* and *Three.*)

Three basic instructional settings facilitate the different kinds of lessons and activities recommended in this guide. Note that the time spans suggested here are for grades 1, 2, and 3. For kindergarten, some of the suggested time spans are a bit shorter.

During math time, the children will work:

- as a *whole class* working together during "mini-lessons" or "shared experiences"
- at *independent stations,* alone or with partners
- with the teacher in a *small group*

Arrange the room to accommodate these three ways of working. You will need to clear a large floor area for gathering the whole class together. For independent-station-work arrange tables or push desks together. You can then work with small groups of children either on a rug on the floor or at the tables.

Whole-Class Work

Mini-Lessons (*Shorter Mini-Lesson:* 5–10 minutes, 3 to 5 times a week; *Longer Mini-Lesson:* 15–25 minutes, as needed)

Mini-lessons provide you with a format for ongoing work with various concepts. You can continually review previously introduced concepts and help children become familiar with new concepts that they will be working with in more depth in the future. A typical math period begins with the class meeting together for a few minutes for a mini-lesson before the children begin work with independent tasks. An activity presented during a mini-lesson should be repeated several times over a period of a few weeks, allowing children to make connections and to internalize the concepts.

You will need to allot more time for those mini-lessons in which the children use manipulatives or other materials. To help you plan your time, the mini-lessons have been designated as "Shorter Mini-Lessons" and "Longer Mini-Lessons."

Shared Experiences (35–50 minutes, 1 or 2 times about every two weeks)

During shared-experience time the whole class works together for the entire math period, usually using manipulatives. This is to ensure that all the children are actively engaged in the lesson. Sometimes the shared experiences will support the development of the concept currently being worked with. Other times, the experiences will be devoted to problem-solving lessons or to additional work from various math strands.

Independent-Station Work

(35–50 minutes, 3 to 5 times a week)

This is the classroom setting that provides children with the greatest opportunity possible to get the practice they need if they are to internalize the math concepts they are working with. New activities are introduced, either to the whole class or to a small group, over a period of about a week. As each activity is introduced, it is put out at an independent station. Then, children choose activities to work with from among eight to ten that deal with a particular concept. The activities for a given concept should be made available for several weeks at a time. You will find that the children become increasingly engaged in the activities as they become more familiar with the tasks. Children can't really learn from an activity until they fully understand how to do the activity. By keeping activities available to them for long periods of time, you ensure that the children will get as much as possible from the experiences.

When you introduce a set of activities, make sure that the children understand:

■ which materials to get
■ how to do the activity

If an activity is new to you, refer to it in the activity book as often as necessary. It is okay to keep the book open in front of you as you work.

These independent-station tasks will meet a variety of needs depending on what the children bring to them. For example, when working on counting tasks, some children may be focused on developing consistency and strength in counting while others may be focused on number sense and discovering relationships. At the same time, still other children may be developing basic counting skills.

When children work independently, you can learn much about their thinking and level of concept development by observing them at work. You will be able to interact with individual children, providing support and challenge as needed. You will also be able to gather children with similar needs to work in small groups with the teacher-directed activities. The children need not be grouped by ability in order to perform the independent activities. Individual needs can be met with children working side by side on many different levels.

After you have introduced a set of activities, you will notice that it usually takes two or three days for the children to really settle in and focus on the tasks. When the tasks are appropriate for them, you will see most children working hard, making a few mistakes, and double-checking their work to see if they did it correctly. After many days or weeks, you will notice that the children are working less intensely as the tasks become easier for them. You will begin to see less concentration and sense some restlessness. When the children know the answers to your questions quickly, without having to figure them out, then it is time to move on.

Teacher-Directed, Small-Group Focus Work

(10–20 minutes, 2 to 3 times a week)

Working with a small group allows you to watch closely, interact with, and respond to individual children. You can use this instructional time in three ways:

- to introduce activities that are difficult to introduce to the whole class
- to assess the needs of children without having to do individual interviews
- to provide experiences to meet the needs of a particular group of children

Rather than setting a permanent schedule for small-group time, work with small groups only when you see a specific need. Call a group together either when certain children need help or when they need a challenge or because a particular activity is most effective when done this way.

Just before beginning work with a small group, ask the children to come to the meeting area and give them something to keep them occupied while you make sure that the rest of the class is working appropriately at independent stations. A simple task, such as writing on individual chalkboards, works well as it takes no introduction and is easily interrupted when it is time to stop and work together.

After working for a short time with the small group, have the children rejoin the others. Then spend the rest of the period observing and interacting with the whole class as they work.

What Does the "MATH-TIME" Routine Look Like?

Usually...MATH TIME is

Whole-Class Time/Mini-Lessons (*Shorter Mini-Lesson:* 5–10 minutes, 3 to 5 times a week; *Longer Mini-Lesson:* 15–25 minutes, as needed)

The math period begins with the whole class meeting together to work with one or two short activities. These activities can give children ongoing practice with concepts previously worked with or they can be used to introduce children to concepts that they will work with in the future. Sometimes you will use this time to introduce the independent activities. On days when you have a longer mini-lesson, you will probably not have time to work with a small group.

Preparation for Independent-Station Time and Small-Group Focus Work

After completing a mini-lesson, you may plan to work with a small group of children during the independent-station time. Call out the names of these children and ask them to gather in one place—the rug area, for example. Give them a task to do so they will be productive while you are making sure that the rest of the children are working appropriately at the independent stations.

Independent-Station Time: (35–50 minutes, 3 to 5 times a week)

Excuse those children who are *not* part of the small group a few at a time to choose their independent activities.

Small-Group Focus Work: (10–20 minutes, 2 to 3 times a week)

Spend a few minutes working with the small group of children who have similar needs. At the end of this lesson, excuse these children to choose their independent activities.

Teacher Observation of Children Working Independently

After the small-group lesson is over, you can move around the room observing and interacting with the children as they work independently.

Cleanup Time

After a period of about 35 to 50 minutes of independent work time, have the children clean up their stations and meet together again as a class.

Brief Discussion of Math Time: (less than 5 minutes)

Spend a few minutes reviewing what went on during independent-station time.

Sometimes...MATH TIME is:

Shared Experiences/Mathematical Events:
(35–50 minutes, 1 or 2 times about every two weeks)

Occasionally vary the usual routine by having the whole class work together on the same task for the entire class period. You may use this time to support the children's current work with a concept, or you may continue work with concepts previously introduced. This is also the time during which you can present mathematical events.

Three types of materials are used throughout the books: basic manipulatives, basic support materials to be used for teacher-directed activities, and concept-development packet materials that are needed for specific activities.

Basic Manipulatives

The basic manipulative materials are listed in each book. These should be stored in a place that is accessible to children so that they can get them, help deliver them to the places at which they are to be used, and put them away at the end of the work time.

Support Materials

Some materials that are to be used over and over again can be stored in a "teacher tub" or on the math shelf.

> Working-Space Papers
>
> Counting Boards, Number cards, and Equation cards
>
> Paper lunch bags
>
> Small plastic bowls or margarine tubs
>
> Number Cubes (dotted/numbered and marked 0–5, 1–6, and 4–9)
>
> Spinners (More-or-Less and Plus-or-Minus)
>
> Individual chalkboards, chalk, and erasers
>
> Containers (of various sorts such as boxes, lids, and small food cartons)

Concept-Development Packet Materials

Particular materials such as task cards, spinners, and game boards will be needed for the individual activities. These can be organized into activity packets which can be stored according to the particular concepts presented in each chapter.

Self-Directed Exploration*

Begin every school year by allowing children to work with the math materials for several weeks using their own ideas. This is the time to teach children the expectations for working independently for the rest of the year. Make it clear to children that the rules you establish at this time will apply whenever they work at the independent stations.

Share the following rules with the children through discussions, role playing, and modeling.

- We work hard during math time.
- We share the materials. (We don't need to keep the materials all to ourselves. We take one thing at a time as we need it.)
- We do not throw things in the classroom. (Our classroom needs to be a safe place.)
- We clean up our stations before moving on to new stations. (Doing this leaves the stations ready for other children to work at them.)
- When we clean up, we take apart our own work only. (When something we create has to be taken apart, we want to take it apart ourselves. If someone else takes it apart, it feels like it is being wrecked.)

Whole-Class Activities

Let the children set up.

If you organize the materials for each independent activity in a tub or a small plastic bag and assign each station to a certain place in the classroom, the children can learn to get the materials, deliver them to the stations, and later return them to where they belong.

Let the children choose where to work.

Allow the children to move from place to place in the classroom whenever they are ready to work at different stations.

Limit the number of children that may work at each station to six.

Establish a signal that the children respond to when you need to get their attention.

Give the children plenty of time to work.

It is important to allow at least 35 to 50 minutes for math time. Children become more involved in activities when they feel they will not be pressured to clean up as soon as they have gotten started.

---

* For more information, see *Math Time: The Learning Environment* by Kathy Richardson. ©1997 Educational Enrichment, Norman OK.

Expect the children to be accountable for working hard.

Get to know your children. Identify and respond to their needs.

Have the children clean up.

The children should be responsible for cleaning up and for putting away materials. Make sure that they know where the materials belong and what they are to do after they have cleaned up.

End math time with a short discussion time.

Remember to gather the children together to discuss how things went. Usually this should be a very brief time, but it is vital.

A balanced math program provides children with experiences covering a wide range of mathematical topics. When planning a balanced program, however, we must take care not to try to do too much. Trying to cover too many topics results in too little time to handle any one topic in depth. The concept development charts will give you an overview of the important concepts that you need to focus on at your particular grade level. The charts begin on these pages: Kindergarten, p. 2; Grade 1, p. 44; Grade 2, p. 102; and Grade 3, p. 158. The following summary will help you decide how to give an appropriate amount of attention to each topic.

Number   What children know and understand about number impacts on their work in all other areas of mathematics. We should not underestimate the importance of building a strong foundation in number, and so we must keep the development of number concepts at the heart of the mathematics program for young children. Children need ongoing and multiple opportunities to develop number sense in ways that ask them to think and reason, to see relationships, and to make connections. The largest proportion of time spent on mathematics in the classroom should be devoted to working with number concepts.

Pattern   The search for pattern should be an ongoing process. It should become a "habit of mind" that children bring to their work in all areas of mathematics. Children need periods of time to focus on developing pattern concepts. In addition to their ongoing work with patterns during mini-lessons, they should work with sets of pattern tasks for three to four weeks at a time at least twice a year.

Measurement   Children can begin their work with measurement during self-directed exploration. They will have experiences in measuring capacity at the measuring-containers station. They will have experiences in comparing weights at the weighing station. These stations can then become part of the science center. This allows children to have ongoing measuring experiences at other-than-math time. In addition, much of the work of measuring is naturally integrated with the work with number. For example, children measure when they work with line or shape puzzles, containers, and yarn.

Geometry   Children begin their work with geometry during self-directed exploration, at which time they work with manipulatives using their own ideas. Then two or three times during the year, the children should focus on geometry for two- to three-week periods at a time.

Sorting   Like the search for patterns, looking for likenesses and differences and seeing which things belong together are naturally an ongoing part of the work children do in all subject areas. Children will benefit from working with sorting activities for several days in a row. This will help them focus on identifying attributes and on looking for similarities and differences in various situations.

Data Collection and Graphing   Generally, children's work with data collection and graphing should be an ongoing part of the math program rather than being treated as a separate topic for several days in a row. Some graphing experiences can be done as mini-lessons. Occasionally, children should have the opportunity to spend an entire math period conducting surveys and organizing the data they collect.

Kindergarten

	Creating the Environment See *Math Time: The Learning Environment.*	**Number** See *Developing Number Concepts: Book One* (Ch. 1 & 3).	**Pattern** See *Developing Number Concepts: Book One* (Ch. 2).
Beginning of the Year: (Sept., Oct., Nov.)	**Exploring Materials** *Provide opportunities for children to work with the math manipulatives in their own ways for about eight weeks. This is the heart of young children's work as it establishes expectations for their work for the whole year.* Children will learn to: ■ work hard ■ make responsible choices ■ work independently ■ share and cooperate ■ stay engaged and focused ■ build and create ■ sort and count ■ clean up	**Estimating to 15** *Present during whole-class lessons.* **Counting Objects to 10** *Provide whole-class counting experiences. Also provide extra counting practice during small-group work for those children who need it.* **Using Numerals** *Model how to write numerals as opportunities come up.*	**Introducing Pattern** *Introduce children to pattern through whole-class experiences. Present simple patterns of motion and color. (Include a variety of patterns. Do not over-emphasize AB patterns.)*

*Adapted from workshop materials presented by Mathematical Perspectives: Kathy Richardson and Associates.

Measurement See *Developing Number Concepts:* Book One (Ch. 1 & 3).	Geometry See *Understanding Geometry.* *	Sorting See *Developing Number Concepts:* Book One (Ch. 1 & 3).	Data Collection See *Developing Number Concepts:* Book One (Ch. 3).
Exploring Volume and Weight During self-directed exploration, children explore the volume of containers and weigh objects using simple scales.	**Exploring Shapes and Three-Dimensional Objects** During self-directed exploration, children work with plane and solid geometric shapes using manipulatives such as Pattern Blocks, geoboards, attribute blocks, geoblocks, Discovery Blocks, and building blocks. **Creating and Recording Designs and Shapes** As an outgrowth of their work exploring the manipulatives, children create designs and shapes and then copy them. Children also work with shapes as they cut and paste to create pictures or designs using lids and various blocks. **Observing and Describing Shapes and Figures** Children become familiar with the attributes of various geometric shapes. They find ways to describe these shapes so that others can identify them. The children also look for geometric shapes in their environment. **Sorting Shapes** Children sort various geometric shapes in different ways according to their attributes.	**Describing Attributes** *Provide opportunities for children to describe attributes during teacher-directed lessons.* **Exploring Sorting** During self-directed exploration, children sort collections and other math manipulatives.	**Gathering and Organizing Data** Children place objects or pictures of things in the appropriate columns of a two-column graph. As a result, the data is automatically organized at the same time that it is collected. Children focus on the idea that lining things up makes it easier to tell which group has more and which has less without having to count each item. **Noticing and Describing Relationships** Children compare groups and tell which group has more or less than the other or whether the two groups have the same number.

* For more information see *Understanding Geometry* by Kathy Richardson, Lummi Bay Publishing Co., ©1999, Bellingham, WA.

	Creating the Environment See *Math Time: The Learning Environment.*	Number See *Developing Number Concepts: Book One (Ch. 1 & 3).*	Pattern See *Developing Number Concepts: Book One (Ch. 2).*
Middle of the Year: (Dec., Jan., Feb., Mar.)	**Exploring Materials** *Continue to provide opportunities for children to work with manipulatives in their own ways, but clearly differentiate between when they are supposed to use their own ideas and when they are supposed to do a specific task.* *Make sure to give children opportunities to explore any new materials you introduce.*	**Estimating to 20** *Through the estimating tasks, provide practice in counting up to 20 (or up to 30 for those children who are ready).* **Counting Objects to 10** Children develop consistency, accuracy, and an awareness of number relationships at independent stations. **Comparing Numbers to 10** *For any children who are ready, provide opportunities to compare numbers.* **Recognizing Numerals** Children use numerals to label their work at independent stations. At the same time they develop a sense of quantity and number relationships. **Writing Numerals** Children practice numeral writing during teacher-directed activities.	**Interpreting Rhythmic Patterns** *Begin by having children interpret color patterns using connecting cubes, Pattern Blocks, and Color Tiles.* **Copying, Extending, and Creating Patterns** Children work with patterns using pattern task cards at the independent-pattern stations. Some children will be able to create their own patterns.

Measurement See *Developing Number Concepts:* Book One (Ch. 1 & 3).	Geometry See *Understanding Geometry.*	Sorting See *Developing Number Concepts:* Book One (Ch. 1 & 3).	Data Collection See *Developing Number Concepts:* Book One (Ch. 3).
Exploring Volume and Weight Children continue to explore containers and scales during self-directed exploration at the science center. **Making Direct Comparisons of Volume and Weight** Children compare two containers directly to see which holds more or less. **Exploring Length and Area** Children determine various lengths and areas by counting during their number work when using materials such as shape puzzles, line puzzles, and yarn.	**Exploring Shapes and Three-Dimensional Objects** *Continue to provide occasional opportunities for children to work with geometric materials using their own ideas.* **Creating and Recording Designs and Shapes** *Continue to provide opportunities for children to build and record the creations they make using various materials.* **Filling in Shapes Using Smaller Shapes** Children discover relationships between shapes. They see how smaller shapes can be used to fill larger shapes by filling in outlines of figures using Pattern Blocks, tangrams, and/or Discovery Blocks. **Observing and Describing Shapes and Figures** Children continue to learn to describe various geometric shapes in ways that help others identify the shapes. Children continue to find shapes in their environment. Then they draw pictures of what they find. **Sorting Shapes** *Help children to continue to become familiar with attributes of various shapes and three-dimensional objects by sorting them in a variety of ways. Model geometric language as appropriate.*	**Sorting by One Attribute** *To help children sort out objects that have a particular attribute say, for example, "Find all the bumpy ones" or "Find all the red ones."*	**Gathering and Organizing Data** Children continue to place objects or pictures of things in the appropriate columns of a two- or three-column graph. **Noticing and Describing Relationships** Children compare groups and tell which has more or less or whether the groups have the same number of items. **Conducting Surveys** Children's first experiences in conducting surveys will have almost a role-playing quality to them. Usually children ask questions and record responses without seeing a need to organize those responses.

	Creating the Environment See *Math Time: The Learning Environment.*	**Number** See *Developing Number Concepts: Book One* (Ch. 1 & 3).	**Pattern** See *Developing Number Concepts: Book One* (Ch. 2).
End of the Year: (Apr., May, June)	**Exploring Materials** *As children work with the manipulatives over time, their creative work evolves.*	**Estimating to 20 and Beyond** *Continue to provide estimating experiences during whole group lessons.* **Comparing Numbers to 10** Children extend their work with numbers to 10 by comparing quantities. This helps them focus on amounts, not just on the process of counting. **Creating Number Arrangements** Children create arrangements using a particular number of objects for each. Those children who are ready should describe the parts of the arrangements. **Adding and Subtracting** Introduce addition and subtraction concepts through the acting out of story problems. **Counting Objects to 20 Through 30** Children practice counting at independent stations. **Writing Numerals** Children practice writing numerals at independent stations.	**Interpreting Rhythmic Patterns** *Present increasingly complex patterns using connecting cubes, Color Tiles, and Pattern Blocks. Most children should be able to interpret such patterns as AABBC and AABC.* **Copying, Extending, Creating, and Interpreting Patterns** *Bring out some activities used at pattern stations earlier in the year. Add some pattern cards, such as ABC cards and rhythmic-patterns cards, that require children to interpret patterns. Also, have children create and record their own patterns.*

Measurement See *Developing Number Concepts:* Book One (Ch. 1 & 3).	Geometry See *Understanding Geometry.*	Sorting See *Developing Number Concepts:* Book One (Ch. 1 & 3).	Data Collection See *Developing Number Concepts:* Book One (Ch. 3).
Comparing Length and Area *Have children compare two lengths to determine which is longer or shorter than the other or if they are about the same. Have children also compare two areas to determine which is larger or smaller than the other or if they are about the same. Integrate this into children's number work when they are using materials such as shape puzzles, line puzzles, and yarn.*	**Exploring Shapes and Three-Dimensional Objects** *Continue to provide occasional opportunities for children to work with geometric materials using their own ideas.* **Creating and Recording Designs and Shapes** *Continue to provide opportunities for children to build and record the creations they make using various materials.* **Filling in Shapes Using Smaller Shapes** Children use their knowledge of relationships between shapes and see how small shapes can be used to make larger ones by filling in shape outlines with Pattern Blocks, tangrams, and/or Discovery Blocks. **Analyzing Three-Dimensional Figures** Children explore boxes in a variety of ways to determine which shapes they are made up of. **Sorting Shapes** *Help children become familiar with attributes of various shapes and three-dimensional objects by sorting them in a variety of ways. Have them use their own language to describe the different ways in which they sorted. Model geometric language as appropriate.* **Observing and Describing Shapes and Figures** Children learn to describe various geometric shapes using their own language but trying to identify the shapes for others. Children look for geometric shapes in their environment and draw pictures of what they find.	**Sorting and Re-Sorting** Children find many different ways to sort a particular set of objects.	**Gathering and Organizing Data** Children continue to place objects or pictures of things in the appropriate columns of a graph. **Noticing and Describing Relationships** Children continue to compare groups and tell which has more or less or whether the groups have the same number of items. **Conducting Surveys** Children continue to conduct informal surveys.

An Overview of the Year's Planning Periods

T his overview highlights the concepts of number and pattern that will form the core of the kindergarten math program. The school year has been divided into five planning periods. The given time periods are offered simply as a point of reference. Adjust them to fit your school calendar and to meet the needs of your particular class. Occasionally spend a day or two on math topics such as sorting, measurement, and geometry. In addition, spend a week or two between planning periods on one of these other topics.

First Planning Period: 8–10 weeks (Sept., Oct., Nov.)

At the beginning of the school year, kindergarten children's focus is on learning to work independently. Children learn independence by working with the math manipulatives during self-directed exploration. At the same time, pattern is introduced and counting experiences are provided. After several weeks, the class is introduced to simple number activities, which are then added to the independent stations.

Second Planning Period: 4–6 weeks (Nov., Dec.)

During this time, the children work at the independent stations with the concept of number in order to develop consistency and accuracy in counting and to develop an understanding of number relationships. After a few weeks, children begin working at the pattern stations. Numeral recognition is presented through teacher-directed activities. Children should also have beginning experiences in interpreting patterns with manipulatives.

Third Planning Period: 5–6 weeks (Jan., Feb.)

The independent activities that the children now work with focus on numeral recognition. Children learn to read numerals and use them to label their work. At the same time, children develop a sense of quantity and number relationships. They continue to have ongoing pattern experiences.

Fourth Planning Period: 5–6 weeks (Feb., Mar.)

The children extend their work with numbers to 10 by comparing quantities. This helps them focus on amounts, not just on the process of counting. Number arrangements are presented as shared experiences. This work helps children develop number sense and may help them learn to describe the parts of numbers. Children will practice writing numerals during teacher-directed activities. They continue to interpret patterns.

Fifth Planning Period: 6–8 weeks (Apr., May, June)

During these last months, children's work with number activities can be extended either by introducing numeral writing or by extending the numbers to which children count to 20 or 30. Children are introduced to addition and subtraction by acting out story problems. If time allows, familiar pattern stations can be brought out again along with new stations.

A Typical Kindergarten "Math Time"

1. Whole-Class Work: *Shorter Mini-Lesson* (5–10 minutes)

The math period begins with a short lesson that provides ongoing practice with concepts previously introduced.

- Rhythmic Clapping
- Estimation (using a container that holds about 12 objects)

2. Preparation for Working with a Small Group

A small group of children stay in the rug area and are given a short task. Today the teacher asks them to practice writing numerals on individual chalkboards while they are waiting for her to make sure that the rest of the children are working appropriately at independent stations.

3. Independent-Station Work (35–40 minutes)*

Having been introduced to the following activities over a period of three or four days, the children now work with them on their own. These activities provide children with opportunities to practice counting while developing a sense of quantities. Both dot cubes and number cubes are included with the activities in order to meet children's various needs.

1: 1–21 Counting Boards, Level 1	**1:** 1–22 Creations Station
1: 1–25 Roll-a-Tower Race	**1:** 1–26 Make-a-Train Race
1: 1–28 Build a City	**1:** 1–30 Shape Puzzles
1: 1–31 Line Puzzles	

4. Teacher-Directed, Small-Group Focus Work (10–15 minutes)

The teacher uses these activities to provide the children with the extra practice they need in counting to 6.

1: 1–1 Slide and Check	**1:** 1–4 Counting Stories
1: 1–7 Grab-Bag Counting	**1:** 1–8 Grow and Shrink

After the small-group lesson is over, the teacher excuses the children to choose an independent-activity station.

5. Teacher Observation of Children Working Independently

The teacher moves around the room observing and interacting with individual children.

6. Cleanup Time

After about 40 minutes of working independently, the children clean up their stations and meet back together again on the rug.

7. Whole-Class Work: Brief Discussion of Math Time (no longer than 5 min.)

The class reviews what went on during math time.

---

* Each activity number refers to book, chapter, and activity. For example, 2: 1–14 means book 2, chapter 1, activity 14. Notice whether each activity appears in Book One (**1:**), Book Two (**2:**), or Book Three (**3:**).

Kindergarten Planning Chart*

First Planning Period: 8–10 Weeks (Sept., Oct., Nov.)

Focus: Learning to Work Independently,
Beginning Counting and Pattern Activities

Whole-Class Work: Mini-Lessons	
Shorter Mini-Lesson (5–10 minutes, 3 to 5 times a week)	**Longer Mini-Lesson** (10–20 minutes, as needed)
Pattern Experiences 1: 2–1 Rhythmic Patterns 1: 2–2 People Patterns 1: 2–3 Patterns in the Environment 1: 2–21 Looking for Patterns on the Calendar **Estimation Experiences to 15** **Informal Rote-Counting Practice**	**Data Collection and Graphing** **Math and Literature** Counting Books

Ongoing Independent-Station Work	
(35–40 minutes, 3 to 5 times a week)	
Self-Directed Exploration of the Math Manipulatives Connecting cubes Color Tiles Wooden cubes Toothpicks Collections *Include any additional math materials you have available, such as Pattern Blocks, geoboards, geoblocks, scales, and containers.* **Introduce Math Manipulatives and Establish Expectations for Independent Work**	*After a few weeks, gradually introduce these activities.* **Independent Counting Experiences** 1: 1–21 Counting Boards, Level 1 1: 1–22 Creations Station, Level 1 1: 1–23 Cover the Dots 1: 1–24 Counting with the Number Shapes 1: 1–25 Roll-a-Tower Race, Level 1 1: 1–26 Make-a-Train Race, Level 1

* Each activity number refers to book, chapter, and activity. For example, 2: 1–14 means book 2, chapter 1, activity 14. Notice whether each activity appears in Book One (1:), Book Two (2:), or Book Three (3:).

Teacher-Directed, Small-Group Focus Work (10–15 minutes, 2 to 3 times a week)

Focus on One-to-One Counting

If you have children who need extra help, choose from the following activities to provide them with focused practice. Choose several activities over time, using two to four of them during any one lesson.

1: 1–1   Slide and Check
1: 1–2   Count and Dump
1: 1–3   Making Towers
1: 1–4   Counting Stories, Level 1
1: 1–5   Creations
1: 1–6   Finger Counting
1: 1–7   Grab-Bag Counting
1: 1–8   Grow and Shrink (focus on small numbers), Levels 1 and 2
1: 1–9   Hide It

If you wish to provide more variation, include some of the following activities.

1: 1–10 Hunt for It, Levels 1 and 2
1: 1–11 Peek and Count, Level 1
1: 1–12 Find a Match, Levels 1 and 2
1: 1–15 Tall and Short, Level 1

OR

Shared Experiences/Mathematical Events
(35–45 minutes, 1 or 2 times about every two weeks)

You will not need to present additional math experiences during this time as self-directed exploration provides children with informal opportunities to work with sorting, geometry, and measurement concepts.

Kindergarten Planning Notes

First Planning Period: 8–10 Weeks (Sept., Oct., Nov.)

Focus: Learning to Work Independently,
Beginning Counting and Pattern Activities

Whole-Class Work: Mini-Lessons

You can present new concepts and review previously taught concepts by
spending just a few minutes at the beginning of each math period on
either a *Shorter Mini-Lesson* (5–10 minutes) or a *Longer Mini-Lesson*
(10–20 minutes).

Shorter Mini-Lesson

(5–10 minutes, 3 to 5 times a week)

Begin math time with a mini-lesson. Choose two to four activities from among
those listed.

Pattern Experiences

Introduce the children to pattern through rhythmic patterns, people patterns,
patterns in the environment, and patterns on the calendar. Present two or three
different pattern experiences several times a week. Provide the appropriate level
of difficulty for your children. Make sure you give the children a variety of experiences to help them develop a broad view of pattern. Be sure to include more
than one type of pattern so that children do not think that the term "pattern"
refers only to AB patterns. Include such patterns as AABB, AAAB, and ABC. Don't
worry if some children do not recognize a pattern right away. Just continue
modeling many different patterns for several weeks using these activities.

> 1: 2–1   Rhythmic Patterns
> 1: 2–2   People Patterns
> 1: 2–3   Patterns in the Environment
> 1: 2–21   Looking for Patterns on the Calendar

Estimation Experiences to 15

Materials: Assorted see-through containers and various objects
with which to fill them.

Once or twice a week, give children the opportunity to estimate the number
of objects that will fill a container. After they have had a chance to guess the
number of objects, have them count with you as you put objects into the
container to determine the actual count.

Informal Rote-Counting Practice

Some children come to kindergarten not yet able to count to ten. It is very important that these children learn this counting sequence so that they can participate fully in other math activities. By just taking a minute or two at a time, you can help them get the practice they need. While everyone can participate in the counting, make sure that the counting sequence fits the needs of those children who need help. Take advantage of all opportunities to count as they come up. For example, the children can count at music time when they are using rhythm sticks and/or when they are marching around the room. Children can also get the practice they need through familiar counting songs and finger plays.

Longer Mini-Lesson
(10–20 minutes, as needed)

Occasionally you will need to spend more than just five to ten minutes on a mini-lesson. This will usually happen when you want the children to use materials. In this case you will teach a longer mini-lesson.

Data Collection and Graphing

Sometime during this planning period, provide opportunities for children to organize data into graphs.

Math and Literature

Provide children with additional counting experiences by reading a variety of counting books to them.

Ongoing Independent-Station Work
(35–40 minutes, 3 to 5 times a week)

During independent-work time, the children are able to practice and internalize the concepts they are learning. Provide frequent ongoing opportunities for them to work at the various stations.

Self-Directed Exploration of the Math Manipulatives

Materials: Connecting cubes, Color Tiles, wooden cubes, toothpicks, and collections. Include any additional math materials that you plan to use for math instruction.

In order for kindergarteners to get the most from their math work time, the focus in the beginning of the year must be on developing routines and expectations. Children need to learn how to make responsible choices, how to get along with the many other children in the class, and what it means to work hard. They can learn this most effectively during a several-week-long period during which they work with and explore the math manipulatives. This time is critical as the children need to work with the manipulatives using their own ideas before they will be able to focus on the tasks you have in mind for them. Having the children explore the manipulatives on their own also allows you to focus on developing the work environment.

Introduce Math Manipulatives and Establish Expectations for Independent Work*

Introduce the various math manipulatives over a period of several days. As you do so, discuss the rules for working with the manipulatives and your expectations for hard work. (See "Establishing the Learning Environment" on p. xxii.)

After the manipulatives have been introduced, have a few children deliver them to the various stations around the room. Then, excuse the rest of the children, a few at a time, to choose where to work. Observe and interact with them while they are at work, commenting and redirecting if necessary. At the end of the math period, spend a minute or two discussing the good hard work you have observed and/or reminding the children of any behaviors that need to be changed.

Make sure you provide sufficient time for the children to work with the math manipulatives. This means that they should work for 35–40 minutes at least three times a week for several weeks. The work children do at this time is very important and will influence how they work with the independent stations throughout the year.

Independent Counting Experiences

Materials: Concept Development Packets—each set up to accommodate six children.

After several weeks, when the children have learned how to work independently with the math manipulatives, you can begin to introduce them to the counting activities in Book One, Chapter One. The first tasks you introduce should be those that are easy for the children to learn so that they can all participate. The purpose of these tasks is not only to give the children practice in counting, but also to help them learn how to follow directions in order to do a specific task, how to choose a task, how to work hard, and how to clean up before moving on to a new task. You can learn much about your children as you observe them at work and engage them in conversation. The tasks can be introduced in a variety of ways by:

■ introducing an activity to half the class or to a small group during self-directed exploration time while the rest of the class is busy working with the math manipulatives.

* See *Math Time: The Learning Environment* for more information about establishing expectations.

- presenting these activities, on occasion, in place of self-directed exploration time.
- adding a few of the counting activities to the self-directed exploration time.

In the beginning, you will want to have enough materials prepared so that all the children being introduced to the activity can participate. The materials needed for the recommended activities are easy to make, so it will not be difficult for you to have many children work with them at one time. Observe the children to determine whether or not they are able to follow the directions and stay on task as they use these activities.

> **1: 1–21** Counting Boards, Level 1
> **1: 1–22** Creations Station, Level 1
> **1: 1–23** Cover the Dots
> **1: 1–24** Counting with the Number Shapes
> **1: 1–25** Roll-a-Tower Race, Level 1
> **1: 1–26** Make-a-Train Race, Level 1

Teacher-Directed, Small-Group Focus Work
(10–15 minutes, 2 to 3 times a week)

It is important for you to work with children having similar needs in order to help them focus on developing concepts. Give children a variety of experiences, choosing from the recommended activities. Spend a few minutes on each of two to four activities during every lesson.

Focus on One-to-One Counting

Materials: Before working with the recommended activities, first assemble your Teacher Tub of Materials and be sure to have connecting cubes, Color Tiles, and collections available to use as needed. This will provide you with the materials you need to do any of the recommended activities.

Teacher Tub of Materials

> Working-space papers (1 per child)
> Counting Boards (1 per child)
> Large dot cubes (1–6 dots)
> Small plastic bowls (10–12)
> Paper lunch bags
> Xylophone (optional)

If you find, through observations or individual assessments, that you have some children who need extra support in learning the counting sequence or one-to-one correspondence, use the following activities for small-group work. These activities provide a lot of repetition for those who need it in a form that young children find intriguing. You may wish to work with these children during another small-group work time if this fits into your day, or you may work with them for a few minutes during the math period before excusing them to join the rest of the class. Do just two or three activities at a time for a total of 10 to 15 minutes.

1: 1–1	Slide and Check
1: 1–2	Count and Dump
1: 1–3	Making Towers
1: 1–4	Counting Stories, Level 1
1: 1–5	Creations
1: 1–6	Finger Counting
1: 1–7	Grab-Bag Counting
1: 1–8	Grow and Shrink (focus on small numbers), Levels 1 and 2
1: 1–9	Hide It

If you wish to provide more variation, include some of the following activities.

1: 1–10	Hunt for It, Levels 1 and 2
1: 1–11	Peek and Count, Level 1
1: 1–12	Find a Match, Levels 1 and 2
1: 1–15	Tall and Short, Level 1

OR

Shared Experiences/Mathematical Events
(35–45 minutes, 1 or 2 times about every two weeks)

You will not need to present additional math experiences during this time as self-directed exploration provides children with informal opportunities to work with sorting, geometry, and measurement concepts.

Kindergarten Planning Chart

Second Planning Period: 4–6 Weeks (Nov., Dec.)

Focus: Beginning Number Concepts, Pattern Stations

Whole-Class Work: Mini-Lessons	
Shorter Mini-Lesson (5–10 minutes, 3 to 5 times a week)	**Longer Mini-Lesson** (10–20 minutes, as needed)

Pattern Experiences 1: 2–1 Rhythmic Patterns 1: 2–2 People Patterns 1: 2–3 Patterns in the Environment 1: 2–21 Looking for Patterns on the Calendar **Estimation Experiences to 15–20** **Informal Rote-Counting Practice** **Number Talks: Instant Recognition** 1: 1–13 Tell Me Fast	**Numeral Recognition** 1: 1–4 Counting Stories, Level 2 1: 1–8 Grow and Shrink, Level 3 1: 1–15 Tall and Short, Level 2 **Data Collection and Graphing** **Math and Literature**

Ongoing Independent-Station Work	
(35–40 minutes, 3 to 5 times a week)	

Additional Counting and Number-Sense Activities *Continue these familiar activities.* 1: 1–21 Counting Boards, Level 1 1: 1–25 Roll-a-Tower Race (1–6), Level 1 1: 1–26 Make-a-Train Race, Level 1 *Gradually phase out the following activities.* 1: 1–22 Creations Station 1: 1–23 Cover the Dots 1: 1–24 Counting with the Number Shapes	*Replace the phased-out activities with these.* 1: 1–27 Build a Staircase, Level 1 1: 1–28 Build a City, Level 1 1: 1–29 Grab-Bag Counting Station, Level 1 *After a few weeks, gradually replace the counting activities with the following.* **Pattern Stations** 1: 2–10 Pattern Trains 1: 2–11 Color-Tile Patterns 1: 2–12 Arrangement Patterns 1: 2–13 Collections Patterns *(For this activity, use any manipulatives you have available, such as buttons, bread tags, or washers and nuts.)*

(Chart continues on next page.)

(Chart continued from previous page.)

Teacher-Directed, Small-Group Focus Work (10–15 minutes, 2 to 3 times a week)

Focus on Numeral Recognition

Choose several activities over time, using two to four of them during any one lesson.

1: 1–4 Counting Stories, Level 2
1: 1–8 Grow and Shrink, Level 3
1: 1–10 Hunt for It, Level 3
1: 1–12 Find a Match, Level 3
1: 1–15 Tall and Short, Level 2

Focus on One-to-One Counting

Work with those children who need extra help. Continue using the activities listed for the First Planning Period.

OR

Shared Experiences/Mathematical Events
(35–45 minutes, 1 or 2 times about every two weeks)

Intersperse work at independent stations with whole-class experiences using this activity.

1: 2–4 Interpreting Rhythmic Patterns with Connecting Cubes or Color Tiles

Later, present this activity.

1: 2–5 Interpreting Rhythmic Patterns with Pattern Blocks

Provide Additional Math Experiences as Time Allows

- Sorting
- Geometry
- Math and Literature

Kindergarten Planning Notes

Second Planning Period: 4–6 Weeks (Nov., Dec.)

Focus: Beginning Number Concepts, Pattern Stations

Whole-Class Work: Mini-Lessons

You can present new concepts and review previously taught concepts by spending just a few minutes at the beginning of each math period on either a *Shorter Mini-Lesson* (5–10 minutes) or a *Longer Mini-Lesson* (10–20 minutes).

Shorter Mini-Lesson
(5–10 minutes, 3 to 5 times a week)

Begin math time with a mini-lesson. Choose two to four activities from among those listed.

Pattern Experiences

Continue to provide opportunities for children to work with pattern activities. Increase the level of complexity of the patterns that the children are asked to work with.

> 1: 2–1 Rhythmic Patterns
> 1: 2–2 People Patterns
> 1: 2–3 Patterns in the Environment
> 1: 2–21 Looking for Patterns on the Calendar

Estimation Experiences to 15–20

Materials: Assorted see-through containers and various objects with which to fill them.

Continue to provide opportunities for children to estimate and check their estimates.

Informal Rote-Counting Practice

Continue to provide opportunities for children to practice counting to ten. Extend the sequence as the children become ready.

Number Talks:* Instant Recognition

1: 1–13   Tell Me Fast

Provide children with opportunities to practice identifying groups of objects or dots.

Longer Mini-Lesson
(10–20 minutes, as needed)

Numeral Recognition

Materials: Connecting cubes, Working-space papers for each child

When the children have developed a strong base of counting skills (specifically, rote sequence and one-to-one counting to 10), they are ready to begin associating the numerals 0 to 9 with corresponding quantities. The numerals can be introduced through teacher-directed activities. Children can then practice reading and writing numerals as they work on the independent activities.

Introduce the numerals as you work with the familiar activities. In this context, children can continue to develop and strengthen their understanding of number concepts at the same time they learn the numerals. Whenever you say a number, write it as well. Replace dot cubes with number cubes. In general, give the children opportunities to see and hear the names of numerals in association with the corresponding sets of objects. Soon the children will be reading the numerals along with you. Presenting all ten numerals at once can be overwhelming. Instead, let children become familiar and confident with just a few at a time.

1: 1–4   Counting Stories, Level 2
1: 1–8   Grow and Shrink, Level 3
1: 1–15   Tall and Short, Level 2

Data Collection and Graphing

Occasionally have the children organize information on a graph.

Math and Literature

---

* Number Talks are experiences that allow children to solve addition, subtraction, multiplication, and division problems in a variety of ways, generally using number relationships. The children should be given opportunities to describe the ways they solve the problems. In kindergarten, this begins with instant recognition of small groups. Make sure you present a variety of problems for children to solve. See the video series *Thinking with Numbers* published by Educational Enrichment, Norman, OK, for more information about number talks.

Ongoing Independent-Station Work
(35–40 minutes, 3 to 5 times a week)

Additional Counting and Number-Sense Activities

Materials: Concept Development Packets—each set up to accommodate six children.

Once children know the rote-counting sequence and can count one-to-one, they need many ongoing opportunities to practice counting. A variety of activities that provides them with this practice will help them to develop accuracy, consistency, and confidence in counting.

Introduce eight to ten activities gradually over a period of several days, and then keep the same activities out for several weeks. You will find that the children become increasingly engaged as they become more and more familiar with the tasks. Children can't really learn from an activity until they know how to do it. By keeping activities out for long periods of time, you ensure that the children get as much as possible from the experiences. The tasks have been designed to meet a variety of needs depending on what the child brings to them. Some children will be working on developing consistency and strength in counting and will be focused on number sense and discovering relationships. Other children will be developing basic counting skills. (You can focus on individual needs by working with small groups as described in the next section.)

Continue these familiar activities.

> **1:** 1–21 Counting Boards, Level 1
> **1:** 1–25 Roll-a-Tower Race, Level 1
> **1:** 1–26 Make-a-Train Race, Level 1

Gradually phase out the following activities.

> **1:** 1–22 Creations Station
> **1:** 1–23 Cover the Dots
> **1:** 1–24 Counting with the Number Shapes

Replace the phased-out activities with these activities.

> **1:** 1–27 Build a Staircase, Level 1
> **1:** 1–28 Build a City, Level 1
> **1:** 1–29 Grab-Bag Counting Station, Level 1

After the children have worked with the counting activities for several weeks, gradually introduce them to the use of pattern task cards, replacing the familiar activities with these new ones. Allow several weeks for the children to work with the pattern stations.

Pattern Stations

Materials: Concept Development Packets—each set up to accommodate six children.

> 1: 2–10   Pattern Trains
> 1: 2–11   Color-Tile Patterns
> 1: 2–12   Arrangement Patterns
> 1: 2–13   Collections Patterns *(For this activity, use any manipulatives you have available, such as buttons, bread tags, or washers and nuts.)*

Teacher-Directed, Small-Group Focus Work
(10–15 minutes, 2 to 3 times a week)

Do two to four activities for a few minutes each during any one lesson.

Focus on Number Sense and Numeral Recognition

Materials: You can choose from any of the recommended activities if you have the following materials available. First assemble your Teacher Tub of Materials and be sure to have connecting cubes, Color Tiles, or collections available to use as needed.

Teacher Tub of Materials

> Working-space papers (1 per child)
> Counting Boards (1 per child)
> Large number cubes (marked 1–6)
> Small plastic bowls (10–12)
> Paper lunch bags
> Xylophone (optional)

The recommended activities can be used to provide extra practice for all of the children. You can vary the size of the numbers to meet children's various needs. Over a period of several weeks, work with the children in a small-group setting whenever you can. Choose two to four activities to do during each 10- to 15-minute period. The activities should be experienced by the children many different times so that they can gain the full benefit from them.

> 1: 1–4   Counting Stories, Level 2
> 1: 1–8   Grow and Shrink, Level 3
> 1: 1–10   Hunt for It, Level 3
> 1: 1–12   Find a Match, Level 3
> 1: 1–15   Tall and Short, Level 2

Focus on One-to-One Counting

Continue to work with those children who need extra help, choosing from the same activities suggested for small-group focus work in the First Planning Period.

OR

Shared Experiences/Mathematical Events
(35–45 minutes, 1 or 2 times about every two weeks)

When you see that many of the children are beginning to get a sense of pattern and are starting to make predictions, begin the interpreting-patterns lessons with the whole class. (Continue to provide experiences with interpreting patterns even after you have moved on to work with other math concepts.)

1: 2–4   Interpreting Rhythmic Patterns with Connecting Cubes or Color Tiles
1: 2–5   Interpreting Rhythmic Patterns with Pattern Blocks

Provide Additional Math Experiences as Time Allows

Sometimes, you will want to break up the routine and do a lesson on another math topic.

- Sorting
- Math and Literature

Kindergarten Planning Chart

Third Planning Period: 5–6 Weeks (Jan., Feb.)

Focus: Numeral Recognition, Developing Number Sense
and Number Relationships

Whole-Class Work: Mini-Lessons

Shorter Mini-Lesson (5–10 minutes, 3 to 5 times a week)	**Longer Mini-Lesson** (10–20 minutes, as needed)

Pattern Experiences

1: 2–1   Rhythmic Patterns
1: 2–2   People Patterns
1: 2–3   Patterns in the Environment
1: 2–21 Looking for Patterns on the
         Calendar

Estimation Experiences to 20

Number Talks: Instant Recognition

1: 1–13 Tell Me Fast

Numeral Recognition

1: 1–4   Counting Stories, Level 2
1: 1–8   Grow and Shrink, Level 3
1: 1–15 Tall and Short, Level 2

Data Collection and Graphing

Sorting

Ongoing Independent-Station Work
(35–40 minutes, 3 to 5 times a week)

Number Sense and Numeral Recognition

Use the familiar activities, but now include numerals.

1: 1–21 Counting Boards, Level 2
1: 1–23 Cover the Dots, Level 2
1: 1–24 Counting with the Number
         Shapes, Level 2
1: 1–25 Roll-a-Tower Race (1–6) and
         (4–9), Level 2
1: 1–26 Make-a-Train Race, Level 2
1: 1–27 Build a Staircase, Level 2
1: 1–28 Build a City, Level 2

Introduce three or four of these new activities.

1: 1–29 Grab-Bag Counting Station,
         Level 1

1: 1–30 Shape Puzzles, Level 1
1: 1–31 Line Puzzles, Level 1
1: 1–32 Pick a Number
1: 1–36 How Long Is It?, Level 1
1: 1–37 How Many Does It Hold?,
         Level 1

Present additional activities and challenges as your children become ready.

1: 1–40 Sorting Shape Puzzles
1: 1–41 Sorting Line Puzzles

Replace some of the familiar activities with any activities listed above that have not yet been introduced.

Teacher-Directed, Small-Group Focus Work (10–15 minutes, 2 to 3 times a week)

Focus on Number Sense and Numeral Recognition

Choose several activities over time, using two to four of them during any one lesson.

1: 1–4   Counting Stories, Level 2
1: 1–8   Grow and Shrink, Level 3
1: 1–10   Hunt for It, Level 3
1: 1–11   Peek and Count, Level 1
1: 1–12   Find a Match, Level 3
1: 1–13   Tell Me Fast
1: 1–14   Break It Up
1: 1–15   Tall and Short, Level 2
1: 1–16   One More/One Less
1: 1–17   Give and Take, Level 1
1: 1–18   Hiding One More
1: 1–19   Hiding One Less
1: 1–20   Towers, Towers, Towers

OR

Shared Experiences/Mathematical Events
(35–45 minutes, 1 or 2 times about every two weeks)

Self-Directed Exploration of the Math Manipulatives

Occasionally give the children additional opportunities to work with the manipulatives using their own ideas.

Number Arrangements

Prepare children for later independent work.

2: 2–16   Number Arrangements: Using Toothpicks, Level 1

Kindergarten Planning Notes

Third Planning Period: 5–6 Weeks (Jan., Feb.)

Focus: Numeral Recognition, Developing Number Sense
and Number Relationships

Whole-Class Work: Mini-Lessons

You can present new concepts and review previously taught concepts by spending just a few minutes at the beginning of each math period on either a *Shorter Mini-Lesson* (5–10 minutes) or a *Longer Mini-Lesson* (10–20 minutes).

Shorter Mini-Lesson

(5–10 minutes, 3 to 5 times a week)

Begin math time with a mini-lesson. Choose two to four activities from among those listed.

Pattern Experiences

Continue to provide ongoing pattern experiences.

      1: 2–1   Rhythmic Patterns
      1: 2–2   People Patterns
      1: 2–3   Patterns in the Environment
      1: 2–21 Looking for Patterns on the Calendar

Estimation Experiences

Materials: Assorted see-through containers and various objects with which to fill them. Yarn and toothpicks and/or large paper clips.

Continue to provide opportunities for the children to estimate and check their estimates. Vary the experience by having them estimate the length of pieces of yarn.

Number Talks: Instant Recognition

Provide children with opportunities to practice identifying groups of objects or dots without counting each one. Add the number shapes to the Tell-Me-Fast cards for the children to identify.

      1: 1–13 Tell Me Fast

Longer Mini-Lesson
(10–20 minutes, as needed)

Occasionally spend a little extra time on lessons that require the children to use materials.

Numeral Recognition

Materials: Connecting cubes, Working-space papers for each child

Continue to provide numeral-recognition practice, as needed.

      1: 1–4   Counting Stories, Level 2
      1: 1–8   Grow and Shrink, Level 3
      1: 1–15 Tall and Short, Level 2

Data Collection and Graphing

Sometime during this planning period, give children opportunities to organize data into graphs.

Sorting

Ongoing Independent-Station Work
(35–40 minutes, 3 to 5 times a week)

Number Sense and Numeral Recognition

Materials: Concept Development Packets—each set up to accommodate six children.

The recommended activities support the development of numeral recognition while they allow children to strengthen their sense of number. You will be using many of the familiar tasks but will be adding numerals to them as your children become ready.

      1: 1–21 Counting Boards, Level 2
      1: 1–23 Cover the Dots, Level 2
      1: 1–24 Counting with the Number Shapes, Level 2
      1: 1–25 Roll-a-Tower Race (1–6) and (4–9), Level 2
      1: 1–26 Make-a-Train Race, Level 2
      1: 1–27 Build a Staircase, Level 2
      1: 1–28 Build a City, Level 2

It is important that you interact with the children while they are working. Children need to be able to do more than simply get a right answer by counting correctly. They also need to develop a sense of quantities and relationships, an understanding of the concept of conservation of number, and instant recognition of the number of a small group of things. Instead of just pointing at the objects they count, one by one, and telling the number they landed on when they counted, children must think about what they are counting. You can focus children's attention and challenge their thinking by asking them to estimate their answers before counting. Do this by posing questions such as the following.

What do you *think* the answer will be?

How many cubes did you think would fit in the shape puzzle? Now that you started to fill the puzzle, do you have a different idea?

How many did you think are in the pile? Are you sure or do you need to count and see?

How many did you have in your biggest handful?

Did the bowl hold more cubes or more walnuts?

Have you rolled that number before?

Keep the activities out for several weeks, gradually replacing some of the old ones with new ones.

Introduce three or four of these new activities.

1: 1–29	Grab-Bag Counting Station, Level 1
1: 1–30	Shape Puzzles, Level 1
1: 1–31	Line Puzzles, Level 1
1: 1–32	Pick a Number
1: 1–36	How Long Is It?, Level 1
1: 1–37	How Many Does It Hold?, Level 1

Present these additional activities and challenges as your children become ready.

1: 1–40	Sorting Shape Puzzles
1: 1–41	Sorting Line Puzzles

Teacher-Directed, Small-Group Focus Work
(10–15 minutes, 2 to 3 times a week)

It is important to work with children having similar needs in order to help them focus on developing concepts. Give children a variety of experiences, choosing from the following activities. Do two to four activities for a few minutes each during every lesson.

Focus on Number Sense and Numeral Recognition

Materials: You can choose from any of the recommended activities if you have the following materials available. First assemble your Teacher Tub of Materials and be sure to have connecting cubes, Color Tiles, or collections available to use as needed.

Teacher Tub of Materials

> Working-space papers (1 per child)
> Counting Boards (1 per child)
> Number cubes (marked 1–6 or 4–9, as needed)
> Small plastic bowls (10–12)
> Paper lunch bags

These activities give children experiences in counting and/or recognizing numerals while they help develop number relationships.

1: 1–4	Counting Stories, Level 2
1: 1–8	Grow and Shrink, Level 3
1: 1–10	Hunt for It, Level 3
1: 1–11	Peek and Count, Level 1
1: 1–12	Find a Match, Level 3
1: 1–13	Tell Me Fast
1: 1–14	Break It Up
1: 1–15	Tall and Short, Level 2
1: 1–16	One More/One Less
1: 1–17	Give and Take, Level 1
1: 1–18	Hiding One More
1: 1–19	Hiding One Less
1: 1–20	Towers, Towers, Towers

OR

Shared Experiences/Mathematical Events
(35–45 minutes, 1 or 2 times about every two weeks)

Self-Directed Exploration of the Math Manipulatives

Occasionally give the children additional opportunities to work with the manipulatives using their own ideas.

Number Arrangements

> **2:** 2–16   Number Arrangements: Using Toothpicks, Level 1

Materials: Toothpicks

Prepare the children for the independent work that they will be asked to do later by having them work with toothpick arrangements. First model some designs and then have the whole class work to create toothpick designs. Help the children to see that there are many different ways in which they can arrange their toothpicks.

Kindergarten Planning Chart

Fourth Planning Period: 5–6 Weeks (Feb., Mar.)

Focus: Numeral Recognition, Developing Number Sense
and Concepts of More and Less

Whole-Class Work: Mini-Lessons

Shorter Mini-Lesson	Longer Mini-Lesson
(5–10 minutes, 3 to 5 times a week)	(10–20 minutes, as needed)

Pattern Experiences	**Practice Writing Numerals**
1: 2–1 Rhythmic Patterns	
1: 2–2 People Patterns	**Data Collection and Graphing**
1: 2–3 Patterns in the Environment	
1: 2–21 Looking for Patterns on the Calendar	**Math and Literature**
Estimation Experiences to 20	
Number Talks: Instant Recognition	
1: 1–13 Tell Me Fast	
2: 3–2 Instant Recognition of Number Arrangements	
2: 3–3 Instant Recognition of Number Shapes	
More* and *Less	
1: 3–1 Is It More or Is It Less?	

Ongoing Independent-Station Work
(35–40 minutes, 3 to 5 times a week)

Number Arrangements	More and Less
2: 2–14 Number Arrangements: Using Cubes, Level 1	**1:** 3–13 Stack, Tell, Spin, and Win
2: 2–15 Number Arrangements: Using Color Tiles, Level 1	**1:** 3–14 Two-Color Grab-Bag Station
	1: 3–15 Comparing Lengths
2: 2–16 Number Arrangements: Using Toothpicks, Level 1	**1:** 3–16 Comparing Shape Puzzles
	1: 3–17 Comparing Line Puzzles
2: 2–17 Number Arrangements: Using Collections, Level 1	**1:** 3–18 Comparing Handfuls
	1: 3–19 Comparing Containers
	1: 3–20 Sort and Compare Colors
After a few weeks, gradually replace the activities above with the following activities.	**1:** 3–22 Counting Boards: Changing Numbers

---

Teacher-Directed, Small-Group Focus Work (10–15 minutes, 2 to 3 times a week)

More and *Less*

1: 3–1 Is It More or Is It Less?, Level 1
1: 3–2 Stacks, Level 1
1: 3–3 Two-Color Grab Bag, Level 1
1: 3–4 Spin and Peek, Level 1
1: 3–5 Graph and See, Level 1
1: 3–7 More-or-Less Spin It, Level 1
1: 3–8 More-or-Less Counting Stories, Level 1

OR

Shared Experiences/Mathematical Events
(35–45 minutes, 1 or 2 times about every two weeks)

Number Arrangements

Interpreting Rhythmic Patterns with Manipulatives

Intersperse work at independent stations with whole-class experiences using these activities.

Number-Arrangements activities, **2:** 2–14 through **2:** 2–17

Interpreting-Rhythmic-Patterns-with-Manipulatives activities,
1: 2–4 through **1:** 2–6

Provide Additional Math Experiences as Time Allows

- Geometry
- Measurement (integrate with science)

Kindergarten Planning Notes

Fourth Planning Period: 5–6 Weeks (Feb., Mar.)

Focus: Numeral Recognition, Developing Number Sense
and Concepts of More and Less

Whole-Class Work: Mini-Lessons

You can present new concepts and review previously taught concepts by
spending just a few minutes at the beginning of each math period on
either a *Shorter Mini-Lesson* (5–10 minutes) or a *Longer Mini-Lesson*
(10–20 minutes).

Shorter Mini-Lesson

(5–10 minutes, 3 to 5 times a week)

It is important to continue to precede independent work time with ongoing
experiences that maintain and extend children's understanding of previously
learned concepts.

Pattern Experiences

1: 2–1	Rhythmic Patterns
1: 2–2	People Patterns
1: 2–3	Patterns in the Environment
1: 2–21	Looking for Patterns on the Calendar

Estimation Experiences to 20

Materials: Assorted see-through containers and various objects with which to
fill them. Yarn and toothpicks and/or large paper clips.

Continue to provide opportunities for the children to estimate and check
their estimates. Vary the experience by having them estimate the length of
pieces of yarn.

Number Talks: Instant Recognition

Materials: Tell-Me-Fast dot cards, number shapes, number-arrangement
recordings made by children

Encourage the children to identify not only the total number in an arrangement
but also the smaller groups that make up the arrangement. For example, rather
than saying, "I see seven!" a child might say, "I see four orange and three red!"

This is a first step in learning number combinations.

     1: 1–13 Tell Me Fast
     2: 3–2   Instant Recognition of Number Arrangements
     2: 3–3   Instant Recognition of Number Shapes

More and *Less*

     1: 3–1   Is It More or Is It Less?

Longer Mini-Lesson

(10–20 minutes, as needed)

Occasionally spend some extra time on lessons that require the use of materials.

Practice Writing Numerals

Materials: Individual chalkboards, chalk, and erasers

Provide opportunities for the children to develop the physical facility to write numerals through directed lessons using individual chalkboards.

Data Collection and Graphing

Sometime during this planning period, provide opportunities for children to organize data into graphs.

Math and Literature

Ongoing Independent-Station Work

(35–40 minutes, 3 to 5 times a week)

Number Arrangements

Materials: Use any of the recommended math manipulatives that you have available. This set of open-ended activities can support children's developing understanding of conservation of number, can help them to develop consistency in counting, and can lead them to seeing the parts of numbers.

     2: 2–14 Number Arrangements: Using Cubes, Level 1
     2: 2–15 Number Arrangements: Using Color Tiles, Level 1
     2: 2–16 Number Arrangements: Using Toothpicks, Level 1
     2: 2–17 Number Arrangements: Using Collections, Level 1

More and Less

Materials: Concept Development Packets—each set up to accommodate six children.

As children develop confidence and consistency with counting, we want them to begin focusing on the quantities that the numbers they are working with represent. Comparing two numbers to see which is more and which is less is one way to support the development of a sense of quantity.

1: 3–13 Stack, Tell, Spin, and Win
1: 3–14 Two-Color Grab-Bag Station
1: 3–15 Comparing Lengths
1: 3–16 Comparing Shape Puzzles
1: 3–17 Comparing Line Puzzles
1: 3–18 Comparing Handfuls
1: 3–19 Comparing Containers
1: 3–20 Sort and Compare Colors
1: 3–22 Counting Boards: Changing Numbers

Teacher-Directed, Small-Group Focus Work
(10–15 minutes, 2 to 3 times a week)

More and Less

Materials: You can choose from any of the recommended activities if you have the following materials available. First assemble your Teacher Tub of Materials and be sure to have connecting cubes, Color Tiles, or collections available to use as needed.

Teacher Tub of Materials

Working-space papers (1 per child)
Counting Boards (1 per child)
Number cubes (marked 1–6 or 4–9, as needed)
Small plastic bowls (10–12)
Paper lunch bags
More-or-Less Spinner

The recommended activities are intended to help the children focus on the concepts of more and less and develop the language used to describe them.

1: 3–1 Is It More or Is It Less?, Level 1
1: 3–2 Stacks, Level 1
1: 3–3 Two-Color Grab Bag, Level 1
1: 3–4 Spin and Peek, Level 1
1: 3–5 Graph and See, Level 1
1: 3–7 More-or-Less Spin It, Level 1
1: 3–8 More-or-Less Counting Stories, Level 1

OR

Number Arrangements

Intersperse the work at independent stations with whole-class experiences with number arrangements if you have enough materials to allow the whole class to work at once. (Toothpicks work well for these activities as it is easy to get lots of them.) You can help focus children and motivate them to work hard independently if you occasionally have them all work together using one kind of material and discussing what they noticed and what they created.

Number-Arrangements activities, **2:** 2–14 through **2:** 2–17

Interpreting Rhythmic Patterns with Manipulatives

Also give the children ongoing experiences interpreting rhythmic patterns.

Interpreting-Rhythmic-Patterns-with-Manipulatives activities,
1: 2–4 through **1:** 2–6

Provide Additional Math Experiences as Time Allows

- Geometry
- Measurement (integrate with science)

Kindergarten Planning Chart
Fifth Planning Period: 6–8 Weeks (Apr., May, June)

Focus: Writing Numerals, Counting to 20–30, Introduction to Addition and Subtraction

Whole-Class Work: Mini-Lessons	
Shorter Mini-Lesson (5–10 minutes, 3 to 5 times a week)	**Longer Mini-Lesson** (10–20 minutes, as needed)

Pattern Experiences

1: 2–1　Rhythmic Patterns
1: 2–2　People Patterns
1: 2–3　Patterns in the Environment
1: 2–21　Looking for Patterns on the Calendar

Estimation Experiences to 20 and Beyond

Number Talks: Instant Recognition

Introduction to Addition and Subtraction

2: 1–1　Acting Out Stories: Using Real Things
2: 1–2　Acting Out Stories: Using Fantasies

Practice Writing Numerals

Counting to 20
Some children will be ready to count to 20 and beyond.

1: 1–7　Grab-Bag Counting, Ext.
1: 1–14　Break It Up, Ext.
1: 1–16　One More /One Less, Ext.
1: 1–17　Give and Take, Ext.

Data Collection and Graphing

1: 3–5　Graph and See

Ongoing Independent-Station Work (35–40 minutes, 3 to 5 times a week)

Counting and Writing Numerals

1: 1–21　Counting Boards, Levels 3 and 4
1: 1–29　Grab-Bag Counting Station, Level 2
1: 1–30　Shape Puzzles, Level 2
1: 1–31　Line Puzzles, Level 2
1: 1–33　Grab a Handful
1: 1–34　Hide-It Station
1: 1–35　Give-and-Take Station, Ext.
1: 1–36　How Long Is It?
1: 1–37　How Many Does It Hold?
1: 1–38　Sorting Colors, Level 2
1: 1–39　Sorting Collections, Level 2

Pattern Stations
Bring out these familiar pattern-station activities.

1: 2–10　Pattern Trains
1: 2–11　Color-Tile Patterns
1: 2–12　Arrangement Patterns
1: 2–13　Collections Patterns

Introduce the more challenging pattern task cards through these activities.

1: 2–14　Rhythmic-Patterns Task Cards
1: 2–15　ABC-Patterns Task Cards

Teacher-Directed, Small-Group Focus Work (10–15 minutes, 2 to 3 times a week)

Counting to 20

Choose several activities over time, using two to three of them during any one lesson.

1: 1–7   Grab-Bag Counting, Ext.
1: 1–14   Break It Up, Ext.
1: 1–16   One More/One Less, Ext.
1: 1–17   Give and Take, Ext.

OR

Shared Experiences/Mathematical Events (35–45 minutes, 1 or 2 times about every two weeks)

Provide Additional Math Experiences as Time Allows
- Sorting
- Geometry
- Math and Literature

Kindergarten Planning Notes

Fifth Planning Period: 6–8 Weeks (Apr., May, June)

Focus: Writing Numerals, Counting to 20–30, Introduction to Addition
and Subtraction

Whole-Class Work: Mini-Lessons

You can present new concepts and review previously taught concepts by
spending just a few minutes at the beginning of each math period on
either a *Shorter Mini-Lesson* (5–10 minutes) or a *Longer Mini-Lesson*
(10–20 minutes).

Shorter Mini-Lesson

(5–10 minutes, 3 to 5 times a week)

Pattern Experiences

      1: 2–1   Rhythmic Patterns
      1: 2–2   People Patterns
      1: 2–3   Patterns in the Environment
      1: 2–21   Looking for Patterns on the Calendar

Estimation Experiences to 20 and Beyond

Materials: Assorted see-through containers and various objects with which to fill
them. Yarn and toothpicks and/or large paper clips.

Continue to provide opportunities for the children to estimate and check their estimates. Vary the experience by having them estimate the length of pieces of yarn.

Number Talks: Instant Recognition

Materials: Tell-Me-Fast Dot Cards, number shapes, number-arrangement
recordings made by children

Continue to encourage the children to identify not only the total number in an
arrangement but also the smaller groups that make up the arrangement.

Introduction to Addition and Subtraction

By the end of the kindergarten year, children will be ready to begin acting out
addition and subtraction story problems. Children need these kinds of experiences to build an understanding of the processes of addition and subtraction and
to provide a meaningful base for later work with symbols.

      2: 1–1   Acting Out Stories: Using Real Things
      2: 1–2   Acting Out Stories: Using Fantasies

Longer Mini-Lesson
(10–20 minutes, as needed)

Numeral Writing

Continue to provide opportunities for children to practice writing numerals during teacher-directed lessons.

Counting to 20

Give those children who are ready to work with larger numbers opportunities to count to 20 and beyond.

> 1: 1–7   Grab-Bag Counting, Ext.
> 1: 1–14 Break It Up, Ext.
> 1: 1–16 One More /One Less, Ext.
> 1: 1–17 Give and Take, Ext.

Data Collection and Graphing

> 1: 3–5   Graph and See

Ongoing Independent-Station Work
(35–40 minutes, 3 to 5 times a week)

Practice Writing Numerals

Materials: Concept Development Packets—each set up to accommodate six children.

After introducing the children to numeral writing during teacher-directed lessons, give them opportunities to practice during independent work time. Continue to provide previously introduced activities that do not require writing to accommodate those children who are not yet ready to write independently.

At this time of year, you will need to have a range of levels for children to work with. For example, if you made the activity How Many Does It Hold? (1: 1–37) available, some children would fill the containers with large objects like walnuts, ending up with small amounts to count. Other children would fill the containers with smaller objects like lima beans, thus ending up with larger numbers to count. If some children are not ready to write, they may use small numeral cards to indicate the number of objects in a container. Those children who are able to write can record the numerals on a worksheet. Initially, allow the children to choose both the size of the objects to use for counting and the way of recording the totals. You can then redirect any children who need help in finding the level that is appropriate for them. The following activities can be easily extended to numbers to 20 and beyond.

1: 1–21   Counting Boards, Levels 3 and 4
1: 1–29   Grab-Bag Counting Station, Level 2
1: 1–30   Shape Puzzles, Level 2
1: 1–31   Line Puzzles, Level 2
1: 1–33   Grab a Handful
1: 1–34   Hide-It Station
1: 1–35   Give-and-Take Station, Ext.
1: 1–36   How Long Is It?
1: 1–37   How Many Does It Hold?
1: 1–38   Sorting Colors, Level 2
1: 1–39   Sorting Collections, Level 2

Pattern Stations

Bring out the familiar pattern stations and then add the activities that call for the more challenging pattern task cards (Rhythmic-Patterns Task Cards and ABC-Patterns Task Cards). Allow the children to work with these stations for several weeks. They will now be able to work with these patterns in a different way than they did earlier in the year.

1: 2–10   Pattern Trains
1: 2–11   Color-Tile Patterns
1: 2–12   Arrangement Patterns
1: 2–13   Collections Patterns
1: 2–14   Rhythmic-Patterns Task Cards
1: 2–15   ABC-Patterns Task Cards

Teacher-Directed, Small-Group Focus Work
(10–15 minutes, 2 to 3 times a week)

Counting to 20

Materials: You can choose from any of the recommended activities if you have the following materials available. First assemble your Teacher Tub of Materials and be sure to have connecting cubes, Color Tiles, or collections available to use as needed.

Teacher Tub of Materials

Small plastic bowls (10–12)
Paper lunch bags

Provide opportunities for children to work in a small group practicing counting to 20.

1: 1–7   Grab-Bag Counting, Ext.
1: 1–14 Break It Up, Ext.
1: 1–16 One More/One Less, Ext.
1: 1–17 Give and Take, Ext.

OR

Continue to work with concepts introduced earlier or present new concepts through an occasional whole-class experience.

Provide Additional Math Experiences as Time Allows

- Sorting
- Geometry
- Math and Literature

First Grade

	Creating the Environment See *Math Time: The Learning Environment.*	Number See *Developing Number Concepts:* Book One (Ch. 1 & 3) and Book Two (Ch. 1).	Pattern See *Developing Number Concepts:* Book One (Ch. 2).
Beginning of the Year: (Sept., Oct., Nov.)	**Self-Directed Exploration** *Provide opportunities for children to work with the math manipulatives in their own ways for about six weeks. This is the heart of young children's work as it establishes expectations for their work for the entire year.* Children will learn to: ■ work hard ■ make responsible choices ■ work independently ■ share and cooperate ■ stay engaged and focused ■ build and create ■ sort and count ■ clean up	**Estimating to 20 or Beyond** *and* **Counting and Comparing Objects to 10 (or 20)** *The activities help prepare children for the number relationships that they will be working with when they add and subtract. Focus not just on counting but on developing a sense of quantity and relationships.* **Adding and Subtracting** *Introduce children to the processes of addition and subtraction by acting out story problems. Model how to write the equation for each story and have children read and interpret it.*	**Interpreting Rhythmic Patterns** Children interpret patterns such as AABC, AAB, and ABBC. They display their patterns using a variety of manipulatives, including connecting cubes, Pattern Blocks, Color Tiles, and collections. **Copying, Extending, and Creating Patterns** Children copy, extend, and create patterns of various levels of complexity at independent-pattern stations. *Introduce growing patterns but do not insist that children work with them independently.* **Introductory Work with Number Patterns** Children are introduced to number patterns through their work with the days-of-school number chart.

* Adapted from workshop materials presented by Mathematical Perspectives: Kathy Richardson and Associates.

Measurement See *Developing Number Concepts: Book One* (Ch. 1 & 3).	Geometry See *Understanding Geometry*.	Sorting See *Developing Number Concepts: Book One* (Ch. 1 & 3).	Data Collection See *Developing Number Concepts: Book One* (Ch. 3).

Exploring Volume and Weight

During self-directed exploration, children explore the capacity of various containers. They compare objects by weighing them on simple scales to find out which weighs more or which weighs less.

Comparing Length and Area

Children compare two lengths to determine which is longer or shorter or whether the two are about the same. They compare two areas to determine which is larger or smaller or whether the two are about the same.

Focus on these concepts during children's work with number when they are using materials such as Shape puzzles, Line puzzles, and yarn.

Exploring Shapes and Three-Dimensional Objects

During self-directed exploration, children work with geometric shapes and solids using materials such as Pattern Blocks, geoboards, attribute blocks, geoblocks, Discovery Blocks, and building blocks and boxes. If mirrors are provided, children can use them to explore reflections and symmetry.

Creating and Recording Designs and Shapes

As an outgrowth of their work with exploring the manipulatives, children create designs and shapes and then copy them. Children also work with shapes as they cut and paste to create pictures or designs using lids and various blocks.

Observing and Describing Shapes and Figures

Children learn to describe various geometric shapes so that others can identify them. They look for geometric shapes in their environment and then draw and/or write about what they find.

Sorting Shapes

Children become familiar with attributes of various geometric shapes and three-dimensional objects by sorting them in a variety of ways. They use their own language to tell how they sorted.

Model geometric language as appropriate.

Describing Attributes

Provide opportunities for children to describe attributes during teacher-directed lessons.

Exploring Sorting

During self-directed exploration, children sort collections and various other math manipulatives.

Gathering and Organizing Data

Children place actual objects or pictures of objects in the appropriate columns of a 2- or 3-column graph.

Focus on the idea that lining things up ("across" and "down") makes it easy to tell which group of objects has more or less without having to count each object.

Noticing and Describing Relationships

Children compare two groups and tell which has more or less than the other or whether the two groups have the same number.

	Creating the Environment See *Math Time: The Learning Environment.*	Number See *Developing Number Concepts:* Book Two (Ch. 1 & 2).	Pattern See *Developing Number Concepts:* Book One (Ch. 2).
Middle of the Year: (Dec., Jan., Feb., Mar.)	**Self-Directed Exploration** *Continue to provide opportunities for children to occasionally work with manipulatives in their own ways, but be sure they understand when they are supposed to use their own ideas and when they are supposed to do a specific task.* *Make sure to give children opportunities to explore any new manipulatives you introduce.*	**Estimating to 30** *Continue to focus on developing a sense of quantity and relationships.* **Adding and Subtracting** Children continue to act out story problems and to practice distinguishing between the plus (+) and minus (–) signs. They work with number combinations for numbers up to 10. (Most children will develop fluency with number combinations up to 6.)	**Interpreting Rhythmic Patterns** *Present increasingly complex patterns using a variety of manipulatives. Occasionally provide a challenge by limiting children to the use of just one color, shape, or kind of counter.* **Exploring Growing Patterns** *Continue to provide opportunities for children to explore growing patterns.* **Exploring Number Patterns** Children continue to work with number patterns using the days-of-school number chart.

Measurement See *Developing Number Concepts:* Book One (Ch. 1 & 3).	Geometry See *Understanding Geometry.*	Sorting See *Developing Number Concepts:* Book One (Ch. 1 & 3).	Data Collection See *Developing Number Concepts:* Book One (Ch. 3).
Making Direct Comparisons of Volume and Weight Children continue to explore containers and scales during self-directed exploration and at the science center. They compare containers directly to see which holds more or less. They weigh and compare objects directly to see which weighs more or less. *Focus on these relationships:* more, less, longer, shorter, about the same. *Challenge children to consider how close two things need to be in length or weight to be considered to be "about the same."* **Using Indirect Measurement** *Introduce indirect measurement by modeling the use of non-standard units for measuring. Use scoops of rice, for example, to compare volume or capacity and ceramic tiles to compare weight.*	**Exploring Shapes and Three-Dimensional Objects** *Continue to provide occasional opportunities for children to use their own ideas in working with the geometry manipulatives.* **Creating and Recording Designs and Shapes** *Continue to provide opportunities for children to build and record the creations they make using various materials.* **Filling in Shapes Using Smaller Shapes** Children discover relationships between shapes. They see how small shapes fill larger ones by filling-in shape outlines with Pattern Blocks, tangrams, or Discovery Blocks. **Describing Shapes and Figures** Children continue to learn to describe various geometric shapes and three-dimensional figures in ways that identify them for others. They begin to use geometric terms to identify the attributes of the shapes. They should also continue to find shapes in their environment and then record what they find. **Sorting Shapes** Children continue to become familiar with the attributes of various shapes and three-dimensional objects by sorting them in a variety of ways. They describe the different ways in which they sorted. **Analyzing Three-Dimensional Figures** Children explore boxes in a variety of ways to discover which geometric shapes the boxes are made up of.	**Sorting by One Attribute** Children sort objects according to one particular attribute. *You can help children begin the sorting by saying, "Find all the bumpy shapes."*	**Gathering and Organizing Data** Children continue to place actual objects, pictures of objects, or symbols in the appropriate columns of a 2- or 3-column graph. **Noticing and Describing Relationships** Children compare two groups and tell which has more or less than the other or whether the two groups have the same number. **Conducting Surveys** Children conduct surveys of their own and organize the data in their own ways.

	Creating the Environment See *Math Time: The Learning Environment.*	**Number** See *Developing Number Concepts:* Book Two (Ch. 1, 2, & 3) and Book Three (Ch. 1).	**Pattern** See *Developing Number Concepts:* Book One (Ch. 2).
End of the Year: (Apr., May, June)	**Self-Directed Exploration** *As children work with the materials over time, you will see how their creative work evolves.*	**Estimating to 50** *Occasionally, during teacher-directed activities, model organizing objects into groups of tens and ones.* **Adding and Subtracting** Children continue practicing addition and subtraction to develop ease and fluency. **Counting to 60 Through 100** Some children will be ready to begin organizing quantities into tens and ones during independent activities. Others will be counting and writing up to 100. **Comparing Quantities** Children compare numbers to 20.	**Creating and Extending Growing Patterns** *Continue to provide opportunities for children to explore growing patterns.* **Extending Number Patterns** *and* **Exploring Counting by Fives and Tens** Children continue to work with number patterns using the days-of-school number chart.

Measurement See *Developing Number Concepts: Book One* (Ch. 1 & 3) and *Book Three* (Ch. 1).	Geometry See *Understanding Geometry.*	Sorting See *Developing Number Concepts: Book One* (Ch. 1 & 3).	Data Collection See *Developing Number Concepts: Book One* (Ch. 3).
Using Non-Standard Units *Children continue to explore the idea of a unit of measure. They measure length, area, and weight using a variety of non-standard measuring tools.*	**Exploring Shapes and Three-Dimensional Objects** Continue to provide occasional opportunities for children to work with the geometry manipulatives using their own ideas. **Creating and Recording Designs and Shapes** Continue to provide opportunities for children to build and record the creations they make using various materials. **Filling in Shapes Using Smaller Shapes** Children use their knowledge of how shapes relate and how smaller shapes fill larger spaces by filling in outlines of figures with Pattern Blocks, tangrams, or Discovery Blocks. **Describing Shapes and Figures** Children describe various shapes and attributes using geometric terms. They continue to find shapes in their environment and then record what they find. **Sorting Shapes** Children continue to become familiar with the attributes of various shapes and three-dimensional objects by sorting them in a variety of ways. They describe the different ways in which they sorted. **Analyzing Three-Dimensional Figures** Children explore blocks in a variety of ways to discover which shapes the blocks are made up of.	**Sorting and Re-Sorting** Children find many different ways to sort a particular set of objects.	**Gathering and Organizing Data** Children participate in organizing data collected by the class. **Noticing and Describing Relationships** Children continue to compare two groups and tell which has more or less than the other or whether the two groups are the same in number. **Conducting Surveys** Children continue to conduct informal surveys and organize their data. Some children will be able to write what they notice about the data they collected.

An Overview of the Year's Planning Periods

T his overview highlights the concepts of number and pattern that will form the core of the first-grade math program. The school year has been divided into seven planning periods. The given time periods are offered simply as a point of reference. Adjust them to fit your own school calendar and the needs of your particular class. During each planning period, spend a day or two on other math experiences such as sorting, measurement, geometry, data collection, and problem solving. Occasionally, spend a week or two between planning periods on one of these other areas of mathematics.

First Planning Period: 6–8 weeks (Sept., Oct.)

It is important to establish the work environment at the beginning of the year through children's self–directed exploration of the math manipulatives. Have children prepare for understanding addition and subtraction by working with numbers to 10, strengthening their sense of number relationships, and developing ease in writing numerals.

Second Planning Period: 6–7 Weeks (Nov., Dec.)

The children work at independent-pattern stations copying, extending, and creating patterns at various levels of complexity. After several weeks, they work with numbers to 20 with an emphasis on developing number sense and writing numerals. They also interpret patterns using various manipulatives.

Third Planning Period: 3–4 Weeks (Dec., Jan.)

The children work to develop an understanding of the concepts of more and less. This helps them to build the sense of the number relationships that they need in order to add and subtract. Children begin to work with addition and subtraction through teacher-directed activities.

Fourth Planning Period: 5–6 Weeks (Jan., Feb.)

From now until the end of the school year, the processes of addition and subtraction become the major focus of the math period. Children read and write addition and subtraction equations and work with activities that help them differentiate between the plus (+) and minus (–) signs.

Fifth Planning Period: 4–6 Weeks (Feb., Mar.)

Through a wide variety of activities, children work to develop facility with number combinations to 10. They focus on particular numbers and learn the combinations that make up each of those numbers.

Sixth Planning Period: 4–6 Weeks (Mar., Apr.)

Children continue to practice addition and subtraction, applying various strategies as they work to develop ease and confidence with these processes.

Seventh Planning Period: 4–6 Weeks (May, June)

As the year comes to an end, children work with somewhat larger numbers, comparing numbers to 20 and, if they are ready, counting objects to 60 through 100. Children also explore growing geometric patterns and begin trying to identify number patterns.

A Typical First-Grade "Math Time"

1. Whole-Class Work: *Shorter Mini-Lesson* (5–10 minutes)

All the children gather on the rug. Math time begins with a short lesson that provides ongoing practice with these previously experienced concepts.

- Estimation (using a container that holds about 12 objects)
- Acting Out Word Problems (The children focus on interpreting the language used in each problem and on the equation that you write to record the problem.)

2. Preparation for Working with a Small Group

The teacher then asks a small group of children to stay in the rug area. She gives them a short task such as writing any of the numerals in their phone number or in their address on individual chalkboards. As they work, the teacher excuses the rest of the class, a few children at a time, to choose an independent-activity station at which to work.

3. Independent-Station Work (35–50 minutes)*

The class has been introduced to the following activities over a period of three or four days. The activities were made available as they were introduced so now they all are familiar to the children.

2: 1–16	Writing Equations with Counting Boards
2: 2–20	Number Shapes: Using Number Cubes
2: 2–23	Number Trains: Using Number Cubes
2: 2–14	Number Arrangements: Using Cubes
2: 2–15	Number Arrangements: Using Color Tiles
2: 2–16	Number Arrangements: Using Toothpicks
2: 3–15	Build-a-Floor Race
2: 3–21	Grab-Bag Addition Station
2: 3–22	Grab-Bag Subtraction Station

4. Teacher-Directed, Small-Group Focus Work (10–20 minutes)

The teacher works with a group of children who need to focus on number combinations of seven. She presents several of the following tasks, spending just three or four minutes on each.

2: 2–1	Snap It
2: 2–3	The Wall Game
2: 2–6	Grab-Bag Subtraction
2: 2–8	Working with Number Shapes

After the small-group lesson is over, the teacher excuses the children to choose an independent-activity station.

---

*Each activity number refers to book, chapter, and activity. For example, 2: 1–14 means book 2, chapter 1, activity 14. Notice whether each activity appears in Book One (1:), Book Two (2:), or Book Three (3:).

5. Teacher Observation of Children Working Independently

The teacher moves around the room observing and interacting with individual children.

6. Cleanup Time

After about 50 minutes of working independently, the children clean up their stations and meet back together again on the rug.

7. Whole-Class Work: Brief Discussion of Math Time (no longer than 5 minutes)

The class reviews what went on during math time.

First-Grade Planning Chart*

First Planning Period: 6–8 Weeks (Sept., Oct.)

Focus: Establishing the Work Environment, Strengthening Understanding of Beginning Number Concepts

Whole-Class Work: Mini-Lessons

Shorter Mini-Lesson	Longer Mini-Lesson
(5–10 minutes, 3 to 5 times a week)	(15–25 minutes, as needed)

Pattern Experiences 1: 2–1 Rhythmic Patterns 1: 2–2 People Patterns 1: 2–3 Patterns in the Environment **Beginning Number Patterns** 1: 2–20 Creating a Number Chart 1: 2–21 Looking for Patterns on the Calendar **Estimation Experiences to 20 and Beyond** **Number Talks: Instant Recognition** *Use the Tell-Me-Fast dot cards and the number shapes.*	**Number Sense and Numeral-Writing Practice** 1: 1–11 Peek and Count, Level 2 1: 1–17 Give and Take, Level 2 1: 1–18 Hiding One More 1: 1–19 Hiding One Less **Data Collection and Graphing** **Math and Literature**

Ongoing Independent-Station Work (35–50 minutes, 3 to 5 times a week)

Self-Directed Exploration Connecting cubes Color Tiles Wooden cubes Toothpicks Collections *Include any additional math materials you have available, such as Pattern Blocks, geoboards, geoblocks, scales, and containers.* **Introduce Math Manipulatives and Establish Expectations for Independent Work**	*After a few weeks, gradually introduce these stations.* **Counting, Writing Numerals, and Number Sense** 1: 1–21 Counting Boards, Levels 3 and 4 1: 1–29 Grab-Bag Counting Station, Level 2 1: 1–33 Grab a Handful 1: 1–36 How Long Is It? 1: 1–37 How Many Does It Hold? 1: 1–38 Sorting Colors 1: 1–39 Sorting Collections

* Each activity number refers to book, chapter, and activity. For example, 2: 1–14 means book 2, chapter 1, activity 14. Notice whether each activity appears in Book One (1:), Book Two (2:), or Book Three (3:).

Teacher-Directed, Small-Group Focus Work (10–20 minutes, 2 to 3 times a week)

Counting, Writing Numerals, and Number Sense
Choose several activities over time, using two to four of them during any one lesson.

Number Relationships

1: 1–8   Grow and Shrink
1: 1–10 Hunt for It
1: 1–13 Tell Me Fast
1: 1–14 Break It Up
1: 1–15 Tall and Short
1: 1–16 One More/One Less
1: 1–17 Give and Take
1: 1–20 Towers, Towers, Towers

Writing Numerals

1: 1–4   Counting Stories, Level 3
1: 1–11 Peek and Count, Level 2
1: 1–17 Give and Take, Level 2
1: 1–18 Hiding One More
1: 1–19 Hiding One Less

OR

Shared Experiences/Mathematical Events
(35–50 minutes, 1 or 2 times about every two weeks)

Intersperse work at independent stations with whole-class experiences.

Interpreting Rhythmic Patterns

1: 2–4   Interpreting Rhythmic Patterns with Connecting Cubes
          or Color Tiles
1: 2–5   Interpreting Rhythmic Patterns with Pattern Blocks
1: 2–6   Interpreting Rhythmic Patterns with Collections

First-Grade Planning Notes

First Planning Period: 6–8 Weeks (Sept., Oct.)

Focus: Establishing the Work Environment, Strengthening Understanding
of Beginning Number Concepts

Whole-Class Work: Mini-Lessons

You can present new concepts and review previously taught concepts by
spending just a few minutes at the beginning of each math period on
either a *Shorter Mini-Lesson* (5–10 minutes) or a *Longer Mini-Lesson*
(15–25 minutes).

Shorter Mini-Lesson

(5–10 minutes, 3 to 5 times a week)

Choose one to three of the following activities each day. Spend just a few minutes
on the activities before dismissing the children to work at independent stations.

Pattern Experiences

Present whole-group pattern experiences beginning on the first day of school.
Spend just two or three minutes on each. Work with a variety of patterns so that
children have the opportunity to generalize about the meaning of "pattern."

Present a variety of patterns. Vary the level of difficulty according to the
children's responses.

      1: 2–1   Rhythmic Patterns
      1: 2–2   People Patterns
      1: 2–3   Patterns in the Environment

Beginning Number Patterns

Each day, add one number to a 10×18 matrix in order to create a number chart.
After several days, the children should begin to see number patterns emerging.
Have them describe the patterns they notice.

      1: 2–20   Creating a Number Chart

Add numbers to the calendar each day, encouraging the children to look for
patterns and to make predictions.

      1: 2–21   Looking for Patterns on the Calendar

Estimation Experiences to 20 and Beyond

Materials: Assorted clear containers and various objects with which to fill them.

Every few weeks, two or three times a week, give the children opportunities to estimate the number of small objects that will fill a container. After children have made their estimates, have them count along with you as you place objects into the container, one by one, to find the actual number needed to fill it. When the container has been partially filled, children may change their estimates.

Number Talks:* Instant Recognition

Provide children with opportunities to practice identifying the number of a group of objects or dots without counting. Hold up the Tell-Me-Fast cards to display groups of dots or show the number shapes, or use the overhead projector to display groups of objects.

> 1: 1–13 Tell Me Fast

Longer Mini-Lesson
(15–25 minutes, as needed)

These lessons take a little more time than do the shorter mini-lessons because they require the children to use manipulatives. (On days in which you teach a longer mini-lesson, you will probably not have time to work with a small group.)

Numeral-Writing Practice

Provide children with opportunities to practice writing numerals while they develop a sense of number and relationships. You may wish to begin with some teacher-directed lessons on numeral formation and then move on to activities that allow children to use this skill to communicate their thinking. Reinforce instant recognition by encouraging the children to quickly identify the number of items in any of the small groups of objects they are working with.

> 1: 1–11 Peek and Count, Level 2
> 1: 1–17 Give and Take, Level 2
> 1: 1–18 Hiding One More
> 1: 1–19 Hiding One Less

Data Collection and Graphing

Occasionally, pose a question that can be answered with data that the children provide. The data should be organized into graphs to highlight relationships.

Math and Literature

---

* Number Talks are experiences that allow children to solve addition, subtraction, multiplication, and division problems in a variety of ways, generally using number relationships. The children should be given opportunities to describe the ways they solve the problems. This begins with instant recognition of small groups. Make sure you present a variety of problems for children to solve. See the video series *Thinking with Numbers* published by Educational Enrichment, Norman, OK, for more information about number talks.

Ongoing Independent-Station Work
(35–50 minutes, 3 to 5 times a week)

Self-Directed Exploration*

Materials: Connecting cubes, wooden cubes, Color Tiles, toothpicks, collections, and Pattern Blocks. Include any additional math materials that you plan to use for instruction.

Establishing routines and expectations is the most important work for the beginning of the school year. If the children are going to accomplish all that they can throughout the year, they need to learn what it means to work hard. They also need to learn how to make choices and how to get along with the other children in the class. Mathematics work time for the young child must start with the exploration of the math manipulatives. Once children are familiar with these they will be prepared for the work they will be asked to do later on. This time is critical to the children as they need to work with manipulatives using their own ideas before they can focus on specific activities. While all the children will be exploring these manipulatives on their own, you will be free to focus on developing the work environment.

Introduce Math Manipulatives and Establish Expectations for Independent Work

Introduce the manipulatives gradually over a period of several days, making sure the children understand how to use them appropriately. Go over the rules and procedures for cleaning up. (See "Establishing the Learning Environment" on p. xxii.)

After the manipulatives have been introduced, have a few children deliver them to the various stations around the room. Excuse the rest of the children, a few at a time, to choose where they would like to work. Observe and interact with them while they are at work, commenting on their work and redirecting them, if necessary. At the end of the math period, spend a minute or two discussing the good, hard work you have observed and/or reminding the children of any behaviors that need to be changed.

Counting, Writing Numerals, and Number Sense

Materials: Concept Development Packets—each set up to accommodate six children.

After several weeks, when the children have learned how to work independently, begin introducing them to activities that allow them to strengthen their counting and numeral-writing skills. While it is true that most children enter first grade capable of counting at least to 20 and capable of writing numerals to 10, it is necessary to make sure that they also have the opportunity to develop a strong

* See *Math Time: The Learning Environment* for a detailed look at self-directed exploration.

sense of number and number relationships. It is also important for them to develop ease in writing numerals. Even when first graders work with tasks they may have experienced in kindergarten, they are now working at a higher level. Generally, kindergarteners focus simply on counting and first-graders pay more attention to the amounts they are working with. These activities can help children move from one-to-one counting to recognizing groups, noticing relationships, and using what they know to figure out what they do not know. The children should work on making reasonable estimates and/or on changing their estimates as they get new information.

1: 1–21   Counting Boards, Levels 3 and 4
1: 1–29   Grab-Bag Counting Station, Level 2
1: 1–33   Grab a Handful
1: 1–36   How Long Is It?
1: 1–37   How Many Does It Hold?
1: 1–38   Sorting Colors
1: 1–39   Sorting Collections

You can provide opportunities for the children to work with the independent counting activities in the following ways.

1. Introduce a few counting activities during the exploration time, allowing children to work with the activities in which they are interested.
2. Work with a small group of children during exploration time while the rest of the class is busy working with the math manipulatives.
3. Occasionally present the counting activities in place of exploration time.

Teacher-Directed, Small-Group Focus Work
(10–20 minutes, 2 to 3 times a week)

It is important to work with children having similar needs in order to help them focus on developing their understanding of math concepts. Give children a variety of experiences, choosing from the following activities. Use two to four activities for a few minutes each during any one lesson.

In the beginning of the year, if you have no other adults in the room to assist you, you may want to work with small groups at another time of day. For example, you may have a time during which the children work in small groups on various projects. One group may be working with clay, another with a cut-and-paste project, while still another group is working with you on math. Later in the year, when the children are better able to work independently, you will be free to work with small groups during math time.

Counting, Writing Numerals, and Number Sense

Materials: You can do any of the recommended activities if you have individual chalkboards, chalk, and erasers on hand along with connecting cubes, Color Tiles, collections (or other counters), and the following items in the Teacher Tub of Materials available to use as needed.

Teacher Tub of Materials

Working-space papers (1 per child)
Counting boards (1 per child)
Large dot cubes (marked with 1–6 dots)
Small plastic bowls (10–12)

Number Relationships

These activities help children focus on number relationships.

1: 1–8	Grow and Shrink
1: 1–10	Hunt for It
1: 1–13	Tell Me Fast
1: 1–14	Break It Up
1: 1–15	Tall and Short
1: 1–16	One More/One Less
1: 1–17	Give and Take
1: 1–20	Towers, Towers, Towers

As you observe the children, make note of how they work with the activities. Some children will rely on counting and will then double-check their answers to make sure they are correct. Others will see the relationships and/or count on.

Writing Numerals

These activities help children focus on writing numerals at the same time they are developing number relationships.

1: 1–4	Counting Stories, Level 3
1: 1–11	Peek and Count, Level 2
1: 1–17	Give and Take, Level 2
1: 1–18	Hiding One More
1: 1–19	Hiding One Less

Shared Experiences/Mathematical Events
(35–50 minutes, 1 or 2 times about every two weeks)

You can vary the usual routine by continuing to work with previously intro-duced concepts or you may present new concepts through occasional whole-class experiences. The following activities generally require the entire math period (since the children work with manipulatives) and so they will occupy the time otherwise spent at independent stations.

Interpreting Rhythmic Patterns

Materials: Connecting cubes, Color Tiles, or Pattern Blocks

Shortly after the beginning of the school year, you can present pattern-interpretation lessons to the children. Continue to give children experiences in occasionally interpreting patterns for many weeks—gradually increasing the level of difficulty.

> 1: 2–4   Interpreting Rhythmic Patterns with Connecting Cubes or Color Tiles
>
> 1: 2–5   Interpreting Rhythmic Patterns with Pattern Blocks
>
> 1: 2–6   Interpreting Rhythmic Patterns with Collections

Provide Additional Math Experiences as Time Allows

This guide focuses on planning for the development of number and pattern concepts. You will also want to provide additional math experiences for your children. On some days, instead of having children work with the independent stations, you may have them work on solving a problem presented through literature. From time to time you may spend a week focusing on geometry or sorting. During this first planning period you will not need to present additional math experiences since self-directed exploration provides children with informal opportunities to work with sorting, geometry, and measurement concepts. Later on in the year, you will need to integrate these other experiences into your math time.

First-Grade Planning Chart

Second Planning Period: 6–7 Weeks (Nov., Dec.)

Focus: Pattern, Numbers to 20

Whole-Class Work: Mini-Lessons	
Shorter Mini-Lesson (5–10 minutes, 3 to 5 times a week)	**Longer Mini-Lesson** (15–25 minutes, as needed)
Pattern Experiences 1: 2–1 Rhythmic Patterns 1: 2–2 People Patterns 1: 2–3 Patterns in the Environment **Number Patterns** 1: 2–20 Creating a Number Chart 1: 2–21 Looking for Patterns on 　　　　　the Calendar **Estimation Experiences to 30** **Number Talks: Instant Recognition** *Use the Tell-Me-Fast dot cards and the number shapes.* **Informal Counting and Recording Numerals to 20**	**Counting and Numeral Recognition to 20** 1: 1–7 Grab-Bag Counting, Ext. 1: 1–14 Break It Up, Ext. 1: 1–16 One More/One Less, Ext. 1: 1–17 Give and Take, Ext. **Data Collection and Graphing**

Ongoing Independent-Station Work (35–50 minutes, 3 to 5 times a week)

Pattern Stations

Begin by having the children use task cards. Later, provide opportunities for them to create and record patterns.

1: 2–10   Pattern Trains
1: 2–11   Color-Tile Patterns
1: 2–12   Arrangement Patterns
1: 2–13   Collections Patterns

For this activity, use whatever manipulatives you have available, such as buttons, bread tags, and washers and nuts.

1: 2–14   Rhythmic-Patterns Task Cards
1: 2–15   ABC-Patterns Task Cards

After a few weeks, gradually replace the pattern stations with the following stations.

Counting and Numeral Recognition to 20

1: 1–22   Creations Station, Ext.
1: 1–30   Shape Puzzles, Ext.
1: 1–31   Line Puzzles, Ext.
1: 1–33   Grab a Handful, Ext.
1: 1–35   Give-and-Take Station, Ext.
1: 1–36   How Long Is It? Ext.
1: 1–37   How Many Does It Hold? Ext.
1: 1–38   Sorting Colors, Ext.
1: 1–39   Sorting Collections, Ext.

Teacher-Directed, Small-Group Focus Work (10–20 minutes, 2 to 3 times a week)

Choose several activities over time, using two to four of them during any one lesson.

Counting and Numeral Recognition to 20

1: 1–7   Grab-Bag Counting, Ext.
1: 1–14 Break It Up, Ext.
1: 1–16 One More/One Less, Ext.
1: 1–17 Give and Take, Ext.

Extending Pattern Experiences

Use these activities for children who are ready for a challenge.

1: 2–9   Creating Patterns, Ext.
1: 2–16 Exploring Growing Patterns

OR

Shared Experiences/Mathematical Events
(35–50 minutes, 1 or 2 times about every two weeks)

Interpreting and Creating Patterns

1: 2–4 through 1: 2–6, the Interpreting Rhythmic Patterns activities

Begin with connecting cubes, Color Tiles, and/or Pattern Blocks. Later, add collections.

1: 2–9   Creating Patterns
1: 2–18 Creating Growing Patterns

Provide Additional Math Experiences as Time Allows

- Problem Solving/Math and Literature
- Sorting
- Geometry

First-Grade Planning Notes
Second Planning Period: 6–7 Weeks (Nov., Dec.)

Focus: Pattern, Number to 20

Whole-Class Work: Mini-Lessons

You can present new concepts and review previously taught concepts by spending just a few minutes at the beginning of each math period on either a *Shorter Mini-Lesson* (5–10 minutes) or a *Longer Mini-Lesson* (15–25 minutes).

Shorter Mini-Lesson
(5–10 minutes, 3 to 5 times a week)

Pattern Experiences

Continue presenting a variety of patterns, varying the level of difficulty over time.

> 1: 2–1   Rhythmic Patterns
> 1: 2–2   People Patterns
> 1: 2–3   Patterns in the Environment

Number Patterns

Continue adding a number each day to a 10×18 matrix in order to create a number chart. Have the children describe the emerging patterns as they notice them.

> 1: 2–20   Creating a Number Chart

Continue adding numbers to the calendar, encouraging children to look for patterns and to make predictions.

> 1: 2–21   Looking for Patterns on the Calendar

Estimation Experiences to 30

Materials: Assorted clear containers and various objects with which to fill them.

Continue providing estimation experiences every few weeks, two or three times a week. As you fill containers to do each actual count, make sure you give the children an opportunity to change their minds and revise their estimates. Make note of their responses. Do their estimates get closer to the actual counts? What do their revised estimates tell you about their sense of number?

Number Talks: Instant Recognition

Continue to provide children with opportunities to practice identifying the number of a group of objects or dots without counting using the overhead projector to display groups of objects, the Tell-Me-Fast cards, and number shapes.

Informal Counting and Recording Numerals to 20

You can help children who need to work on counting to 20 by taking advantage of counting opportunities as they arise. While everyone can participate in the counting, be sure that the counting sequence fits the needs of those children who need the help.

Longer Mini-Lesson

(15–25 minutes, as needed)

Counting and Numeral Recognition to 20

Give the children the counting practice they need by providing them with the listed activities. When children first learn to count, they focus more on the action of counting and less on developing a sense of number or number relationships. These teacher-directed activities will help focus children on the relationships.

> 1: 1–7   Grab-Bag Counting, Ext.
> 1: 1–14   Break It Up, Ext.
> 1: 1–16   One More, One Less, Ext.
> 1: 1–17   Give and Take, Ext.

Data Collection and Graphing

Sometime during this planning period, give the children opportunities to collect data and to organize their data into graphs.

Ongoing Independent-Station Work

(35–50 minutes, 3 to 5 times a week)

Introduce Pattern Stations

Materials: Concept Development Packets—each set up to accommodate six children.

The amount of time during which children will benefit from exploring pattern through the pattern stations will vary depending on children's past experiences. Watch to make sure that your children are challenged by the activities. At first, have the children work with the task cards alone. For some children, simply copying and extending the patterns will be challenging enough. As they become ready for more challenging work, encourage them to choose the more complex pattern task cards and to create their own patterns. Occasionally, children can record their patterns. Some will be ready to extend a task by labeling the patterns with ABCs.

1: 2–10	Pattern Trains
1: 2–11	Color-Tile Patterns
1: 2–12	Arrangement Patterns
1: 2–13	Collections Patterns
1: 2–14	Rhythmic-Patterns Task Cards
1: 2–15	ABC-Patterns Task Cards

Counting and Numeral Recognition to 20

Materials: Concept Development Packets—each set up to accommodate six children.

After the children have worked with pattern for several weeks, gradually replace the pattern stations with extensions to the familiar number stations that they worked with earlier in the year. During the earlier part of the year, children worked with numbers to 10. Now they should work with numbers to 20.

Many of the children will already be able to count to 20. The purpose of these tasks is to go beyond simply counting to make sure that children are accurate, confident, and able to write the numerals to 20 with ease. They should also begin developing a sense of quantities and number relationships. Estimating answers and then checking results will help develop a sense of quantity and relationships. (You can also extend some of these activities by asking the children to make comparisons. See Book One, Chapter Three.)

1: 1–22	Creations Station, Ext.
1: 1–30	Shape Puzzles, Ext.
1: 1–31	Line Puzzles, Ext.
1: 1–33	Grab a Handful, Ext.
1: 1–35	Give-and-Take Station, Ext.
1: 1–36	How Long Is It? Ext.
1: 1–37	How Many Does It Hold? Ext.
1: 1–38	Sorting Colors, Ext.
1: 1–39	Sorting Collections, Ext.

Teacher-Directed, Small-Group Focus Work
(10–20 minutes, 2 to 3 times a week)

Materials: You can do any of the recommended activities if you have individual chalkboards, chalk, and erasers on hand along with connecting cubes, Color Tiles, collections (or other counters), and the following items in the Teacher Tub of Materials available to use as needed.

Teacher Tub of Materials

> Working-space papers (1 per child)
> Counting boards (1 per child)
> Paper lunch bags
> Small plastic bowls (8–10)

Counting and Numeral Recognition to 20

Provide extra practice for those children who need to develop facility in counting to 20. Give children a variety of experiences, choosing from the recommended activities. Spend a few minutes on each of two or three activities during any one lesson.

> 1: 1–7   Grab-Bag Counting, Ext.
> 1: 1–14 Break It Up, Ext.
> 1: 1–16 One More/One Less, Ext.
> 1: 1–17 Give and Take, Ext.

Extending Pattern Experiences

Some children will be ready for more challenging pattern activities during small-group lessons.

> 1: 2–9   Creating Patterns, Ext.
> 1: 2–16 Exploring Growing Patterns

> **OR**

Shared Experiences/Mathematical Events
(35–50 minutes, 1 or 2 times about every two weeks)

Interpreting and Creating Patterns

Materials: Connecting cubes, Pattern Blocks, Color Tiles, and collections

Provide opportunities for the children to use the materials worked with previously, (Color Tiles, connecting cubes, and Pattern Blocks), but also add collections to provide them with a greater challenge.

> 1: 2–4 through 1: 2–6, the Interpreting Rhythmic Patterns activities

Give children opportunities to create their own patterns—either repeating patterns or growing patterns. Model growing patterns for them and encourage those children who can create their own growing patterns to do so. (Do not worry if some children do not yet understand the difference between the two kinds of patterns.)

> 1: 2–9   Creating Patterns
> 1: 2–18 Creating Growing Patterns

Provide Additional Math Experiences as Time Allows

- Problem Solving/Math and Literature
- Sorting
- Geometry

First-Grade Planning Chart

Third Planning Period: 3–4 Weeks (Dec., Jan.)

Focus: The Concepts of More and Less

Whole-Class Work: Mini-Lessons	
Shorter Mini-Lesson (5–10 minutes, 3 to 5 times a week)	**Longer Mini-Lesson** (15–25 minutes, as needed)

Pattern Experiences 1: 2–1 Rhythmic Patterns **Number Patterns** 1: 2–20 Creating a Number Chart 1: 2–21 Looking for Patterns on the Calendar **Estimation Experiences to 30** **Number Talks: Instant Recognition, Plus or Minus 1 or 2** *Use the Tell-Me-Fast dot cards and the number shapes.* ***More* and *Less*** 1: 3–1 Is It More or Is It Less? 1: 3–6 Number Cards **Addition and Subtraction Stories** 2: 1–1 Acting Out Stories: Using Real Things 2: 1–2 Acting Out Stories: Using Fantasies 2: 1–4 Modeling Addition and Subtraction Equations	***More* and *Less*** 1: 3–8 More-or-Less Counting Stories 1: 3–9 Build a Stack 1: 3–10 Grow, Shrink, and Compare **Addition and Subtraction Stories** 2: 1–3 Acting Out Stories: Using Counters 2: 1–4 Modeling Addition and Subtraction Equations **Data Collection and Graphing** 1: 3–5 Graph and See

Ongoing Independent-Station Work (35–50 minutes, 3 to 5 times a week)	
***More-and-Less* Stations** *Begin by having children use more/less/same cards to label the groups. Later, allow those who are ready to record on worksheets.* 1: 3–13 Stack, Tell, Spin, and Win 1: 3–14 Two-Color Grab-Bag Station 1: 3–15 Comparing Lengths	1: 3–16 Comparing Shape Puzzles 1: 3–17 Comparing Line Puzzles 1: 3–18 Comparing Handfuls 1: 3–19 Comparing Containers 1: 3–20 Sort and Compare Colors 1: 3–21 Comparing Numbers 1: 3–22 Counting Boards: Changing Numbers

Teacher-Directed, Small-Group Focus Work (10–20 minutes, 2 to 3 times a week)

Choose several activities over time, using two to four of them during any one lesson.

More and Less

1: 3–1   Is It More or Is It Less?
1: 3–2   Stacks
1: 3–3   Two-Color Grab Bag
1: 3–4   Spin and Peek
1: 3–5   Graph and See
1: 3–7   More-or-Less Spin It
1: 3–8   More-or-Less Counting Stories
1: 3–10 Grow, Shrink, and Compare

Practicing Writing More and Less Using Natural Language

1: 3–11 More or Less
1: 3–12 Roll and Spin

OR

Shared Experiences/Mathematical Events
(35–50 minutes, 1 or 2 times about every two weeks)

Intersperse work at independent stations with whole-class experiences.

Interpreting and Creating Patterns

1: 2–4 through 1: 2–6, the Interpreting Rhythmic Patterns activities
1: 2–9   Creating Patterns
1: 2–18 Creating Growing Patterns

Provide Additional Math Experiences as Time Allows

- Problem Solving/Math and Literature
- Sorting
- Geometry

First-Grade Planning Notes
Third Planning Period: 3–4 Weeks (Dec., Jan.)

Focus: The Concepts of More and Less

Whole-Class Work: Mini-Lessons

You can present new concepts and review previously taught concepts by spending just a few minutes at the beginning of each math period on either a *Shorter Mini-Lesson* (5–10 minutes) or a *Longer Mini-Lesson* (15–25 minutes).

Shorter Mini-Lesson
(5–10 minutes, 3 to 5 times a week)

Pattern Experiences

Continue presenting a variety of patterns, varying the level of difficulty over time.

> 1: 2–1   Rhythmic Patterns

Number Patterns

Continue adding a number each day to a 10 × 18 matrix in order to create a number chart. Have the children describe the emerging patterns as they notice them.

> 1: 2–20   Creating a Number Chart

Continue adding numbers to the calendar, encouraging children to look for patterns and to make predictions.

> 1: 2–21   Looking for Patterns on the Calendar

Estimation Experiences to 30

Materials: Assorted clear containers and various objects with which to fill them. Assorted lengths of yarn, Color Tiles, toothpicks, and/or large paper clips.

Continue to provide opportunities for the children to estimate and check their estimates. Vary the experience by having children estimate the length of a piece of yarn in terms of a number of objects such as toothpicks, Color Tiles, or large paper clips. Then, after you measure a portion of the yarn with the chosen object, allow children to revise their estimates of the length of the whole piece of yarn.

Number Talks: Instant Recognition, Plus or Minus 1 or 2

Continue to provide children with opportunities to practice identifying the number of a group of objects, dots, or number shapes without counting. For each group, ask the children to tell how many there would be if you added one more, took one away, added two more, or took two away. Write the symbols to record what the children describe so that they begin to associate numbers with these arrangements. For example, if a child said, "I knew it was five because I saw three dots and two dots and that makes five," you would write "3 + 2 = 5." Then if you asked, "How many would there be if we added one more?" and a child responded, "Five and one more makes six," you would write "5 + 1 = 6."

More and _Less_

Ask children to compare quantities by identifying which is more and which is less.

        1: 3–1   Is It More or Is It Less?
        1: 3–6   Number Cards

Addition and Subtraction Stories

Introduce children to the processes of addition and subtraction through the acting out of word problems. When most of the children can easily act out simple addition and subtraction problems, begin modeling the writing of addition and subtraction equations.

        2: 1–1   Acting Out Stories: Using Real Things
        2: 1–2   Acting Out Stories: Using Fantasies
        2: 1–4   Modeling Addition and Subtraction Equations

Longer Mini-Lesson

(15–25 minutes, as needed)

More and _Less_

Give children opportunities to compare numbers and develop the language used to describe number relationships using activities that involve the use of manipulatives.

        1: 3–8   More-or-Less Counting Stories
        1: 3–9   Build a Stack
        1: 3–10 Grow, Shrink, and Compare

Addition and Subtraction Stories

Occasionally have the children act out addition and subtraction stories using counters.

        2: 1–3   Acting Out Stories: Using Counters
        2: 1–4   Modeling Addition and Subtraction Equations

Data Collection and Graphing

Sometime during this planning period, give the children opportunities to collect data and to organize their data into graphs. Such graphs provide children with important opportunities to compare real-world numerical data.

> 1: 3–5   Graph and See

Ongoing Independent-Station Work

(35–50 minutes, 3 to 5 times a week)

More-and-*Less* Stations

Materials: Concept Development Packets—each set up to accommodate six children.

During this time, the children will focus on the relationships between numbers by working with the more-and-less activities. At first, the children will use the more/less/same cards to compare the groups. Later, those who are ready can record their findings on worksheets.

> 1: 3–13   Stack, Tell, Spin, and Win
> 1: 3–14   Two-Color Grab-Bag Station
> 1: 3–15   Comparing Lengths
> 1: 3–16   Comparing Shape Puzzles
> 1: 3–17   Comparing Line Puzzles
> 1: 3–18   Comparing Handfuls
> 1: 3–19   Comparing Containers
> 1: 3–20   Sort and Compare Colors
> 1: 3–21   Comparing Numbers
> 1: 3–22   Counting Boards: Changing Numbers

Teacher-Directed, Small-Group Focus Work

(10–20 minutes, 2 to 3 times a week)

You can use the following activities to help children focus their attention on the relationships between numbers. These activities can be appropriate for all of your children if you vary the size of the numbers and/or vary the kind of questions you ask. Some children will be focused on determining which quantities are more or less than others. A few children will be ready to answer the questions "How many more?" and "How many less?"

More **and** *Less*

Materials: You can do any of the recommended activities if you have connecting cubes, Color Tiles, collections (or other counters), and the Teacher Tub of Materials available to use as needed.

Teacher Tub of Materials

Working-space papers (1 per child)
Counting boards (1 per child)
Small plastic bowls (1 per child)
Paper lunch bags
More-or-Less Spinner

1: 3–1   Is It More or Is It Less?
1: 3–2   Stacks
1: 3–3   Two-Color Grab Bag
1: 3–4   Spin and Peek
1: 3–5   Graph and See
1: 3–7   More-or-Less Spin It
1: 3–8   More-or-Less Counting Stories
1: 3–10 Grow, Shrink, and Compare

Practicing Writing *More* and *Less* Using Natural Language

Children can practice using informal language to record the relationships between numbers using these activities. Rather than writing the more-than and less-than symbols, the children should write the words "is more than" and "is less than" to record the comparisons.

1: 3–11 More or Less
1: 3–12 Roll and Spin

Shared Experiences/Mathematical Events
(35–50 minutes, 1 or 2 times about every two weeks)

Continue to work with previously introduced concepts or present new concepts through occasional whole-class experiences.

Interpreting and Creating Patterns

1: 2–4 through 1: 2–6, the Interpreting Rhythmic Patterns activities
1: 2–9 Creating Patterns
1: 2–18 Creating Growing Patterns

Provide Additional Math Experiences as Time Allows

- Problem Solving/Math and Literature
- Sorting
- Measurement

First-Grade Planning Chart

Fourth Planning Period: 5–6 Weeks (Jan., Feb.)

Focus: The Processes of Addition and Subtraction, Distinguishing Between the Plus (+) and Minus (–) Signs

Whole-Class Work: Mini-Lessons	
Shorter Mini-Lesson (5–10 minutes, 3 to 5 times a week)	**Longer Mini-Lesson** (15–25 minutes, as needed)

Pattern Experiences 1: 2–1 Rhythmic Patterns	**Addition and Subtraction Stories** 2: 1–3 Acting Out Stories: Using Counters 2: 1–5 Acting Out Stories To Go with Equations 2: 1–10 Writing Stories To Go with Equations
Number Patterns 1: 2–20 Creating a Number Chart 1: 2–21 Looking for Patterns on the Calendar	
Estimation Experiences to 30	**Distinguishing Between the Plus (+) and Minus (–) Signs** 2: 1–6 Roll and Count 2: 1–7 Listen and Count 2: 1–8 Grow and Shrink: Using the Plus (+) and Minus (–) Signs
Number Talks: Instant Recognition, Plus or Minus 1 or 2 *Use the Tell-Me-Fast dot cards and the number shapes.*	
More* and *Less 1: 3–1 Is It More or Is It Less? 1: 3–6 Number Cards	**Adding and Subtracting** 2: 2–8 Working with Number Shapes 2: 2–9 Number Shapes: On and Off 2: 2–10 Working with Number Trains 2: 2–11 Number Trains: On and Off 2: 2–12 Counting Boards: Number-Combination Stories
Addition and Subtraction Stories 2: 1–1 Acting Out Stories: Using Real Things 2: 1–2 Acting Out Stories: Using Fantasies 2: 1–4 Modeling Addition and Subtraction Equations	**Learning to Write Equations** 2: 1–9 Writing Equations To Label Addition and Subtraction Stories *Begin with Level 1. After a few days, move to Level 2.*
	Data Collection and Graphing

Ongoing Independent-Station Work (35–50 minutes, 3 to 5 times a week)

Distinguishing Between the Plus (+) and Minus (–) Signs

2: 1–12   Counting Boards: Reading Equations
2: 1–13   Race to Ten
2: 1–14   Plus-and-Minus Train
2: 1–15   Clear the Deck

Finding Number Combinations

2: 2–18   Counting Boards: Making Up Number-Combination Stories, Level 1
2: 2–19   Number-Shape Arrangements, Level 1
2: 2–20   Number Shapes: Using Number Cubes, Level 1
2: 2–22   Number-Train Arrangements, Level 1
2: 2–23   Number Trains: Using Number Cubes

Writing Equations Independently

2: 1–16   Writing Equations with Counting Boards

If you have children who are ready for a challenge, use some of these activities:

2: 1–17   Writing Stories To Match Equations
2: 2–18   Counting Boards: Making Up Number-Combination Stories, Level 2
2: 2–19   Number-Shape Arrangements, Level 2
2: 2–20   Number Shapes: Using Number Cubes, Level 2
2: 2–23   Number Trains: Using Number Cubes, Level 2
2: 3–20   Counting Boards: Think and Write

Teacher-Directed, Small-Group Focus Work (10–20 minutes, 2 to 3 times a week)

Choose several activities over time, using two to four of them during any one lesson.

Distinguishing Between the Plus (+) and Minus (–) Signs

2: 1–6   Roll and Count
2: 1–7   Listen and Count
2: 1–8   Grow and Shrink: Using the Plus (+) and Minus (–) Signs

Finding Number Combinations

2: 2–8   Working with Number Shapes
2: 2–9   Number Shapes: On and Off
2: 2–10   Working with Number Trains
2: 2–11   Number Trains: On and Off
2: 2–12   Counting Boards: Number-Combination Stories

If you have children who are ready for a challenge, work with them using some of the following:

Reviewing Number Combinations

2: 3–6   What Do You Think? Using Counting Boards
2: 3–7   What Do You Think? Using Grab Bags
2: 3–8   What Do You Think? Using Tubs
2: 3–9   Let's Pretend: Grab Bags
2: 3–10   Let's Pretend: Counting Boards
2: 3–11   Let's Pretend: Number Trains
2: 3–12   Let's Pretend: Number Shapes

OR

Shared Experiences/Mathematical Events
(35–50 minutes, 1 or 2 times about every two weeks)

Intersperse work at independent stations with whole-class experiences.

Provide Additional Math Experiences as Time Allows

■ Problem Solving/Math and Literature   ■ Geometry

First-Grade Planning Notes

Fourth Planning Period: 5–6 Weeks (Jan., Feb.)

Focus: The Processes of Addition and Subtraction, Distinguishing Between the Plus (+) and Minus (–) Signs, Finding Number Combinations

Whole-Class Work: Mini-Lessons

You can present new concepts and review previously taught concepts by spending just a few minutes at the beginning of each math period on either a *Shorter Mini-Lesson* (5–10 minutes) or a *Longer Mini-Lesson* (15–25 minutes).

Shorter Mini-Lesson

Pattern Experiences

Continue presenting a variety of patterns, varying the level of difficulty over time.

> 1: 2–1   Rhythmic Patterns

Number Patterns

Continue adding a number each day to a 10×18 matrix in order to create a number chart. Have the children describe the emerging patterns as they notice them.

> 1: 2–20   Creating a Number Chart

Continue adding numbers to the calendar, encouraging children to look for patterns and to make predictions about the next numbers in each pattern.

> 1: 2–21   Looking for Patterns on the Calendar

Estimation Experiences to 30

Materials: Assorted clear containers and various objects with which to fill them. Assorted lengths of yarn, Color Tiles, and toothpicks and/or large paper clips.

Continue to provide opportunities for the children to estimate and check their estimates. Sometimes, have them estimate how much a container will hold. Other times, have them estimate the length of a piece of yarn in terms of a number of small objects.

Number Talks: Instant Recognition, Plus or Minus 1 or 2

Continue to provide children with opportunities to practice identifying the number of a group of objects, dots, or number shapes without counting. Also continue asking the children to add one or two more to each group and to take away one or two. Write the symbols to record what the children describe so that they begin to associate numbers with these arrangements.

More* and *Less

Continue to focus the children's attention on the relationships between numbers by having them compare quantities.

       1: 3–1   Is It More or Is It Less?
       1: 3–6   Number Cards

Addition and Subtraction Stories

Continue to provide opportunities for children to act out addition and subtraction stories. Record the related addition and subtraction equations.

       2: 1–1   Acting Out Stories: Using Real Things
       2: 1–2   Acting Out Stories: Using Fantasies
       2: 1–4   Modeling Addition and Subtraction Equations

Longer Mini-Lesson
(15–25 minutes, as needed)

Occasionally spend a little extra time on those lessons that require the children to use manipulatives.

Addition and Subtraction Stories

The children will experience addition and subtraction in a variety of ways. They will act out stories using counters and they will become familiar with addition and subtraction signs and equations.

       2: 1–3   Acting Out Stories: Using Counters
       2: 1–5   Acting Out Stories To Go with Equations
       2: 1–10   Writing Stories To Go with Equations

Distinguishing Between the Plus (+) and Minus (–) Signs

       2: 1–6   Roll and Count
       2: 1–7   Listen and Count
       2: 1–8   Grow and Shrink: Using the Plus (+) and Minus (–) Signs

Finding Number Combinations

2: 2–8   Working with Number Shapes
2: 2–9   Number Shapes: On and Off
2: 2–10 Working with Number Trains
2: 2–11 Number Trains: On and Off
2: 2–12 Counting Boards: Number-Combination Stories

Learning to Write Equations

Prepare the children for the reading and interpreting of addition and subtraction equations that they will do during independent-station time.

2: 1–9   Writing Equations To Label Addition and Subtraction Stories

Data Collection and Graphing

Sometime during this planning period, give the children opportunities to collect data and to organize their data into graphs.

Ongoing Independent-Station Work
(35–50 minutes, 3 to 5 times a week)

Distinguishing Between the Plus (+) and Minus (–) Signs

Have the children practice reading and interpreting equations using the counting boards. Gradually introduce other activities designed to focus the children's attention on the plus and minus signs.

2: 1–12 Counting Boards: Reading Equations
2: 1–13 Race to Ten
2: 1–14 Plus-and-Minus Train
2: 1–15 Clear the Deck

Finding Number Combinations

2: 2–18 Counting Boards: Making Up Number-Combination Stories, Level 1
2: 2–19 Number-Shape Arrangements, Level 1
2: 2–20 Number Shapes: Using Number Cubes, Level 1
2: 2–22 Number-Train Arrangements, Level 1
2: 2–23 Number Trains: Using Number Cubes

Writing Equations Independently

Once the children know how to write equations independently, you can add the following activities to the independent stations.

2: 1–16 Writing Equations with Counting Boards
2: 1–17 Writing Stories To Match Equations
2: 2–18 Counting Boards: Making Up Number-Combination Stories, Level 2

2: 2–19 Number-Shape Arrangements, Level 2
2: 2–20 Number Shapes: Using Number Cubes, Level 2
2: 2–23 Number Trains: Using Number Cubes, Level 2
2: 3–20 Counting Boards: Think and Write

Teacher-Directed, Small-Group Focus Work
(10–20 minutes, 2 to 3 times a week)

Distinguishing Between the Plus (+) and Minus (–) Signs

Materials: You can do any of the recommended activities if you have connecting cubes, Color Tiles, collections (or other counters), and the Teacher Tub of Materials available to use as needed.

Teacher Tub of Materials

Working-space papers (1 per child)
Large number cubes (marked 1–6)
Bell or xylophone
Counting Boards (1 per child)
Number Shapes
Paper lunch bags
Small plastic bowls or margarine tubs

2: 1–6   Roll and Count
2: 1–7   Listen and Count
2: 1–8   Grow and Shrink: Using the Plus (+) and Minus (–) Signs
2: 2–8   Working with Number Shapes
2: 2–9   Number Shapes: On and Off
2: 2–10 Working with Number Trains
2: 2–11 Number Trains: On and Off
2: 2–12 Counting Boards: Number-Combination Stories
2: 3–6   What Do You Think? Using Counting Boards
2: 3–7   What Do You Think? Using Grab Bags
2: 3–8   What Do You Think? Using Tubs
2: 3–9   Let's Pretend: Grab Bags
2: 3–10 Let's Pretend: Counting Boards
2: 3–11 Let's Pretend: Number Trains
2: 3–12 Let's Pretend: Number Shapes

Shared Experiences/Mathematical Events
(35–50 minutes, 1 or 2 times about every two weeks)

Provide Additional Math Experiences as Time Allows

- Problem Solving/Math and Literature
- Geometry

First-Grade Planning Chart

Fifth Planning Period: 4–6 Weeks (Feb., Mar.)

Focus: Number Combinations

Whole-Class Work: Mini-Lessons	
Shorter Mini-Lesson (5–10 minutes, 3 to 5 times a week)	**Longer Mini-Lesson** (15–25 minutes, as needed)
Pattern Experiences 1: 2–1 Rhythmic Patterns **Number Patterns** 1: 2–20 Creating a Number Chart 1: 2–21 Looking for Patterns on the Calendar **Estimation Experiences to 30 or Beyond** **Number Talks: Instant Recognition of Number Combinations** 2: 3–2 Instant Recognition of Number Arrangements 2: 3–3 Instant Recognition of Number Shapes 2: 3–4 Instant Recognition of Number Trains 2: 3–7 What Do You Think? Using Grab Bags 2: 3–8 What Do You Think? Using Tubs	**Addition and Subtraction Equations** 2: 1–10 Writing Stories To Go with Equations **Data Collection and Graphing**

Ongoing Independent-Station Work (35–50 minutes, 3 to 5 times a week)

Number Combinations: Using Arrangements

Begin at Level 1, but move to Level 2 after a few weeks.

2: 2–14   Number Arrangements: Using Cubes, Level 1

2: 2–15   Number Arrangements: Using Color Tiles, Level 1

2: 2–16   Number Arrangements: Using Toothpicks, Level 1

2: 2–17   Number Arrangements: Using Collections, Level 1

2: 2–22   Number-Train Arrangements, Level 1

Occasionally, do the extensions for the above.

Number Combinations: Reading and Writing Equations

Add the following activities.

2: 2–18   Counting Boards: Making Up Number-Combination Stories, Level 2

2: 2–21   Number Shapes: Using Spinners

2: 2–24   Number Trains: Using Spinners

Occasionally, work with the following activities.

2: 2–25   How Many Ways?

2: 2–26   Number-Train Graph

2: 2–27   Building and Rebuilding

Teacher-Directed, Small-Group Focus Work (10–20 minutes, 2 to 3 times a week)

Number Combinations

Choose several activities over time, using two to four of them during any one lesson. Work with the children according to the information you gathered from the Hiding Assessment.

(Level 1 or Level 2, as needed)

2: 2–1   Snap It

2: 2–2   The Tub Game

2: 2–3   The Wall Game

2: 2–4   Bulldozer

2: 2–5   The Cave Game

2: 2–6   Grab-Bag Subtraction

2: 2–7   Finger Combinations

2: 2–8   Working with Number Shapes

2: 2–9   Number Shapes: On and Off

2: 2–10   Working with Number Trains

2: 2–11   Number Trains: On and Off

2: 2–12   Counting Boards: Number-Combination Stories

If you have children who are ready for a challenge, work with them using any of the following activities:

2: 3–6   What Do You Think? Using Counting Boards

2: 3–7   What Do You Think? Using Grab Bags

2: 3–8   What Do You Think? Using Tubs

2: 3–9   Let's Pretend: Grab Bags

2: 3–10   Let's Pretend: Counting Boards

2: 3–11   Let's Pretend: Number Trains

2: 3–12   Let's Pretend: Number Shapes

OR

Shared Experiences/Mathematical Events
(35–50 minutes, 1 or 2 times about every two weeks)

Addition and Subtraction

2: 1–17   Writing Stories To Match Equations

2: 2–27   Building and Rebuilding

Provide Additional Math Experiences as Time Allows

- Problem Solving/Math and Literature
- Sorting
- Data Collection

First-Grade Planning Notes

Fifth Planning Period: 4–6 Weeks (Feb., Mar.)

Focus: Number Combinations

Whole-Class Work: Mini-Lessons

You can present new concepts and review previously taught concepts by spending just a few minutes at the beginning of each math period on either a *Shorter Mini-Lesson* (5–10 minutes) or a *Longer Mini-Lesson* (15–25 minutes).

Shorter Mini-Lesson

Pattern Experiences

Continue presenting a variety of patterns, varying the level of difficulty over time.

> 1: 2–1   Rhythmic Patterns

Number Patterns

Continue adding a number each day to a 10×18 matrix in order to create a number chart. Have the children describe the emerging patterns as they notice them.

> 1: 2–20   Creating a Number Chart

Continue adding numbers to the calendar, encouraging children to look for patterns and to make predictions.

> 1: 2–21   Looking for Patterns on the Calendar

Estimation Experiences to 30 or Beyond

Materials: Assorted clear containers and various objects with which to fill them. Assorted lengths of yarn, Color Tiles, and toothpicks and/or large paper clips.

Continue to provide opportunities for the children to estimate and check their estimates. Sometimes, have them estimate how much a container will hold. Other times, have them estimate the length of a piece of yarn in terms of a number of small objects.

Number Talks: Instant Recognition of Number Combinations

After the children have been working independently for some time with the various number-combination tasks, begin using their recordings of number arrangements as "meaningful flash cards." (This replaces traditional work with flash cards. It gives the children the same kind of practice but also helps them to understand the number relationships instead of just memorizing them.) The children can also begin working with the "What Do You Think?" activities (Book Two, Chapter Three) at this time.

2: 3–2   Instant Recognition of Number Arrangements
2: 3–3   Instant Recognition of Number Shapes
2: 3–4   Instant Recognition of Number Trains
2: 3–7   What Do You Think? Using Grab Bags
2: 3–8   What Do You Think? Using Tubs

Longer Mini-Lesson
(15–25 minutes, as needed)

Addition and Subtraction Equations

Give the children opportunities to connect the equations they are working with to familiar situations. Do this by having them write stories that correspond to particular equations.

2: 1–10   Writing Stories To Go with Equations

Data Collection and Graphing

Sometime during this planning period, give the children opportunities to collect data and to organize their data into graphs.

Ongoing Independent-Station Work
(35–50 minutes, 3 to 5 times a week)

Number Combinations: Using Arrangements

Gradually introduce the independent number-arrangements activities (Book Two, Chapter Two) over several days. The activities are intended to be used for several weeks as the children's understanding of number combinations increases. Begin by using the Hiding Assessment (Book Two, page 45) to determine which numbers the children need to work with. After children have experienced these activities, use the Hiding Assessment again to check their progress. Most of children's time should be spent on creating and describing number combinations using the various manipulatives. Occasionally, give the children opportunities to make recordings of their creations as described in the extensions of the activities.

> **2: 2–14** Number Arrangements: Using Cubes, Level 1
> **2: 2–15** Number Arrangements: Using Color Tiles, Level 1
> **2: 2–16** Number Arrangements: Using Toothpicks, Level 1
> **2: 2–17** Number Arrangements: Using Collections, Level 1
> **2: 2–22** Number-Train Arrangements, Level 1

Number Combinations: Reading and Writing Equations

After the children have spent several weeks creating and describing number arrangements, have them use the addition and subtraction cards and/or write equations to label their work.

> **2: 2–14** Number Arrangements: Using Cubes, Level 2
> **2: 2–15** Number Arrangements: Using Color Tiles, Level 2
> **2: 2–16** Number Arrangements: Using Toothpicks, Level 2
> **2: 2–17** Number Arrangements: Using Collections, Level 2
> **2: 2–18** Counting Boards: Making Up Number-Combination Stories, Level 2
> **2: 2–21** Number Shapes: Using Spinners
> **2: 2–22** Number-Train Arrangements, Level 2
> **2: 2–24** Number Trains: Using Spinners

After having had many experiences with number arrangements, the children should occasionally work with these activities.

> **2: 2–25** How Many Ways?
> **2: 2–26** Number-Train Graph
> **2: 2–27** Building and Rebuilding

Teacher-Directed, Small-Group Focus Work
(10–20 minutes, 2 to 3 times a week)

Number Combinations

While the class is working independently, you will be able to work with small groups of children, focusing on the particular number(s) each child needs to work with. Work either with Level 1 (describing the parts) of each activity or with Level 2 (telling the missing part), according to the children's needs. Choose two to four activities at a time, spending five minutes or so on each.

Materials: You can do any of the recommended activities if you have connecting cubes, Color Tiles, collections (or other counters), and the Teacher Tub of Materials available to use as needed.

Teacher Tub of Materials

> Plastic bowls
> Working-space papers
> Paper lunch bag
> Number Shapes (4–10)
> Number Trains (4–10)
> Counting Boards

Focus children on number combinations using Level 1 or 2, as needed.

2: 2–1	Snap It
2: 2–2	The Tub Game
2: 2–3	The Wall Game
2: 2–4	Bulldozer
2: 2–5	The Cave Game
2: 2–6	Grab-Bag Subtraction
2: 2–7	Finger Combinations
2: 2–8	Working with Number Shapes
2: 2–9	Number Shapes: On and Off
2: 2–10	Working with Number Trains
2: 2–11	Number Trains: On and Off
2: 2–12	Counting Boards: Number-Combination Stories

If any children are ready for a challenge, work with them using the following activities.

2: 3–6	What Do You Think? Using Counting Boards
2: 3–7	What Do You Think? Using Grab Bags
2: 3–8	What Do You Think? Using Tubs
2: 3–9	Let's Pretend: Grab Bags
2: 3–10	Let's Pretend: Counting Boards
2: 3–11	Let's Pretend: Number Trains
2: 3–12	Let's Pretend: Number Shapes

Shared Experiences/Mathematical Events
(35–50 minutes, 1 or 2 times about every two weeks)

Addition and Subtraction

At times you will want to spend an entire period working with these activities.

2: 2–17	Writing Stories To Match Equations
2: 2–27	Building and Rebuilding

Provide Additional Math Experiences as Time Allows

- Problem Solving/Math and Literature
- Sorting
- Data Collection

First-Grade Planning Chart
Sixth Planning Period: 4–6 Weeks (Mar., Apr.)

Focus: Practicing Addition and Subtraction, Developing Strategies for
Adding and Subtracting

Whole-Class Work: Mini-Lessons	
Shorter Mini-Lesson (5–10 minutes, 3 to 5 times a week)	**Longer Mini-Lesson** (15–25 minutes, as needed)

Pattern Experiences
 	
1: 2–1   Rhythmic Patterns
 	
Number Patterns
 	
1: 2–20 Creating a Number Chart
1: 2–21 Looking for Patterns on
          the Calendar
 	
Estimation Experiences to 50
 	
Number Talks: Instant Recognition of Number Combinations
 	
2: 3–2 Instant Recognition of
         Number Arrangements
2: 3–3 Instant Recognition of
         Number Shapes
2: 3–4 Instant Recognition of
         Number Trains
2: 3–6 What Do You Think?
         Using Counting Boards
2: 3–7 What Do You Think? Using
         Grab Bags
2: 3–8 What Do You Think?
         Using Tubs
	Addition and Subtraction
	Take advantage of opportunities for addition and subtraction practice as they arise.
	
	Data Collection and Graphing

Ongoing Independent-Station Work
(35–50 minutes, 3 to 5 times a week)

Meaningful Addition and Subtraction Practice

Number Combinations

Begin with familiar stations.

2: 2–14 Number Arrangements: Using Cubes, Level 2

2: 2–15 Number Arrangements: Using Color Tiles, Level 2

2: 2–16 Number Arrangements: Using Toothpicks, Level 2

2: 2–17 Number Arrangements: Using Collections, Level 2

2: 2–18 Counting Boards: Making Up Number-Combination Stories, Level 2

2: 2–21 Number Shapes: Using Spinners

2: 2–22 Number-Train Arrangements, Level 2

2: 2–24 Number Trains: Using Spinners

2: 2–25 How Many Ways?

2: 2–26 Number-Train Graph

Addition and Subtraction Stations

Gradually add or replace with these activities.

2: 1–16 Writing Equations with Counting Boards

2: 3–14 Combination Toss

2: 3–15 Build-a-Floor Race

2: 3–16 Apartment Buildings

2: 3–21 Grab-Bag Addition Station

2: 3–22 Grab-Bag Subtraction Station

2: 3–26 What's Missing?

Additional Addition and Subtraction Stations

Over time, replace some number-arrangements activities and/or addition and subtraction stations with these stations.

2: 3–17 Describing Shape Puzzles

2: 3–18 What Numbers Can You Make?

2: 3–19 Addition-and-Subtraction Spin-It

2: 3–20 Counting Boards: Think and Write

2: 3–27 Comparing Combinations

Solving Addition and Subtraction Problems Using Numbers to 20

If you have children who are ready to work with numbers to 20, use these activities.

2: 1–16 Writing Equations with Counting Boards

2: 3–17 Describing Shape Puzzles

2: 3–21 Grab-Bag Addition Station

2: 3–22 Grab-Bag Subtraction Station

(Chart continues on next page.)

(Continued from previous page.)

Teacher-Directed, Small-Group Focus Work (10–20 minutes, 2 to 3 times a week)

Number Combinations

Choose several activities over time, using two to four of them during any one lesson. Vary the size of the numbers according to the information you get from the Hiding Assessment.

2: 2–1   Snap It
2: 2–2   The Tub Game
2: 2–3   The Wall Game
2: 2–4   Bulldozer
2: 2–5   The Cave Game
2: 2–6   Grab-Bag Subtraction
2: 2–7   Finger Combinations
2: 2–8   Working with Number Shapes
2: 2–9   Number Shapes: On and Off
2: 2–10 Working with Number Trains
2: 2–11 Number Trains: On and Off

Review of Number Combinations

2: 3–5   Related Combinations: Short Stacks
2: 3–6   What Do You Think? Using Counting Boards
2: 3–7   What Do You Think? Using Grab Bags
2: 3–8   What Do You Think? Using Tubs
2: 3–9   Let's Pretend: Grab Bags
2: 3–10 Let's Pretend: Counting Boards
2: 3–11 Let's Pretend: Number Trains
2: 3–12 Let's Pretend: Number Shapes

Number Combinations to 20

If you have children who are ready to work with numbers to 20, use these activities.

2: 3–28 Related Combinations: Tall Stacks
2: 3–29 How Do You See It? Adding Number Shapes
2: 3–32 Exploring Number Relationships with the Magic Box

OR

Shared Experiences/Mathematical Events
(35–50 minutes, 1 or 2 times about every two weeks)

Exploring and Creating Patterns

Give children opportunities to create their own patterns working either with repeating patterns or growing patterns.

1: 2–9   Creating Patterns
1: 2–18 Creating Growing Patterns

Addition and Subtraction

2: 2–17 Writing Stories To Match Equations

2: 2–25 How Many Ways?
2: 2–27 Building and Rebuilding

Provide Additional Math Experiences as Time Allows

- Problem Solving/Math and Literature
- Measurement

First-Grade Planning Notes

Sixth Planning Period: 4–6 Weeks (Mar., Apr.)

Focus: Practicing Addition and Subtraction, Developing Strategies for Adding and Subtracting

---

Whole-Class Work: Mini-Lessons

You can present new concepts and review previously taught concepts by spending just a few minutes at the beginning of each math period on either a *Shorter Mini-Lesson* (5–10 minutes) or a *Longer Mini-Lesson* (15–25 minutes).

Shorter Mini-Lesson

Pattern Experiences

Continue to occasionally present more complex rhythmic patterns.

> **1:** 2–1   Rhythmic Patterns

Number Patterns

Continue adding a number each day to a 10×18 matrix in order to create a number chart. Have the children describe the emerging patterns as they notice them.

> **1:** 2–20   Creating a Number Chart

Continue adding numbers to the calendar, encouraging children to look for patterns and to make predictions.

> **1:** 2–21   Looking for Patterns on the Calendar

Estimation Experiences to 50

Continue to give children opportunities to estimate two or three times a week every few weeks. Note how their sense of number relationships develops.

Number Talks: Instant Recognition of Number Combinations

Continue to work with the "meaningful flash cards" and the "What Do You Think" activities (Book Two, Chapter Three). Occasionally, write problems to help children make the connection between numbers of real things and the symbols that represent them.

> **2:** 3–2   Instant Recognition of Number Arrangements
> **2:** 3–3   Instant Recognition of Number Shapes
> **2:** 3–4   Instant Recognition of Number Trains
> **2:** 3–6   What Do You Think? Using Counting Boards
> **2:** 3–7   What Do You Think? Using Grab Bags
> **2:** 3–8   What Do You Think? Using Tubs

> ## Longer Mini-Lesson
> (15–25 minutes, as needed)

Addition and Subtraction

Once children are able to interpret addition and subtraction problems and read and write the equations that describe them, they should use these skills to solve a variety of problems that come up in other situations. You can encourage this by posing questions such as the following.

> How many days are in a week? (7) Today is Wednesday. How many days of this week are over? (3) How many days are left? (4, 7 – 3 = 4)
>
> We brought 6 carrots for our rabbit to eat. There are 2 left. How many did the rabbit eat? (4, 6 – 4 = 2)
>
> How can you record the number of crackers you ate at snack time this week? (2 + 2 +1 + 3 + 0 = 8)
>
> When we read *Mouse Count* (by Ellen Stoll Walsh), we saw three mice in the jar. Then four more mice were put into the jar. How many mice were in the jar?
> (7, 3 + 4 = 7)

Data Collection and Graphing

Sometime during this planning period, give the children opportunities to collect data and to organize their data into graphs.

> ## Ongoing Independent-Station Work
> (35–50 minutes, 3 to 5 times a week)

Meaningful Addition and Subtraction Practice

The next several weeks are an important practice time for the children as they work to develop ease and confidence in adding and subtracting. How children practice is very important because it influences how much benefit they get from the practice. Some children may look at an equation such as 3 + 4, count out three counters and then four more counters, count all the counters together, and then write the answer. Then, if they see the same equation a few minutes later, they may repeat the counting procedure as though they had never done it before. While this may be appropriate for a child who is just beginning to learn to add and subtract, we need to help children move beyond this. We need to help them pay attention to what they are doing and begin to internalize number combinations. Asking questions such as the following helps to keep children thinking about what they are doing and creates in them an attitude different from one that is concerned only with getting the task done.

What do you *think* the answer is going to be?

Now that you can see the group of (three) and the group of (four), how can you tell how many there are all together without counting each one?

How did you find out?

Are you sure? How do you know (seven) is correct?

Have you seen this problem before? Do you remember how many there were when you figured it out?

Continue working with the number-combination activities used during the fifth planning period.

Number Combinations

2: 2–14 Number Arrangements: Using Cubes, Level 2
2: 2–15 Number Arrangements: Using Color Tiles, Level 2
2: 2–16 Number Arrangements: Using Toothpicks, Level 2
2: 2–17 Number Arrangements: Using Collections, Level 2
2: 2–18 Counting Boards: Making Up Number-Combination
         Stories, Level 2
2: 2–21 Number Shapes: Using Spinners
2: 2–22 Number-Train Arrangements, Level 2
2: 2–24 Number Trains: Using Spinners
2: 2–25 How Many Ways?
2: 2–26 Number-Train Graph

Addition and Subtraction Stations

Continue with the number-arrangement and counting-boards activities, gradually introducing additional addition and subtraction stations.

2: 1–16 Writing Equations with Counting Boards
2: 3–14 Combination Toss
2: 3–15 Build-a-Floor Race
2: 3–16 Apartment Buildings
2: 3–21 Grab-Bag Addition Station
2: 3–22 Grab-Bag Subtraction Station
2: 3–26 What's Missing?

Additional Addition and Subtraction Stations

As children become ready, replace some of the familiar activities with new activities.

2: 3–17 Describing Shape Puzzles
2: 3–18 What Numbers Can You Make?
2: 3–19 Addition-and-Subtraction Spin-It
2: 3–20 Counting Boards: Think and Write
2: 3–27 Comparing Combinations

Solving Addition and Subtraction Problems Using Numbers to 20

By the end of first grade many children are eager to add and subtract larger numbers even though they may need to count by ones in order to figure out the answers.

2: 1–16   Writing Equations with Counting Boards
2: 3–17   Describing Shape Puzzles
2: 3–21   Grab-Bag Addition Station
2: 3–22   Grab-Bag Subtraction Station

Teacher-Directed, Small-Group Focus Work
(10–20 minutes, 2 to 3 times a week)

Continue to provide small groups with focused work according to their needs.

Number Combinations

Materials: You can do any of the recommended activities if you have connecting cubes, Color Tiles, collections (or other counters), and the Teacher Tub of Materials available to use as needed.

Teacher Tub of Materials

Plastic bowls
Working-space papers
Paper lunch bags
Number Shapes (4–10)
Number Trains (4–10)
Counting Boards
Magic Box and Cards (for children who are ready)

2: 2–1   Snap It
2: 2–2   The Tub Game
2: 2–3   The Wall Game
2: 2–4   Bulldozer
2: 2–5   The Cave Game
2: 2–6   Grab-Bag Subtraction
2: 2–7   Finger Combinations
2: 2–8   Working with Number Shapes
2: 2–9   Number Shapes: On and Off
2: 2–10   Working with Number Trains
2: 2–11   Number Trains: On and Off

Review of Number Combinations

Children often count to find answers even when they already know them. Help the children recognize what they already know by working with the activities listed.

2: 3–5   Related Combinations: Short Stacks
2: 3–6   What Do You Think? Using Counting Boards
2: 3–7   What Do You Think? Using Grab Bags
2: 3–8   What Do You Think? Using Tubs
2: 3–9   Let's Pretend: Grab Bags
2: 3–10 Let's Pretend: Counting Boards
2: 3–11 Let's Pretend: Number Trains
2: 3–12 Let's Pretend: Number Shapes
2: 3–28 Related Combinations: Tall Stacks
2: 3–29 How Do You See It? Adding Number Shapes
2: 3–32 Exploring Number Relationships with the Magic Box

Shared Experiences/Mathematical Events
(35–50 minutes, 1 or 2 times about every two weeks)

Provide opportunities for children to continue to explore pattern in a variety of ways.

Exploring and Creating Patterns

Allow children to create their own repeating patterns or growing patterns.

1: 2–9   Creating Patterns
1: 2–18 Creating Growing Patterns

Addition and Subtraction

Continue to give children a chance to work with these activities.

2: 2–17 Writing Stories To Match Equations
2: 2–25 How Many Ways?
2: 2–27 Building and Rebuilding

Provide Additional Math Experiences as Time Allows

- Problem Solving/Math and Literature
- Measurement

First-Grade Planning Chart

Seventh Planning Period: 4–6 Weeks (May, June)

Focus: Comparing Numbers to 20, Counting Numbers to 60–100, Extending Pattern Experiences

Whole-Class Work: Mini-Lessons	
Shorter Mini-Lesson (5–10 minutes, 3 to 5 times a week)	**Longer Mini-Lesson** (15–25 minutes, as needed)
Pattern Experiences 1: 2–1　Rhythmic Patterns 1: 2–21　Looking for Patterns on 　　　　the Calendar **Number Patterns** 1: 2–20　Creating a Number Chart 3: 1–12　Patterns on the 00–99 Chart **Estimation Experiences to 50** **Number Talks: Instant Recognition of Number Combinations** 2: 3–2　Instant Recognition of 　　　　Number Arrangements 2: 3–3　Instant Recognition of 　　　　Number Shapes 2: 3-4　Instant Recognition of 　　　　Number Trains 2: 3–7　What Do You Think? Using 　　　　Grab Bags 2: 3–8　What Do You Think? Using Tubs	**Addition and Subtraction** *Take advantage of addition and subtraction opportunities as they arise.* **Data Collection and Graphing**

Ongoing Independent-Station Work (35–50 minutes, 3 to 5 times a week)

Counting Numbers to 60–100	Counting and Comparing Numbers to 20
1: 1–30　Shape Puzzles, Ext. 1: 1–31　Line Puzzles, Ext. 1: 1–33　Grab a Handful, Ext. 1: 1–35　Give-and-Take Station, Ext. 1: 1–36　How Long Is It? Ext. 1: 1–37　How Many Does It Hold? Ext. 1: 1–39　Sorting Collections, Ext. 3: 1–32　Lots of Lines 3: 1–33　Paper Shapes 3: 1–34　Yarn 3: 1–35　Yarn Shapes 3: 1–36　Containers	1: 1–35　Give-and-Take Station, Ext. 1: 3–15　Comparing Lengths, Ext. 1: 3–16　Comparing Shape Puzzles, Ext. 1: 3–17　Comparing Line Puzzles, Ext. 1: 3–18　Comparing Handfuls, Ext. 1: 3–19　Comparing Containers, Ext. 1: 3–20　Sort and Compare Colors, Ext.

Teacher-Directed, Small-Group Focus Work (10–20 minutes, 2 to 3 times a week)

Review of Number Combinations

Choose several activities over time, using two to four of them during any one lesson.

2: 3–5   Related Combinations: Short Stacks
2: 3–6   What Do You Think? Using Counting Boards
2: 3–7   What Do You Think? Using Grab Bags
2: 3–8   What Do You Think? Using Tubs
2: 3–9   Let's Pretend: Grab Bags
2: 3–10 Let's Pretend: Counting Boards
2: 3–11 Let's Pretend: Number Trains
2: 3–12 Let's Pretend: Number Shapes

OR

Shared Experiences/Mathematical Events
(35–50 minutes, 1 or 2 times about every two weeks)

Exploring and Creating Patterns

Provide opportunities for children to continue to explore pattern in a variety of ways.

1: 2–8   How Many Ways?
1: 2–9   Creating Patterns, Ext.
1: 2–16 Exploring Growing Patterns
3: 1–19 Number Patterns in Growing Patterns
3: 1–20 Margie's Grid Pictures
3: 1–21 Looking for Patterns on the 00–99 Chart

Provide Additional Math Experiences as Time Allows

- Problem Solving/Math and Literature
- Geometry

First-Grade Planning Notes
Seventh Planning Period: 4–6 Weeks (May, June)

Focus: Comparing Numbers to 20, Counting Numbers to 60–100,
Extending Pattern Experiences

Whole-Class Work: Mini-Lessons

You can present new concepts and review previously taught concepts by
spending just a few minutes at the beginning of each math period on
either a *Shorter Mini-Lesson* (5–10 minutes) or a *Longer Mini-Lesson*
(15–25 minutes).

Shorter Mini-Lesson

Pattern Experiences

Continue presenting a variety of patterns, varying the level of difficulty
over time.

> **1:** 2–1   Rhythmic Patterns

Number Patterns

Continue adding a number each day to a 10 × 18 matrix in order to create
a number chart. Have the children describe the emerging patterns as they
notice them.

> **1:** 2–20   Creating a Number Chart
> **3:** 1–12   Patterns on the 00–99 Chart

Continue adding numbers to the calendar, encouraging children to look for
patterns and to make predictions.

> **1:** 2–21   Looking for Patterns on the Calendar

Estimation Experiences to 50

Continue to provide opportunities for the children to estimate volume and
length and to check their estimates sometimes using containers and sometimes
using yarn.

Number Talks: Instant Recognition of Number Combinations

Continue to work with the "meaningful flash cards" and the "What Do You
Think" activities (Book Two, Chapter Three). Occasionally write problems on the
board to help children make the connection between numbers of real things and
the symbols that represent them.

2: 3–2   Instant Recognition of Number Arrangements
2: 3–3   Instant Recognition of Number Shapes
2: 3–4   Instant Recognition of Number Trains
2: 3–7   What Do You Think? Using Grab Bags
2: 3–8   What Do You Think? Using Tubs

Longer Mini-Lesson
(15–25 minutes, as needed)

Data Collection and Graphing

Sometime during this period, give the children opportunities to collect data and to organize their data into graphs.

Ongoing Independent-Station Work
(35–50 minutes, 3 to 5 times a week)

Addition and Subtraction Stations

Continue these stations, as needed.

Counting Numbers to 60–100

Materials: Concept Development Packets—each set up to accommodate six children.

Provide opportunities for the children to count to 100. You can provide a range of numbers and meet a range of needs by including Book One, Chapter One activities, which limit the numbers to 20–30 and Book Three, Chapter One activities, which give children opportunities to count to 100. A few children may be able to count by organizing quantities into tens, but most first graders will count by ones.

1: 1–30   Shape Puzzles, Ext.
1: 1–31   Line Puzzles, Ext.
1: 1–33   Grab a Handful, Ext.
1: 1–35   Give-and-Take Station, Ext.
1: 1–36   How Long Is It? Ext.
1: 1–37   How Many Does It Hold? Ext.
1: 1–39   Sorting Collections, Ext.
3: 1–32   Lots of Lines
3: 1–33   Paper Shapes
3: 1–34   Yarn
3: 1–35   Yarn Shapes
3: 1–36   Containers

Counting and Comparing Numbers to 20

Materials: Concept Development Packets—each set up to accommodate six children.

You can add a challenge to those activities that deal with numbers to 20 by asking children to make comparisons.

> 1: 1–35 Give-and-Take Station, Ext.
> 1: 3–15 Comparing Lengths, Ext.
> 1: 3–16 Comparing Shape Puzzles, Ext.
> 1: 3–17 Comparing Line Puzzles, Ext.
> 1: 3–18 Comparing Handfuls, Ext.
> 1: 3–19 Comparing Containers, Ext.
> 1: 3–20 Sort and Compare Colors, Ext.

Teacher-Directed, Small-Group Focus Work
(10–20 minutes, 2 to 3 times a week)

Review of Number Combinations

Materials: You can do any of the recommended activities if you have connecting cubes, Color Tiles, collections (or other counters), and the Teacher Tub of Materials available to use as needed.

Teacher Tub of Materials

> Counting Boards (1 per child)
> Large dot cubes (1–6 dots)
> Paper lunch bags
> Plastic bowls

Continue to provide opportunities for children to review number combinations with the following activities.

> 2: 3–5   Related Combinations: Short Stacks
> 2: 3–6   What Do You Think? Using Counting Boards
> 2: 3–7   What Do You Think? Using Grab Bags
> 2: 3–8   What Do You Think? Using Tubs
> 2: 3–9   Let's Pretend: Grab Bags
> 2: 3–10 Let's Pretend: Counting Boards
> 2: 3–11 Let's Pretend: Number Trains
> 2: 3–12 Let's Pretend: Number Shapes

Shared Experiences/Mathematical Events
(35–50 minutes, 1 or 2 times about every two weeks)

Exploring and Creating Patterns

Materials: Connecting cubes, Color Tiles, Pattern Blocks, wooden cubes, collections, 00–99 charts, Margie's Grid Pictures activity packet.

Provide opportunities for children to continue to explore the concept of pattern in a variety of ways. Most of them will be able to make growing patterns. Allow them to create a variety of patterns on their own.

      1: 2–8   How Many Ways?
      1: 2–9   Creating Patterns, Ext.
      1: 2–16 Exploring Growing Patterns
      3: 1–19 Number Patterns in Growing Patterns
      3: 1–20 Margie's Grid Pictures
      3: 1–21 Looking for Patterns on the 00–99 Chart

Provide Additional Math Experiences as Time Allows

■ Problem Solving/Math and Literature
■ Geometry

Second Grade

···

	Creating the Environment See *Math Time: The Learning Environment.*	Number See *Developing Number Concepts:* Book One (Ch. 3) and Book Two (Ch. 1, 2, & 3).	Pattern See *Developing Number Concepts:* Book One (Ch. 2) and Book Three (Ch. 1).
Beginning of the Year: (Sept., Oct., Nov.)	**Self-Directed Exploration** *Allow children time to work with the manipulatives in their own ways for four to five weeks. Use this time to establish the classroom environment and the work ethic.* Children will learn to: ■ work hard ■ make responsible choices ■ work independently ■ share and cooperate ■ stay engaged and focused ■ build and create ■ sort and count ■ clean up	**Estimating to 50** *and* **Counting by Twos, Fives, and Tens** *Work with the above concepts during ongoing mini-lessons.* **Adding and Subtracting** *Provide meaningful practice with number combinations to help children develop fluency with combinations to 10. Also provide practice in developing increasingly efficient strategies for adding and subtracting numbers to 20.* *Introduce children to word problems that require them to use comparative subtraction and missing addends.* **Comparing Numbers to 20** Children compare numbers to 20 to answer the question "How many more?"	**Interpreting Rhythmic Patterns** *Determine which levels of complexity children can interpret. Use a variety of materials, including collections.* **Working with Repeating Patterns** After creating repeating patterns, children analyze them using ABCs. Children sort the patterns according to their underlying structures. **Exploring Growing Patterns** Children create a variety of growing patterns using Color Tiles, wooden cubes, or connecting cubes.

* Adapted from workshop materials presented by Mathematical Perspectives: Kathy Richardson and Associates.

Measurement See *Developing Number Concepts:* Book One (Ch. 3) and Book Three (Ch. 1).	Geometry See *Understanding Geometry.*	Sorting See *Developing Number Concepts:* Book One (Ch. 1 & 3).	Data Collection See *Developing Number Concepts:* Book One (Ch. 3).
Exploring Volume and Weight During self-directed exploration, children explore the capacity of various containers. They compare objects by weighing them on simple scales to find out which weighs more or which weighs less. *Introduce indirect measures as well. For example, have children find the number of scoopfuls of rice that are needed to fill a container or the number of ceramic tiles needed to equal the weigh of an object.*	**Exploring Shapes and Three-Dimensional Objects** During self-directed exploration, children work with geometric shapes and solids using materials such as Pattern Blocks, geoboards, attribute blocks, geoblocks, Discovery Blocks, and building blocks and boxes. If mirrors are provided, children can use them to explore reflections and symmetry. **Creating and Recording Designs and Shapes** Children create designs and shapes and copy them. Children also work with shapes as they cut and paste to create pictures or designs using lids and various blocks. **Observing and Describing Shapes and Figures** Children look for geometric shapes in their environment and record what they find. **Sorting Shapes** Children become familiar with attributes of various geometric shapes and three-dimensional objects by sorting them in a variety of ways. They use their own language to tell how they sorted. *Model geometric language, as appropriate.*	**Exploring Sorting** During self-directed exploration, children sort collections and other math manipulatives. They identify and label the categories into which these things are sorted.	**Organizing and Describing Data** Children participate in class activities during which they organize data into graphs and then describe the information they get from looking at the graphs.

	Creating the Environment See *Math Time: The Learning Environment.*	**Number** See *Developing Number Concepts:* Book Two (Ch. 2 & 3) and Book Three (Ch. 1).	**Pattern** See *Developing Number Concepts:* Book One (Ch. 2) and Book Three (Ch. 1).
Middle of the Year: (Dec., Jan., Feb., Mar.)	**Self-Directed Exploration** *Continue to provide occasional opportunities for children to work with manipulatives in their own ways.* *Make sure to give children opportunities to explore any new materials you introduce.*	**Estimating to 100** *and* **Counting by Twos, Fives, and Tens** *Continue working with these concepts during ongoing mini-lessons.* **Developing Place-Value Concepts** Children form and count groups of objects and record the patterns that emerge from this process. They spend several weeks working at independent stations organizing numbers into tens and ones. **Adding and Subtracting Two-Digit Numbers** Children begin to work on developing strategies for adding and subtracting two-digit numbers.	**Exploring Number Patterns** Children work with a variety of number patterns at independent stations. **Analyzing and Describing Growing Patterns** Children create growing patterns and describe how they grow.

| Measurement
See *Developing Number Concepts: Book One* (Ch. 1 & 3) and Book Three (Ch. 1). | Geometry
See *Understanding Geometry.* | Sorting
See *Developing Number Concepts: Book One* (Ch. 3). | Data Collection
See *Developing Number Concepts: Book One* (Ch. 3). |
|---|---|---|---|
| **Making Indirect Comparisons of Volume and Weight**

As children work at the science center they continue to explore containers and weigh objects.

Exploring Length and Area

Children determine lengths and areas at the place-value stations using materials such as Paper Shapes, Lots-of-Lines task cards, and yarn.

Begin working with the idea of precision. Ask questions such as "When Alex measured the table with paper clips why do you think he got 27 while Lee got 31?" | **Exploring Shapes and Three-Dimensional Objects**

Continue to provide occasional opportunities for children to work with the geometric materials using their own ideas.

Creating and Recording Designs and Shapes

Continue to provide opportunities for children to build designs and shapes but emphasize the recording of their creations.

Filling in Shapes Using Smaller Shapes

Children discover relationships between shapes. They see how small shapes can be used to make larger ones by filling in shape outlines with Pattern Blocks, tangrams, or Discovery Blocks.

Analyzing Solids: Using Boxes and Blocks

Children discover that some geometric solids are composed of faces. They identify these faces as plane geometric shapes.

Describing Shapes and Figures

Children begin to use geometric terms to identify the attributes of various shapes so that others can identify those shapes.

Sorting Shapes

Children continue to become familiar with attributes of various geometric shapes and three-dimensional objects by sorting them in a variety of ways. They use geometric terms to identify the attributes. | **Sorting and Re-sorting**

Children find many different ways to sort a particular set of objects.

Using Sorting

Children use sorting to create categories for graphing. They also use sorting to explore the attributes of geometric shapes and solids. | **Gathering and Organizing Data**

Children continue to collect data and organize them into categories. They display the categories in graphs and then make comparisons such as how many more objects there are in one group than in another.

Conducting Surveys

Children conduct simple surveys and organize their data into graphs. |

	Creating the Environment See *Math Time: The Learning Environment.*	Number See *Developing Number Concepts: Book Three* (Ch. 1, 2, & 3).	Pattern See *Developing Number Concepts: Book Three* (Ch. 1).
End of the Year: (Apr., May, June)	**Self-Directed Exploration** *As children work with the materials over time, you will see how their creative work evolves.*	**Estimating to 100 and Beyond** *and* **Counting by Twos, Fives, and Tens** *Continue working with these concepts during ongoing mini-lessons.* **Adding and Subtracting Two-Digit Numbers** Children continue to work to develop increasingly efficient strategies for adding and subtracting two-digit numbers. **Comparing Two-Digit Numbers** Children compare two two-digit numbers to determine how much more one number is than the other.	**Exploring Growing Patterns** Connect number patterns to growing patterns. **Searching for Patterns** Children investigate real-world patterns that they record and sort. For example, they work with patterns such as the number of ears for growing numbers of people (2, 4, 6, 8, ...) and the number of sides for growing numbers of squares (4, 8, 12, 16, ...).

Measurement See *Developing Number Concepts:* Book Three (Ch. 1).	Geometry See *Understanding Geometry.*	Sorting See *Developing Number Concepts:* Book One (Ch. 1 & 3).	Data Collection See *Developing Number Concepts:* Book One (Ch. 3).
Making Indirect Comparisons of Volume and Weight Children continue to explore volumes of containers and weigh objects on scales at the science center. **Comparing Length and Area** Children continue to compare lengths and areas at the place-value stations, using materials such as shape puzzles, line puzzles, and yarn.	**Filling-In Shapes Using Smaller Shapes** Children discover relationships between shapes and see how small shapes can be used to fill larger spaces by filling in outlines with Pattern Blocks, tangrams, or Discovery Blocks. **Analyzing Solids: Using Boxes and Blocks** Children continue to see that some geometric solids are composed of faces. They identify those faces. **Describing Shapes and Figures** Children continue to use geometric terms to identify the attributes of various shapes in ways that identify those shapes for others. **Sorting Shapes** Children continue to become familiar with attributes of various geometric shapes and three-dimensional objects by sorting them in a variety of ways. **Measuring Area** Children determine the area of simple shapes built on the geoboard. They express the area in terms of square units and half-square units. **Using Quilting** Children explore the ideas of rotation and symmetry through their work with quilting.	**Using Sorting** Children use sorting to form categories for graphing and to explore the attributes of geometric shapes and solids. **Exploring the Idea of Overlapping Categories (Venn Diagram)s** Children consider how to sort objects that belong to two categories at the same time.	**Collecting and Organizing Data** Children continue to collect data in order to answer questions. They conduct surveys and then organize their data into graphs that others can interpret.

An Overview of the Year's Planning Periods

T his overview highlights the concepts of number and pattern that will form the core of the second-grade math program. The school year has been divided into seven planning periods. The given time periods are offered simply as a point of reference. Adjust them to fit your own school calendar and the needs of your particular class. During each planning period, spend a day or two on other math experiences such as sorting, measurement, geometry, data collection, and problem solving. Occasionally spend a week or two between planning periods on one of these other areas of mathematics.

First Planning Period: 6–8 weeks (Sept., Oct.)

It is important to establish the work environment at the beginning of the year through children's self–directed exploration of the math manipulatives. Observe children as they work with number combinations to 10 to determine their level of facility. Provide them with interpreting-patterns experiences to determine their understanding of pattern.

Second Planning Period: 3–4 Weeks (Oct., Nov.)

The children continue to work with addition and subtraction of numbers to 10. Most second graders will need several weeks to internalize number combinations to 10. Then they move on to addition and subtraction to 20.

Third Planning Period: 3–4 Weeks (Nov., Dec.)

The emphasis during this period is on developing children's understanding of pattern concepts. The interpreting-patterns work that children did previously will help you decide whether to provide additional opportunities for them to work with basic patterns or to have them move on to more challenging work. If children show that they still need to work with beginning pattern experiences, have them use the pattern-station task cards, which require them to copy and extend patterns at the independent-pattern stations. If children are able to interpret a variety of patterns with ease, have them create their own patterns and then analyze and sort them. Then have the children begin work with growing patterns. Later in the year, they will work with number patterns.

Fourth Planning Period: 4–6 Weeks (Jan., Feb.)

Children's work with place value will continue to be a major focus for the rest of the year. At first, children form groups of objects and then count them, discovering patterns that emerge from this process. After working with the teacher-directed grouping games for two to three weeks, children work at independent-pattern stations exploring number patterns in different ways.

Fifth Planning Period: 5–6 Weeks (Feb., Mar.)

The place-value activities that children experience during this period help them to develop a sense of quantity, to recognize the value of grouping numbers into tens and ones, and to learn how to take numbers apart in different ways. As the children become ready, the tasks can be extended to include comparing numbers to determine how much more one quantity is than another.

Sixth Planning Period: 3–4 Weeks (Mar., Apr.)

The children use their knowledge of place value to work with addition and subtraction of two-digit numbers. They develop their own strategies for determining sums and differences.

Seventh Planning Period: 8–10 Weeks (May, June)

Children can be introduced to multiplication during this time period. They will also continue to work with addition and subtraction of large numbers. They will have opportunities to explore number patterns through pattern searches. This will be useful to them in their study of multiplication.

A Typical Second-Grade "Math Time"

1. Whole-Class Work: *Shorter Mini-Lesson* (5–10 minutes)*

All the children gather on the rug. Math time begins with a short lesson that provides review of number combinations to 20 using one or more of these activities.

> 2: 3–28   Related Combinations: Tall Stacks
> 2: 3–29   How Do You See It? Adding Number Shapes
> 2: 3–31   A Ten-Shape and More: Subtraction, Level 1

2. Preparation for Working with a Small Group

A small group of children stay in the rug area and are given a short task—to practice writing numerals, starting with 57—to occupy them while they are waiting for the teacher to make sure that the rest of the children are working appropriately at independent stations.

3. Independent-Station Work (35–50 minutes)

Having been introduced to the following activities over a period of three or four days, the children are now excused to work with them on their own. These activities help children develop a sense of the meaning of larger numbers, organize counters into groups of tens and ones, and write numerals to 100.

> 3: 1–32   Lots of Lines
> 3: 1–33   Paper Shapes
> 3: 1–34   Yarn
> 3: 1–35   Yarn Shapes
> 3: 1–36   Containers
> 3: 1–37   Cover It Up
> 3: 1–38   Measuring Things in the Room
> 3: 1–39   Measuring Myself
> 3: 1–42   Cube Stacks
> 3: 1–43   Race to 100

*Each activity number refers to book, chapter, and activity. For example, 2: 1–14 means book 2, chapter 1, activity 14. Notice whether each activity appears in Book One (1:), Book Two (2:), or Book Three (3:).

4. Teacher-Directed, Small-Group Focus Work (10–20 minutes)

The teacher uses these activities to provide a particular group of children with the extra practice they need in working with number combinations to ten.

        2: 3–6   What Do You Think? Using Counting Boards
        2: 3–7   What Do You Think? Using Grab Bags
        2: 3–8   What Do You Think? Using Tubs
        2: 3–12 Let's Pretend: Number Shapes

After the small-group lesson is over, the teacher excuses the children to choose an independent activity.

5. Teacher Observation of Children Working Independently

The teacher moves around the room observing and interacting with individual children.

6. Cleanup Time

After about 50 minutes of working independently, the children clean up their stations and meet back together again on the rug.

7. Whole-Class Work: Brief Discussion of Math Time (no longer than 5 minutes)

The class reviews what went on during math time.

Second-Grade Planning Chart*

First Planning Period: 6–8 Weeks (Sept., Oct.)

Focus: Establishing the Work Environment, Determining Children's Needs, Reviewing Number Combinations

Whole-Class Work: Mini-Lessons	
Shorter Mini-Lesson (5–10 minutes, 3 to 5 times a week)	**Longer Mini-Lesson** (15–25 minutes, as needed)

Pattern Experiences 1: 2–1 Rhythmic Patterns 1: 2–20 Creating a Number Chart 1: 2–21 Looking for Patterns on the Calendar **Estimation Experiences to 50** **Number Talks: Review of Number Combinations** 2: 3–2 Instant Recognition of Number Arrangements 2: 3–3 Instant Recognition of Number Shapes	**Addition and Subtraction Stories** 2: 1–3 Acting Out Stories: Using Counters 2: 1–5 Acting Out Stories To Go with Equations **Data Collection and Graphing**

Ongoing Independent-Station Work (35–50 minutes, 3 to 5 times a week)	

Self-Directed Exploration Connecting cubes Toothpicks Color Tiles Collections Wooden cubes Pattern Blocks *Include any additional math materials you have available, such as geoboards, geoblocks, scales, and containers.* **Introduce Math Manipulatives and Establish Expectations for Independent Work** *After a few weeks, gradually introduce the following stations.*	**Number Combinations** *Introduce Number Arrangements first. Begin at Level 1, but move to Level 2 after a few days.* 2: 2–14 Number Arrangements: Using Cubes 2: 2–15 Number Arrangements: Using Color Tiles 2: 2–16 Number Arrangements: Using Toothpicks 2: 2–17 Number Arrangements: Using Collections *Also introduce the following activities.* 2: 1–16 Writing Equations with Counting Boards, level 2 2: 3–16 Apartment Buildings *Use these activities to provide extensions and challenges.* 2: 2–25 How Many Ways? 2: 2–26 Number Train Graph 2: 2–27 Building and Rebuilding

* Each activity number refers to book, chapter, and activity. For example, 2: 1–14 means book 2, chapter 1, activity 14. Notice whether each activity appears in Book One (1:), Book Two (2:), or Book Three (3:).

Teacher-Directed, Small-Group Focus Work (10–20 minutes, 2 to 3 times a week)

Number Combinations

Continue to provide review for those children who need it. Choose several activities over time, using two to four of them during any one lesson.

2: 2–1   Snap It, Level 2
2: 2–2   The Tub Game, Level 2
2: 2–3   The Wall Game, Level 2
2: 2–4   Bulldozer, Level 2
2: 2–5   The Cave Game, Level 2
2: 2–6   Grab-Bag Subtraction, Level 2
2: 3–2   Instant Recognition of Number Arrangements
2: 3–3   Instant Recognition of Number Shapes

OR

Shared Experiences/Mathematical Events
(35–50 minutes, 1 or 2 times about every two weeks)

Interpreting Rhythmic Patterns

Intersperse work at independent stations with whole-class experiences.

1: 2–4   Interpreting Rhythmic Patterns with Connecting Cubes or Color Tiles
1: 2–5   Interpreting Rhythmic Patterns with Pattern Blocks
1: 2–6   Interpreting Rhythmic Patterns with Collections

Provide Additional Math Experiences as Time Allows

Self-directed exploration provides informal opportunities for children to work with sorting, measuring, and geometry.

Second-Grade Planning Notes

First Planning Period: 6–8 Weeks (Sept., Oct.)

Focus: Establishing the Work Environment, Determining Children's Needs, Reviewing Number Combinations

Whole-Class Work: Mini-Lessons

You can present new concepts and review previously taught concepts by spending just a few minutes at the beginning of each math period on either a *Shorter Mini-Lesson* (5–10 minutes) or a *Longer Mini-Lesson* (15–25 minutes).

Shorter Mini-Lesson
(5–10 minutes, 3 to 5 times a week)

Choose one to three of the following activities each day. Observe the children closely as their responses to these activities can give you information about their instructional needs. Spend just a few minutes on each activity before dismissing the children to work at the independent stations.

Pattern Experiences

Present whole-group pattern experiences beginning on the first day of school. Begin by presenting a variety of patterns. Vary the level of difficulty according to the children's responses.

> 1: 2–1   Rhythmic Patterns

Each day, add one number to a 10 × 18 matrix in order to create a number chart. After several days, the children should begin to see number patterns emerging. Have them describe the ones they notice.

> 1: 2–20   Creating a Number Chart

Add numbers to the calendar each day. Encourage the children to look for patterns and make predictions.

> 1: 2–21   Looking for Patterns on the Calendar

Estimation Experiences to 50

Materials: Assorted clear containers and various objects with which to fill them.

Every few weeks, once or twice a week, give the children opportunities to estimate the number of small objects needed to fill a container. After children have estimated, have them count along with you as you place the objects into the container, one by one. After the container has been partially filled, allow the children to revise their estimates. Continue adding objects to the container and counting along until the container is full.

Number Talks:* Review of Number Combinations

Using teacher-made recordings of number arrangements, number shapes, and the Tell-Me-Fast Dot Cards (Book One BLMs #20–27), review the number combinations to 10. This will provide children with important practice and can also help you determine if the children know the combinations instantly or if they need to count. (Later in the year, the children will be able to make their own number-arrangement recordings.)

2: 3–2   Instant Recognition of Number Arrangements
2: 3–3   Instant Recognition of Number Shapes

Longer Mini-Lesson
(15–25 minutes, as needed)

These lessons take a little more time than do the shorter mini-lessons because they require the children to use manipulatives. (On those days that you teach the longer mini-lessons, you will probably not have time to work with a small group.)

Addition and Subtraction Stories

These activities give children opportunities to act out story problems using manipulatives and then write equations for the problems. Observe the children as they work so that you can determine how well they understand the processes of addition and subtraction.

2: 1–3   Acting Out Stories: Using Counters
2: 1–5   Acting Out Stories To Go with Equations

Data Collection and Graphing

Sometime during this planning period, give the children opportunities to collect data and to organize their data into graphs.

---

* Number Talks are experiences that allow children to solve addition, subtraction, multiplication, and division problems in a variety of ways, generally using number relationships. The children should be given opportunities to describe the ways they solve the problems. Make sure you present a variety of problems for children to solve. See the video series *Thinking with Numbers* published by Educational Enrichment, Norman, OK, for more information about number talks.

Ongoing Independent-Station Work
(35–50 minutes, 3 to 5 times a week)

Self-Directed Exploration

Materials: Connecting cubes, wooden cubes, Color Tiles, toothpicks, collections, and Pattern Blocks. Include any additional math materials that you plan to use for instruction.

Establishing routines and expectations is the most important work for the beginning of the school year. If the children are going to accomplish all that they can throughout the year, they need to learn how to work hard, how to make choices, and how to get along with the other children in the class. This time is critical for the children as they need to work with manipulatives using their own ideas before they can focus on specific activities. While all the children will be exploring these manipulatives on their own, you will be free to focus on helping to develop the work environment.

Introduce Math Manipulatives and Establish Expectations for Independent Work

Introduce the manipulatives gradually over a period of several days, making sure that the children understand how to use them appropriately. Go over the rules for using the manipulatives and the procedures for cleaning up. (See "Establishing the Learning Environment" on p. xxii.)

After the manipulatives have been introduced, have a few children deliver them to the various stations around the room. Excuse the rest of the children, a few at a time, to choose where they will work. Observe and interact with them while they are at work, commenting on their work and redirecting them, if necessary. At the end of the math period, spend a minute or two discussing the good hard work you observed and/or reminding the children of any behaviors that need to be changed.

Addition and Subtraction Stations

Materials: Concept Development Packets—each set up to accommodate six children.

After several weeks, when the children are focused and working well independently, begin introducing them to the addition and subtraction activities that will strengthen their knowledge of number combinations to 10. Gradually replace the self-directed exploration stations with these activities. Provide frequent ongoing opportunities for the children to work at the various stations. Observe them at work, making note of the particular strategies they use to do these tasks.

Number Combinations

Have the children begin by creating as many number arrangements as they can. Then have them give verbal descriptions of the parts of their arrangements. After several days of doing this, children can use equation cards to label their arrangements or they can write the equations on small pieces of paper.

> 2: 2–14   Number Arrangements: Using Cubes
> 2: 2–15   Number Arrangements: Using Color Tiles
> 2: 2–16   Number Arrangements: Using Toothpicks
> 2: 2–17   Number Arrangements: Using Collections

Also introduce the following stations.

> 2: 1–16   Writing Equations with Counting Boards, Level 2
> 2: 3–16   Apartment Buildings

When the children are ready for more challenging work, introduce the following extension activities.

> 2: 2–25   How Many Ways?
> 2: 2–26   Number Train Graph
> 2: 2–27   Building and Rebuilding

Teacher-Directed, Small-Group Focus Work
(10–20 minutes, 2 to 3 times a week)

When the class is able to work independently, you can work with small groups of children, taking the time to focus on the particular number(s) that each group needs to work with. Use the Hiding Assessment (Book Two, page 45) to determine children's needs. Give children a variety of experiences, choosing the appropriate level of each of the listed activities—Level 1 (describing the parts) or Level 2 (telling the missing part). Spend a few minutes on each of two to four activities during any one lesson.

Materials: You can do any of the recommended activities if you have individual chalkboards, chalk, and erasers on hand along with connecting cubes, Color Tiles, collections (or other counters), and the following items in the Teacher Tub of Materials available to use as needed.

Teacher Tub of Materials

> Working-space papers (1 per child)
> Small plastic bowls (1 per child)
> Paper lunch bags
> Number shapes
> Recordings of number arrangements (See Book Two, page 77.)

Number Combinations

> 2: 2–1   Snap It, Level 2
> 2: 2–2   The Tub Game, Level 2

2: 2–3	The Wall Game, Level 2
2: 2–4	Bulldozer, Level 2
2: 2–5	The Cave Game, Level 2
2: 2–6	Grab-Bag Subtraction, Level 2
2: 3–2	Instant Recognition of Number Arrangements

OR

Shared Experiences/Mathematical Events
(35–50 minutes, 1 or 2 times about every two weeks)

You can vary the usual routine through occasional whole-class experiences. The listed activities generally require the entire math period as they involve the children in working with manipulatives and will replace the time otherwise spent at independent stations.

Interpreting Rhythmic Patterns

Give children experiences with these patterns early in the year. This will give you information about the level at which children are ready to work.

1: 2–4	Interpreting Rhythmic Patterns with Connecting Cubes or Color Tiles
1: 2–5	Interpreting Rhythmic Patterns with Pattern Blocks
1: 2–6	Interpreting Rhythmic Patterns with Collections

Provide Additional Math Experiences as Time Allows

This guide focuses on planning for the development of number and pattern concepts. You will also want to provide additional math experiences for your children. Sometimes, instead of having the children work with the independent stations, you may have them spend a day solving a problem presented through literature. Other times, you may have them spend a week focusing on another math strand, such as geometry or sorting. During this first planning period, you will not need to present additional math experiences since self-directed exploration provides children with informal opportunities to work with sorting, geometry, and measurement concepts. Later on in the year, you will need to integrate these other experiences into your math time.

Second-Grade Planning Chart

Second Planning Period: 3–4 Weeks (Oct., Nov.)

Focus: Strengthening Understanding of Addition and Subtraction, Number Combinations to 10

Whole-Class Work: Mini-Lessons	
Shorter Mini-Lesson (5–10 minutes, 3 to 5 times a week)	**Longer Mini-Lesson** (15–25 minutes, as needed)
Pattern Experiences 1: 2–20 Creating a Number Chart 1: 2–21 Looking for Patterns on the Calendar **Estimation Experiences to 50** **Number Talks: Review of Number Combinations** 2: 3–2 Instant Recognition of Number Arrangements 2: 3–3 Instant Recognition of Number Shapes 2: 3–4 Instant Recognition of Number Trains 2: 3–7 What Do You Think? Using Grab Bags	**Addition and Subtraction Stories** 2: 1–11 Working with Complex Addition and Subtraction Stories **Data Collection and Graphing**

Ongoing Independent-Station Work (35–50 minutes, 3 to 5 times a week)

Addition and Subtraction Stations

2: 2–15 Number Arrangements: Using Color Tiles, Level 2
2: 2–16 Number Arrangements: Using Toothpicks, Level 2
2: 2–17 Number Arrangements: Using Collections, Level 2
2: 2–20 Number Shapes: Using Number Cubes, Level 2 (Use BLMs #83–89.)
2: 2–21 Number Shapes: Using Spinners (Use BLMs #83–89.)
2: 2–22 Number-Train Arrangements, Level 2 (Use BLMs #99–106.)
2: 2–23 Number Trains: Using Number Cubes, Level 2 (Use BLMs #99–106.)
2: 2–24 Number Trains: Using Spinners
2: 3–14 Combination Toss, Level 2
2: 3–15 Build-a-Floor Race, Level 2

Gradually replace the activities listed above with the following activities.

2: 1–17 Writing Stories To Match Equations, Var.
2: 3–17 Describing Shape Puzzles
2: 3–18 What Numbers Can You Make?
2: 3–19 Addition-and-Subtraction Spin-It
2: 3–20 Counting Boards: Think and Write
2: 3–21 Grab-Bag Addition Station
2: 3–22 Grab-Bag Subtraction Station
2: 3–27 Comparing Combinations

Number Combinations to 20

Use the following activities for those children who need the challenge of working with larger numbers.

2: 3–17 Describing Shape Puzzles, Ext.
2: 3–33 Number-Shape Pairs
2: 3–34 Two Ten-Shapes: Addition and Subtraction
2: 3–35 A Ten-Shape and More: Subtraction Station
2: 3–36 Roll and Double, Var.
2: 3–37 Wipe Out

(Chart continues on next page.)

(Continued from previous page.)

Teacher-Directed, Small-Group Focus Work (10–20 minutes, 2 to 3 times a week)

Depending on the needs of the particular group, choose from the following activities, using two to four of them during any one lesson.

Number Combinations

2: 2–1 Snap It
2: 2–2 The Tub Game
2: 2–3 The Wall Game
2: 2–4 Bulldozer
2: 2–5 The Cave Game
2: 2–6 Grab-Bag Subtraction
2: 2–8 Working with Number Shapes
2: 2–9 Number Shapes: On and Off
2: 2–10 Working with Number Trains
2: 2–11 Number Trains: On and Off

Developing Strategies for Adding and Subtracting

2: 3–5 Related Combinations: Short Stacks
2: 3–6 What Do You Think? Using Counting Boards
2: 3–7 What Do You Think? Using Grab Bags
2: 3–8 What Do You Think? Using Tubs
2: 3–10 Let's Pretend: Counting Boards
2: 3–11 Let's Pretend: Number Trains
2: 3–12 Let's Pretend: Number Shapes

OR

Shared Experiences/Mathematical Events
(35–50 minutes, 1 or 2 times about every two weeks)

Intersperse work at independent stations with whole-class experiences.

Interpreting Rhythmic Patterns

1: 2–4 Interpreting Rhythmic Patterns with Connecting Cubes or Color Tiles
1: 2–5 Interpreting Rhythmic Patterns with Pattern Blocks
1: 2–6 Interpreting Rhythmic Patterns with Collections

Addition and Subtraction Stories

2: 1–17 Writing Stories To Match Equations

Number Arrangements

2: 2–27 Building and Rebuilding

Provide Additional Math Experiences as Time Allows

- Problem Solving/Math and Literature
- Geometry

Second-Grade Planning Notes

Second Planning Period: 3–4 Weeks (Oct., Nov.)

Focus: Strengthening Understanding of Addition and Subtraction, Number Combinations to 10

Whole-Class Work: Mini-Lessons

You can present new concepts and review previously taught concepts by spending just a few minutes at the beginning of each math period on either a *Shorter Mini-Lesson* (5–10 minutes) or a *Longer Mini-Lesson* (15–25 minutes).

Shorter Mini-Lesson
(5–10 minutes, 3 to 5 times a week)

Pattern Experiences

Continue adding a number each day to a 10×18 matrix in order to create a number chart. Have the children describe the emerging patterns as they notice them.

> 1: 2–20 Creating a Number Chart

Continue adding numbers to the calendar, encouraging children to look for patterns and make predictions.

> 1: 2–21 Looking for Patterns on the Calendar

Estimation Experiences

Materials: Assorted clear containers and various objects with which to fill them.

Continue presenting opportunities for children to estimate the number of objects a container will hold and then count to see how many it actually holds. Over time, vary the size of the containers and the size of the objects used to fill them. At some point during each count, allow the children to change their estimates if they like.

Number Talks: Review of Number Combinations

Regularly take a few minutes at a time to practice and review basic facts using the recommended activities and a variety of manipulatives. (This gives the children the same kind of practice they would get from using flash cards but in a more meaningful setting.)

2: 3–2   Instant Recognition of Number Arrangements
2: 3–3   Instant Recognition of Number Shapes
2: 3–4   Instant Recognition of Number Trains
2: 3–7   What Do You Think? Using Grab Bags

Longer Mini-Lesson
(15–25 minutes, as needed)

Addition and Subtraction Stories

Provide a variety of addition and subtraction word problems which require children to interpret the language of:

- Equalizing
- Missing Addends
- Comparative Subtraction

These concepts and the language used to describe them are quite difficult for young children to interpret. The connection between the actions of a problem and their symbolic representation may not be apparent to children. It is important to allow children to make sense of these situations in their own ways. These types of problems are most appropriate for second graders to grapple with in both whole-class and small-group work.

2: 1–11   Working with Complex Addition and Subtraction Stories

Data Collection and Graphing

At some time during this planning period, give the children opportunities to collect data and to organize their data into graphs.

Ongoing Independent-Station Work
(35–50 minutes, 3 to 5 times a week)

If children are to work with confidence and efficiency with larger numbers, they must be able to take smaller numbers apart and put them back together with ease. Too often we rush children to work with larger numbers before they have the necessary foundation. The list of recommended activities is designed to give children the opportunity to internalize these basic number relationships. The amount of time you need to spend with these activities will depend in large part on your children's previous experiences and the results of the Hiding Assessment (Book Two, page 45). These sets of activities provide two different kinds of experiences for the children. The number-arrangement activities focus on describing the parts of numbers and the other addition and subtraction stations help children learn to combine and separate numbers with ease.

Addition and Subtraction Stations

Materials: Concept Development Packets—each set up to accommodate six children.

> 2: 2–14 Number Arrangements: Using Cubes, Level 2
> 2: 2–15 Number Arrangements: Using Color Tiles, Level 2
> 2: 2–16 Number Arrangements: Using Toothpicks, Level 2
> 2: 2–17 Number Arrangements: Using Collections, Level 2
> 2: 2–20 Number Shapes: Using Number Cubes, Level 2
>   (Use BLMs #83–89.)
> 2: 2–21 Number Shapes: Using Spinners (Use BLMs #83–89.)
> 2: 2–22 Number-Train Arrangements, Level 2 (Use BLMs #99–106.)
> 2: 2–23 Number Trains: Using Number Cubes, Level 2
>   (Use BLMs #99–106.)
> 2: 2–24 Number Trains: Using Spinners
> 2: 3–14 Combination Toss, Level 2
> 2: 3–15 Build-a-Floor Race, Level 2

Gradually replace the above activities with the following.

These activities provide children with practice in applying various strategies as they work to develop ease and confidence in adding and subtracting. Children should have several weeks to practice using these activities.

> 2: 1–17 Writing Stories To Match Equations, Var.
> 2: 3–17 Describing Shape Puzzles
> 2: 3–18 What Numbers Can You Make?
> 2: 3–19 Addition-and-Subtraction Spin-It
> 2: 3–20 Counting Boards: Think and Write
> 2: 3–21 Grab-Bag Addition Station
> 2: 3–22 Grab-Bag Subtraction Station
> 2: 3–27 Comparing Combinations

Number Combinations to 20

If you have children who need the challenge of working with larger numbers, choose from these activities, adding them to the independent stations. (These tasks will be appropriate for most children later in the year after they have experienced the mini-lessons that focus on numbers to 20.)

> 2: 3–17 Describing Shape Puzzles, Ext.
> 2: 3–33 Number-Shape Pairs
> 2: 3–34 Two Ten-Shapes: Addition and Subtraction
> 2: 3–35 A Ten-Shape and More: Subtraction Station
> 2: 3–36 Roll and Double, Var.
> 2: 3–37 Wipe Out

> ## Teacher-Directed, Small-Group Focus Work
> (10–20 minutes, 2 to 3 times a week)

When the class is able to work independently, you can work with small groups of children, taking the time to focus on the particular number(s) that each group needs to work with. Use the Hiding Assessment, (Book Two, page 45) to determine children's needs. Give children a variety of experiences, choosing the appropriate level of each of the listed activities—Level 1 (describing the parts) or Level 2 (telling the missing part). Spend a few minutes on each of two to four activities during any one lesson.

Materials: You can do any of the recommended activities if you have individual chalkboards, chalk, and erasers on hand along with connecting cubes, Color Tiles, collections (or other counters), and the following items in the Teacher Tub of Materials available to use as needed.

Teacher Tub of Materials

Working-space papers (1 per child)
Small plastic bowls (1 per child)
Paper lunch bags
Number shapes
Recordings of number arrangements (See Book Two, page 77.)
Plus-or-Minus Spinner
Number cubes (marked 0–5, 1–6, and 4–9)

Number Combinations

2: 2–1 Snap It
2: 2–2 The Tub Game
2: 2–3 The Wall Game
2: 2–4 Bulldozer
2: 2–5 The Cave Game
2: 2–6 Grab-Bag Subtraction
2: 2–8 Working with Number Shapes
2: 2–9 Number Shapes: On and Off
2: 2–10 Working with Number Trains
2: 2–11 Number Trains: On and Off

Developing Strategies for Adding and Subtracting

Some children will benefit from the activities that focus on developing strategies. The following activities help children to move beyond counting. The "What Do You Think?" activities ask them to make predictions before figuring out the answers. The "Let's Pretend" activities ask them to figure out the combinations without using manipulatives.

OR

Shared Experiences/Mathematical Events
(35–50 minutes, 1 or 2 times about every two weeks)

You can vary the usual routine through occasional whole-class experiences. The listed activities generally require the entire math period as they involve the children in working with manipulatives and will replace the time otherwise spent at independent stations.

Interpreting Rhythmic Patterns

Addition and Subtraction Stories

Provide continuing opportunities for children to write addition and subtraction stories.

Number Arrangements

Occasionally have the whole class work with this independent-station activity.

Provide Additional Math Experiences as Time Allows

- Problem Solving and/or Math and Literature
- Measurement

Second-Grade Planning Chart

Third Planning Period: 3–4 Weeks (Dec., Jan.)

Focus: Strengthening and Extending Pattern Experiences, Strengthening Understanding of Addition and Subtraction

Whole-Class Work: Mini-Lessons	
Shorter Mini-Lesson (5–10 minutes, 3 to 5 times a week)	**Longer Mini-Lesson** (15–25 minutes, as needed)
Pattern Experiences 1: 2–20 Creating a Number Chart 1: 2–21 Looking for Patterns on the Calendar **Estimation Experiences to 50** **Number Talks: Addition and Subtraction of Numbers to 20** *Teacher models.* 2: 3–29 How Do You See It? Adding Number Shapes, Level 1 2: 3–30 Working with Ten-Shapes 2: 3–31 A Ten-Shape and More: Subtraction	**Number Talks: Addition and Subtraction of Numbers to 20** *Children use manipulatives and record equations.* 2: 3–29 How Do You See It? Adding Number Shapes 2: 3–30 Working with Ten-Shapes 2: 3–31 A Ten-Shape and More: Subtraction **Addition and Subtraction Stories** 2: 1–10 Writing Stories To Go With Equations 2: 1–11 Working with Complex Addition and Subtraction Stories **Data Collection and Graphing**

Ongoing Independent-Station Work (35–50 minutes, 3 to 5 times a week)
Repeating-Patterns Stations 1: 2–10 Pattern Trains 1: 2–11 Color-Tile Patterns 1: 2–12 Arrangement Patterns 1: 2–13 Collections Patterns 1: 2–14 Rhythmic-Patterns Task Cards 1: 2–15 ABC-Patterns Task Cards **Growing-Patterns Stations** 1: 2–16 Exploring Growing Patterns 1: 2–17 Growing-Patterns Task Cards 1: 2–18 Creating Growing Patterns

Teacher-Directed, Small-Group Focus Work (10–20 minutes, 2 to 3 times a week)

Review of Number Combinations to 10

2: 3–5   Related Combinations: Short Stacks
2: 3–6 through 2: 3–8, the "What Do You Think?" activities
2: 3–9 through 2: 3–12, the "Let's Pretend" activities

Number Combinations to 20

2: 3–28   Related Combinations: Tall Stacks
2: 3–29   How Do You See It? Adding Number Shapes
2: 3–30   Working with Ten-Shapes
2: 3–31   A Ten-Shape and More: Subtraction

Number Relationships

2: 3–32   Exploring Number Relationships with the Magic Box

Pattern Experiences

1: 2–19   Break-Aparts

OR

Shared Experiences/Mathematical Events
(35–50 minutes, 1 or 2 times about every two weeks)

Pattern Experiences

1: 2–6   Interpreting Rhythmic Patterns with Collections
1: 2–8   How Many Ways?
1: 2–9   Creating Patterns

Addition and Subtraction Stories

2: 1–10   Writing Stories To Go with Equations

Provide Additional Math Experiences as Time Allows

- Problem Solving and/or Math and Literature
- Data Collection and Graphing
- Sorting
- Geometry

Second-Grade Planning Notes
Third Planning Period: 3–4 Weeks (Nov., Dec.)

Focus: Strengthening and Extending Pattern Experiences, Strengthening Understanding of Addition and Subtraction

---

Whole-Class Work: Mini-Lessons

You can present new concepts and review previously taught concepts by spending just a few minutes at the beginning of each math period on either a *Shorter Mini-Lesson* (5–10 minutes) or a *Longer Mini-Lesson* (15–25 minutes).

Shorter Mini-Lesson
(5–10 minutes, 3 to 5 times a week)

Pattern Experiences

Continue adding a number each day to a 10 × 18 matrix in order to create a number chart. Have the children describe the emerging patterns as they notice them.

> 1: 2–20   Creating a Number Chart

Continue adding numbers to the calendar, encouraging children to look for patterns and make predictions.

> 1: 2–21   Looking for Patterns on the Calendar

Estimation Experiences to 50

Materials: Assorted clear containers and various objects with which to fill them and lengths of yarn and various objects with which to measure them.

Continue to present opportunities for children to estimate the number of objects a container will hold. Encourage children to think about number relationships in determining the amounts. Vary the experiences by asking children to estimate the length of a piece of yarn in terms of numbers of paper clips, toothpicks, or other small objects.

Number Talks: Addition and Subtraction of Numbers to 20

Provide opportunities for the children to solve problems using number shapes and cube trains involving numbers to 20. Hold up models for the children to see, but do not give them manipulatives.

> 2: 3–29   How Do You See It? Adding Number Shapes, Level 1
> 2: 3–30   Working with Ten-Shapes
> 2: 3–31   A Ten-Shape and More: Subtraction

Longer Mini-Lesson
(15–25 minutes, as needed)

Number Talks: Addition and Subtraction of Numbers to 20

Provide opportunities for children to work with addition and subtraction problems using manipulatives to discover relationships and to figure out answers. Have them record the corresponding equations for the problems.

> 2: 3–29 How Do You See It? Adding Number Shapes
> 2: 3–30 Working with Ten-Shapes
> 2: 3–31 A Ten-Shape and More: Subtraction

Addition and Subtraction Stories

Begin giving the children opportunities to solve addition and subtraction problems involving equalizing, finding missing addends, and comparative subtraction.

> 2: 1–10 Writing Stories To Go With Equations
> 2: 1–11 Working with Complex Addition and Subtraction Stories

Data Collection and Graphing

Sometime during this planning period, give the children opportunities to collect data and to organize their data into graphs.

Ongoing Independent-Station Work
(35–50 minutes, 3 to 5 times a week)

Materials: Concept-Development Packets—each set up to accommodate six children.

Repeating-Patterns Stations

Provide opportunities for your children to create repeating patterns. This work, along with children's work in interpreting rhythmic patterns (see "Shared Experiences/Mathematical Events" below) will give you information about their level of understanding of pattern. Use the pattern task cards only if children seem to need more direction.

> 1: 2–10 Pattern Trains
> 1: 2–11 Color-Tile Patterns
> 1: 2–12 Arrangement Patterns
> 1: 2–13 Collections Patterns
> 1: 2–14 Rhythmic-Patterns Task Cards
> 1: 2–15 ABC-Patterns Task Cards

Growing-Patterns Stations

Introduce the children to the growing patterns and then provide them with opportunities to work with both repeating and growing patterns.

> 1: 2–16 Exploring Growing Patterns
> 1: 2–17 Growing-Patterns Task Cards
> 1: 2–18 Creating Growing Patterns

Teacher-Directed, Small-Group Focus Work
(10–20 minutes, 2 to 3 times a week)

Materials: You can do any of the recommended activities if you have individual chalkboards, chalk, and erasers on hand along with connecting cubes, Color Tiles, collections (or other counters), and the following items in the Teacher Tub of Materials available to use as needed.

Teacher Tub of Materials

> Working-space papers (1 per child)
> Clear-the-Deck game boards (1 per child)
> Paper lunch bags
> Number shapes
> Recordings of number arrangements (See Book Two, page 77.)
> Number cubes (marked 0–5, 1–6, and 4–9)
> Magic Box, Magic-Box cards, and Magic-Box number lines

Review of Number Combinations to 10 or 20

It is important to occasionally work with groups of children having similar needs. Give each group a variety of experiences, choosing from the recommended activities. Some children will need additional work with combinations to 10.

> 2: 3–5   Related Combinations: Short Stacks
> 2: 3–6 through 2: 3–8, the "What Do You Think?" activities
> 2: 3–9 through 2: 3–12, the "Let's Pretend" activities

Other children will be ready to add and subtract numbers to 20.

> 2: 3–28 Related Combinations: Tall Stacks
> 2: 3–29 How Do You See It? Adding Number Shapes
> 2: 3–30 Working with Ten-Shapes
> 2: 3–31 A Ten-Shape and More: Subtraction

Number Relationships

Give everyone the opportunity to explore number relationships using the Magic Box.

> 2: 3–32   Exploring Number Relationships with the Magic Box

Pattern Experiences

When the children are working at the independent stations, have small groups explore the activity "Break-Aparts" with you.

> 1: 2–19   Break-Aparts

OR

Shared Experiences/Mathematical Events
(35–50 minutes, 1 or 2 times about every two weeks)

You can vary the usual routine and by continuing to work with previously introduced concepts or you can present new concepts through occasional whole-class experiences. The listed activities generally require the entire math period as they involve the children in working with manipulatives.

Pattern Experiences

> 1: 2–6   Interpreting Rhythmic Patterns with Collections
> 1: 2–8   How Many Ways?
> 1: 2–9   Creating Patterns

Addition and Subtraction Stories

> 2: 1–10   Writing Stories To Go with Equations

Provide Additional Math Experiences as Time Allows

- Problem Solving and/or Math and Literature
- Data Collection and Graphing
- Sorting
- Geometry

Second-Grade Planning Chart

Fourth Planning Period: 4–6 Weeks (Jan., Feb.)

Focus: The Process of Regrouping, Patterns that Emerge from Regrouping

Whole-Class Work: Mini-Lessons	
Shorter Mini-Lesson (5–10 minutes, 3 to 5 times a week)	**Longer Mini-Lesson** (15–25 minutes, as needed)
Pattern Experiences 1: 2–20 Creating a Number Chart 1: 2–21 Looking for Patterns on the Calendar **Estimation Experiences to 100** **Number Talks: Addition and Subtraction of Numbers to 20** 2: 3–28 Related Combinations: Tall Stacks 2: 3–29 How Do You See It? Adding Number Shapes, Level 1 2: 3–31 A Ten-Shape and More: Subtraction	*For this planning period alone, the longer mini-lessons have been replaced with the series of teacher-directed, whole-class lessons that follows.*

Teacher-Directed, Whole-Class Lesson (40–50 minutes, as needed)

The Grouping Games

The following activities should be introduced in order.

3: 1–1 Introducing the Plus-One and Minus-One Games
3: 1–2 The Grouping Games with Groups of Other Sizes
3: 1–3 Plus or Minus Any Number
3: 1–5 Number Patterns in the Plus-One and Minus-One Games
3: 1–6 Recording the Plus-One and Minus-One Patterns
3: 1–7 Introducing Number Patterns in a Matrix
3: 1–8 Recording Number Patterns in a Matrix

Use these activities to provide work with tens and ones.

3: 1–9   Introducing Grouping by Tens
3: 1–10 Writing Base-Ten Patterns on a Strip
3: 1–11 Creating a 00–99 Chart
3: 1–13 Naming Patterns with Colors

Growing Patterns

3: 1–14 Analyzing Growing Patterns
3: 1–15 Finding the Number Patterns in Growing Patterns

Ongoing Independent-Station Work (35–50 minutes, 3 to 5 times a week)

Number-Pattern Stations

3: 1–17 Recording Various Number Patterns on Strips

3: 1–18 Grab and Add

3: 1–19 Number Patterns in Growing Patterns

3: 1–20 Margie's Grid Pictures

3: 1–21 Looking for Patterns on the 00–99 Chart

3: 1–22 The 00–99 Chart Puzzles

Teacher-Directed, Small-Group Focus Work (10–20 minutes, 2 to 3 times a week)

Choose several activities over time, using two to four of them during any one lesson.

Addition and Subtraction of Numbers to 20

2: 3–28 Related Combinations: Tall Stacks

2: 3–29 How Do You See It? Adding Number Shapes

2: 3–30 Working with Ten-Shapes

2: 3–31 A Ten-Shape and More: Subtraction

Review of Number Combinations

2: 3–5 Related Combinations: Short Stacks

2: 3–6 What Do You Think? Using Counting Boards

2: 3–7 What Do You Think? Using Grab Bags

2: 3–8 What Do You Think? Using Tubs

2: 3–9 Let's Pretend: Grab Bags

2: 3–10 Let's Pretend: Counting Boards

2: 3–11 Let's Pretend: Number Trains

2: 3–12 Let's Pretend: Number Shapes

Number Relationships

2: 3–32 Exploring Number Relationships with the Magic Box

OR

Shared Experiences/Mathematical Events
(35–50 minutes, 1 or 2 times about every two weeks)

Because of the time needed for the teacher-directed, whole-class activities during this planning period, there will be little time left for additional math experiences.

Second-Grade Planning Notes
Fourth Planning Period: 4–6 Weeks (Jan., Feb.)

Focus: The Process of Regrouping, Patterns that Emerge from Regrouping

---

Whole-Class Work: Mini-Lessons

You can present new concepts and review previously taught concepts by spending just a few minutes at the beginning of each math period on either a *Shorter Mini-Lesson* (5–10 minutes) or a *Longer Mini-Lesson* (15–25 minutes).

Shorter Mini-Lesson
(5–10 minutes, 3 to 5 times a week)

Pattern Experiences

Continue adding a number each day to a 10 × 18 matrix in order to create a number chart. Have the children describe the emerging patterns as they notice them.

> 1: 2–20   Creating a Number Chart

Continue adding numbers to the calendar, encouraging children to look for patterns and make predictions.

> 1: 2–21   Looking for Patterns on the Calendar

Estimation Experiences to 100

Materials: Assorted clear containers and various objects with which to fill them.

Use estimation to reinforce the number facts to 20. Find a container that holds about 20 small objects of one kind. Place a few of those objects into the container and then ask the children to estimate how many more of these objects would be needed to fill the container. Alternatively, begin by filling the container, then remove some of the objects, challenging the children to estimate how many are now left in the container.

Number Talks: Addition and Subtraction of Numbers to 20

Use various number shapes and recordings of number arrangements to review the number combinations to 20. Also write addition and subtraction problems on the board for the children to solve.

> 2: 3–28   Related Combinations: Tall Stacks
> 2: 3–29   How Do You See It? Adding Number Shapes
> 2: 3–31   A Ten-Shape and More: Subtraction

For this planning period alone, the longer mini-lessons have been replaced with the series of teacher-directed, whole-class lessons that follows.

Teacher-Directed, Whole-Class Lesson
(40–50 minutes, as needed)

Present the underlying concepts of place value to the whole class. Many of the activities will be repeated several times but should be introduced in sequential order.

Place Value/The Grouping Games

The grouping games give the children practice in forming and counting groups, recording groups and leftovers, and looking for the number patterns that emerge.

3: 1–1   Introducing the Plus-One and Minus-One Games
3: 1–2   Grouping Games with Groups of Other Sizes
3: 1–3   Plus or Minus Any Number
3: 1–5   Number Patterns in the Plus-One and Minus-One Games
3: 1–6   Recording the Plus-One and Minus-One Patterns
3: 1–7   Introducing Number Patterns in a Matrix
3: 1–8   Recording Number Patterns in a Matrix

The children can apply what they learned from the grouping games as they search for number patterns in base ten. Introduce the children to grouping by tens and then have them work independently.

3: 1–9   Introducing Grouping by Tens
3: 1–10   Writing Base-Ten Patterns on a Strip
3: 1–11   Creating a 00–99 Chart
3: 1–13   Naming Patterns with Colors

Growing Patterns

Once the children have begun working with tens and ones, you can provide opportunities for them to explore growing patterns. This work will prepare them for the number-pattern stations described below.

3: 1–14   Analyzing Growing Patterns
3: 1–15   Finding the Number Patterns in Growing Patterns

Ongoing Independent-Station Work
(35–50 minutes, 3 to 5 times a week)

Number-Pattern Stations

Materials: Concept Development Packets—each set up to accommodate six children.

Introduce children to a variety of the pattern-exploration activities and have them spend several days exploring them independently at the number-pattern stations.

3: 1–17   Recording Various Number Patterns on Strips
3: 1–18   Grab and Add
3: 1–19   Number Patterns in Growing Patterns
3: 1–20   Margie's Grid Pictures
3: 1–21   Looking for Patterns on the 00–99 Chart
3: 1–22   The 00–99 Chart Puzzles

Teacher-Directed, Small-Group Focus Work
(10–20 minutes, 2 to 3 times a week)

Materials: You can do any of the recommended activities if you have individual chalkboards, chalk, and erasers on hand along with connecting cubes, Color Tiles, collections (or other counters), and the following items in the Teacher Tub of Materials available to use as needed.

Teacher Tub of Materials

Working-space papers (1 per child)
Counting boards (1 per child)
Number shapes
Clear-the-Deck game boards (1 per child)
Small plastic bowls (10–12)
Paper lunch bags
Number cubes (marked 0–5, 1–6, and 4–9)
Magic Box, Magic-Box cards, and Magic-Box number lines

Addition and Subtraction of Numbers to 20

Continue to provide opportunities for children to work with addition and subtraction. Some children will continue to need practice in adding and subtracting to 10. Others will need to focus on adding and subtracting to 20. Choose several activities over time, using two to four of them during any one lesson.

2: 3–28   Related Combinations: Tall Stacks
2: 3–29   How Do You See It? Adding Number Shapes
2: 3–30   Working with Ten-Shapes
2: 3–31   A Ten-Shape and More: Subtraction

Review of Number Combinations

2: 3–5   Related Combinations: Short Stacks
2: 3–6   What Do You Think? Using Counting Boards
2: 3–7   What Do You Think? Using Grab Bags
2: 3–8   What Do You Think? Using Tubs
2: 3–9   Let's Pretend: Grab Bags
2: 3–10   Let's Pretend: Counting Boards
2: 3–11   Let's Pretend: Number Trains
2: 3–12   Let's Pretend: Number Shapes

Number Relationships

Continue to give everyone the opportunity to explore number relationships using the Magic Box.

2: 3–32   Exploring Number Relationships with the Magic Box

Shared Experiences/Mathematical Events
(35–50 minutes, 1 or 2 times about every two weeks)

Because so much time will be needed for the teacher-directed, whole-class activities during this planning period, there will be little time left for additional math experiences.

Second-Grade Planning Chart

Fifth Planning Period: 5–6 Weeks (Feb., Mar.)

Focus: Developing a Sense of Quantity,
Grouping Numbers as Tens and Ones

Whole-Class Work: Mini-Lessons	
Shorter Mini-Lesson (5–10 minutes, 3 to 5 times a week)	**Longer Mini-Lesson** (15–25 minutes, as needed)
Pattern Experiences 1: 2–20 Creating a Number Chart 1: 2–21 Looking for Patterns on the Calendar 3: 1–21 Looking for Patterns on the 00–99 Chart **Estimation Experiences to 100** **Number Talks: Addition and Subtraction of Numbers to 20** 2: 3–28 Related Combinations: Tall Stacks 2: 3–29 How Do You See It? Adding Number Shapes 2: 3–31 A Ten-Shape and More: Subtraction **Working with Tens and Ones** 3: 1–30 Give-and-Take with Tens and Ones **Acting Out Complex Story Problems** 2: 1–11 Working with Complex Addition and Subtraction Stories	**Working with Tens and Ones** 3: 1–24 Rearrange It: Arranging Loose Counters into Tens and Ones 3: 1–25 Rearrange It: Breaking Up Trains into Tens and Ones 3: 1–26 Rearrange It: Finding All the Ways 3: 1–27 Rearrange It: How Many Cubes? 3: 1–28 Rearrange It: Breaking up Tens 3: 1–29 Build It Fast 3: 1–30 Give-and-Take with Tens and Ones 3: 1–31 Think About the Symbols **Data Collection and Graphing**

Ongoing Independent-Station Work
(35–50 minutes, 3 to 5 times a week)

Working with Tens and Ones

3: 1–32 Lots of Lines
3: 1–33 Paper Shapes
3: 1–34 Yarn
3: 1–35 Yarn Shapes
3: 1–36 Containers
3: 1–37 Cover It Up
3: 1–38 Measuring Things in the Room
3: 1–39 Measuring Myself
3: 1–40 Comparing Myself
3: 1–41 Making Trails
3: 1–42 Building Stacks
3: 1–43 Race to 100
3: 1–44 Race to Zero

Comparing Quantities

As children become ready, have them work with Level 3 of the following activities.

3: 1–32 Lots of Lines, Level 3
3: 1–33 Paper Shapes, Level 3
3: 1–34 Yarn, Level 3
3: 1–36 Containers, Level 3
3: 1–37 Cover It Up, Level 3
3: 1–38 Measuring Things in the Room, Level 3

If you have children who would benefit from comparing smaller numbers up to 20 or 30, include the following Book-One activities.

1: 3–3   Two-Color Grab Bag
1: 3–15 Comparing Lengths
1: 3–16 Comparing Shape Puzzles
1: 3–17 Comparing Line Puzzles
1: 3–18 Comparing Handfuls
1: 3–19 Comparing Containers
1: 3–20 Sort and Compare Colors

Teacher-Directed, Small-Group Focus Work (10–20 minutes, 2 to 3 times a week)

Choose several activities over time, using two to four of them during any one lesson.

Addition and Subtraction of Numbers to 20

2: 3–30 Working with Ten-Shapes
2: 3–31 A Ten-Shape and More: Subtraction

Working with Tens and Ones

3: 1–24 Rearrange It: Arranging Loose Counters into Tens and Ones

3: 1–25 Rearrange It: Breaking Up Trains into Tens and Ones
3: 1–26 Rearrange It: Finding All the Ways
3: 1–27 Rearrange It: How Many Cubes?
3: 1–28 Rearrange It: Breaking up Tens
3: 1–29 Build It Fast
3: 1–30 Give-and-Take with Tens and Ones
3: 1–31 Think About the Symbols

OR

Shared Experiences/Mathematical Events
(35–50 minutes, 1 or 2 times about every two weeks)

Provide Additional Math Experiences as Time Allows

■ Problem Solving and/or Math and Literature
■ Data Collection and Graphing
■ Sorting
■ Geometry

Second-Grade Planning Notes
Fifth Planning Period: 5–6 Weeks (Feb., Mar.)

Focus: Developing a Sense of Quantity,
  Grouping Numbers as Tens and Ones

Whole-Class Work: Mini-Lessons

You can present new concepts and review previously taught concepts by spending just a few minutes at the beginning of each math period on either a *Shorter Mini-Lesson* (5–10 minutes) or a *Longer Mini-Lesson* (15–25 minutes).

Shorter Mini-Lesson
(5–10 minutes, 3 to 5 times a week)

Pattern Experiences

Continue adding a number each day to a 10×18 matrix in order to create a number chart. Have the children describe the emerging patterns as they notice them. Have the children look for similarities between the number chart and the 00–99 chart.

> **1: 2–20** Creating a Number Chart
> **1: 2–21** Looking for Patterns on the Calendar

Continue adding numbers to the calendar, encouraging children to look for patterns and make predictions about the next numbers in each pattern.

> **3: 1–21** Looking for Patterns on the 00–99 Chart

Estimation Experiences to 100

Materials: Assorted clear containers and various objects with which to fill them. Lengths of yarn and paper clips of two sizes.

Emphasize experiences in which children estimate the number of objects needed to fill a container after seeing it filled halfway. Use the language of "doubling" as children discuss their estimates. For example, you might say, "When Jason told us that halfway is eleven and so all the way would be twenty-two, he was doubling eleven. Eleven and eleven make twenty-two."

Also provide opportunities for children to estimate the lengths of pieces of yarn—first as a number of small paper clips and then as a number of large paper clips. Encourage the children to compare how many clips of each size are needed to measure each piece of yarn.

Number Talks: Addition and Subtraction of Numbers to 20

Provide ongoing practice in addition and subtraction to 20 in which children use various number shapes and recordings of number arrangements.

    2: 3–28 Related Combinations: Tall Stacks
    2: 3–29 How Do You See It? Adding Number Shapes
    2: 3–31 A Ten-Shape and More: Subtraction

Working with Tens and Ones

Give the children practice in adding and subtracting tens and ones using this activity.

    3: 1–30 Give-and-Take with Tens and Ones

Acting Out Complex Story Problems

Occasionally, have children act out addition and subtraction stories that describe situations related to equalizing, missing addends, and comparative subtraction.

    2: 1–11 Working with Complex Addition and Subtraction Stories

---

Longer Mini-Lesson
(15–25 minutes, as needed)

Working with Tens and Ones

The recommended activities focus the children on regrouping numbers as tens and ones and on taking numbers apart in a variety of ways. The children practice partitioning large numbers in order to develop flexibility with numbers and to develop an understanding of conservation of large numbers. Choose one or two of these activities at a time. Spend just a few minutes on each before having the children go on to work with the independent activities.

    3: 1–24 Rearrange It: Arranging Loose Counters into Tens and Ones
    3: 1–25 Rearrange It: Breaking Up Trains into Tens and Ones
    3: 1–26 Rearrange It: Finding All the Ways
    3: 1–27 Rearrange It: How Many Cubes?
    3: 1–28 Rearrange It: Breaking up Tens
    3: 1–29 Build It Fast
    3: 1–30 Give-and-Take with Tens and Ones
    3: 1–31 Think About the Symbols

Data Collection and Graphing

Sometime during this planning period, give the children opportunities to collect data and to organize their data into graphs.

Ongoing Independent-Station Work
(35–50 minutes, 3 to 5 times a week)

Working with Tens and Ones

Materials: Concept Development Packets—each set up for six children.

Have the children work with the place-value stations for several weeks. This will give them experiences in counting large numbers and in organizing them into tens and ones.

3: 1–32 Lots of Lines
3: 1–33 Paper Shapes
3: 1–34 Yarn
3: 1–35 Yarn Shapes
3: 1–36 Containers
3: 1–37 Cover It Up
3: 1–38 Measuring Things in the Room
3: 1–39 Measuring Myself
3: 1–40 Comparing Myself
3: 1–41 Making Trails
3: 1–42 Building Stacks
3: 1–43 Race to 100
3: 1–44 Race to Zero

Comparing Quantities

Gradually have the children begin to work with Level 3 for the following activities. They will focus on determining how many more one quantity is than another. You may want to have them begin by comparing numbers to 20. You can facilitate this by adapting the materials; for example, by making smaller paper shapes or by providing shorter pieces of yarn. If you have access to the comparing activities in Book One, you could use those having the children work with the More/Less/ Same Worksheets [BLM #63]. When the children can do these tasks with ease, they will be more able to compare numbers to 100.

3: 1–32 Lots of Lines, Level 3
3: 1–33 Paper Shapes, Level 3
3: 1–34 Yarn, Level 3
3: 1–36 Containers, Level 3
3: 1–37 Cover It Up, Level 3
3: 1–38 Measuring Things in the Room, Level 3
3: 1–39 Measuring Myself
1: 3–3   Two-Color Grab Bag
1: 3–15 Comparing Lengths
1: 3–16 Comparing Shape Puzzles
1: 3–17 Comparing Line Puzzles
1: 3–18 Comparing Handfuls
1: 3–19 Comparing Containers
1: 3–20 Sort and Compare Colors

Teacher-Directed, Small-Group Focus Work
(10–20 minutes, 2 to 3 times a week)

Materials: You can do any of the recommended activities if you have individual chalkboards, chalk, and erasers on hand along with connecting cubes, Color Tiles, collections (or other counters), and the following items in the Teacher Tub of Materials available to use as needed.

Teacher Tub of Materials

Number cubes (marked 0–5, 1–6, and 4–9)
Number shapes
Clear-the-Deck game boards (1 per child)

Addition and Subtraction of Numbers to 20

Continue to have those children who need additional work with combinations to 10 work with activities used in previous planning periods. Others will be ready to work with combinations to 20 using the following activities.

2: 3–30 Working with Ten-Shapes
2: 3–31 A Ten-Shape and More: Subtraction

Working with Tens and Ones

Materials: Connecting cubes, beans and portion cups

Give those children who need it extra practice in organizing and reorganizing groups of manipulatives into tens and ones in a variety of ways.

3: 1–24 Rearrange It: Arranging Loose Counters into Tens and Ones
3: 1–25 Rearrange It: Breaking Up Trains into Tens and Ones
3: 1–26 Rearrange It: Finding All the Ways
3: 1–27 Rearrange It: How Many Cubes?
3: 1–28 Rearrange It: Breaking up Tens
3: 1–29 Build It Fast
3: 1–30 Give-and-Take with Tens and Ones

Shared Experiences/Mathematical Events
(35–50 minutes, 1 or 2 times about every two weeks)

Provide Additional Math Experiences as Time Allows

- Problem Solving and/or Math and Literature
- Data Collection and Graphing
- Sorting
- Geometry

Second-Grade Planning Chart
Sixth Planning Period: 3–4 Weeks (Mar., Apr.)

Focus: Addition and Subtraction of Large Numbers

Whole-Class Work: Mini-Lessons	
Shorter Mini-Lesson (5–10 minutes, 3 to 5 times a week)	**Longer Mini-Lesson** (15–25 minutes, as needed)
Pattern Experiences 1: 2–20 Creating a Number Chart 1: 2–21 Looking for Patterns on the Calendar **Estimation Experiences to 100**	**Number Talks: Addition and Subtraction of Numbers to 20** 2: 3–28 Related Combinations: Tall Stacks 2: 3–29 How Do You See It? Adding Number Shapes 2: 3–31 A Ten-Shape and More: Subtraction **Number Talks: Addition and Subtraction of Two-Digit Numbers** *Problems Posed by the Teacher* 3: 1–45 Addition and Subtraction of Two-Digit Numbers 3: 1–46 Story Problems 3: 1–47 Figure It Out

Ongoing Independent-Station Work
(35–50 minutes, 3 to 5 times a week)

Choose from the following activities to provide ongoing practice according to the needs of your class.

Addition and Subtraction Stations (to 20)

2: 3–17 Describing Shape Puzzles, Ext.
2: 3–21 Grab-Bag Addition Station
2: 3–22 Grab-Bag Subtraction Station
2: 3–31 A Ten-Shape and More: Subtraction
2: 3–33 Number-Shape Pairs
2: 3–34 Two Ten-Shapes: Addition and Subtraction
2: 3–36 Roll and Double, Var.
2: 3–37 Wipe Out

(to 100)

3: 1–48 Partner Add-It
3: 1–49 Partner Take-Away
3: 1–50 Roll and Add
3: 1–51 Roll and Subtract
3: 1–52 Add 'Em Up: Lots of Lines

3: 1–53 Add 'Em Up: Paper Shapes
3: 1–54 Add 'Em Up: Yarn
3: 1–55 Add 'Em Up: Yarn Shapes
3: 1–56 Add 'Em Up: Containers
3: 1–57 Add 'Em Up: Cover It Up
3: 1–58 Add 'Em Up: Measuring Things in the Room
3: 1–59 Solving Story Problems

Comparing Quantities

Continue working with the following activities.

3: 1–32 Lots of Lines, Level 3
3: 1–33 Paper Shapes, Level 3
3: 1–34 Yarn, Level 3
3: 1–36 Containers, Level 3
3: 1–37 Cover It Up, Level 3
3: 1–38 Measuring Things in the Room, Level 3

Teacher-Directed, Small-Group Focus Work (10–20 minutes, 2 to 3 times a week)

Addition and Subtraction of Numbers to 20

2: 3–28 Related Combinations: Tall Stacks
2: 3–29 How Do You See It? Adding Number Shapes
2: 3–31 A Ten-Shape and More: Subtraction

Working with Tens and Ones

3: 1–30 Give-and-Take with Tens and Ones

Addition and Subtraction of Two-Digit Numbers

3: 1–45 Addition and Subtraction of Two-Digit Numbers
3: 1–46 Story Problems
3: 1–47 Figure It Out

OR

Shared Experiences/Mathematical Events
(35–50 minutes, 1 or 2 times about every two weeks)

Provide Additional Math Experiences as Time Allows

- Problem Solving and/or Math and Literature
- Sorting
- Geometry

Second-Grade Planning Notes

Sixth Planning Period: 3–4 Weeks (Mar., Apr.)

Focus: Addition and Subtraction of Large Numbers

Whole-Class Work: Mini-Lessons

You can present new concepts and review previously taught concepts by spending just a few minutes at the beginning of each math period on either a *Shorter Mini-Lesson* (5–10 minutes) or a *Longer Mini-Lesson* (15–25 minutes).

Shorter Mini-Lesson

(5–10 minutes, 3 to 5 times a week)

Pattern Experiences

Continue adding a number each day to a 10 × 18 matrix in order to create a number chart. Have the children describe the emerging patterns as they notice them.

> 1: 2–20   Creating a Number Chart

Continue adding numbers to the calendar, encouraging children to look for patterns and make predictions.

> 1: 2–21   Looking for Patterns on the Calendar

Estimation Experiences to 100

Materials: Assorted clear containers and various objects with which to fill them.

Provide opportunities for the class to estimate the number of small objects that will fill given containers. Begin counting out the objects as you place them into the containers. Allow the children to change their estimates when the containers are filled with just one or two layers of counters.

Longer Mini-Lesson
(15–25 minutes, as needed)

Number Talks: Addition and Subtraction of Numbers to 20

In order to meet the range of needs in your classroom and to provide ongoing practice in addition and subtraction to 20, be sure to include daily work with one-digit numbers as well as two-digit numbers.

> 2: 3–28   Related Combinations: Tall Stacks
> 2: 3–29   How Do You See It? Adding Number Shapes
> 2: 3–31   A Ten-Shape and More: Subtraction

Number Talks: Addition and Subtraction of Two-Digit Numbers

Number Talks become very important at this time of year and should occur almost daily. Give the children a variety of problems to solve, writing some of the problems on the board and presenting others in the context of story problems. Make sure you make manipulatives available and follow the procedure outlined in this activity.

> 3: 1–45   Addition and Subtraction of Two-Digit Numbers

Also provide story problems and work with symbols as described in these activities.

> 3: 1–46   Story Problems
> 3: 1–47   Figure It Out

Ongoing Independent-Station Work
(35–50 minutes, 3 to 5 times a week)

Materials: Concept Development Packets—each set up to accommodate six children.

Addition and Subtraction Stations

You can provide for a range of needs and give children the practice they need using the following activities. Some of the activities involve addition to 20 only. Others involve addition and subtraction to 100. Begin by choosing only a few activities from each group that meet the needs of your particular class. Add more activities or replace activities introduced earlier as the needs change.

(to 20)

2: 3–17   Describing Shape Puzzles, Ext.
2: 3–21   Grab-Bag Addition Station
2: 3–22   Grab-Bag Subtraction Station
2: 3–31   A Ten-Shape and More: Subtraction
2: 3–33   Number-Shape Pairs
2: 3–34   Two Ten-Shapes: Addition and Subtraction
2: 3–36   Roll and Double, Var.
2: 3–37   Wipe Out

(to 100)

3: 1–48   Partner Add-It
3: 1–49   Partner Take-Away
3: 1–50   Roll and Add
3: 1–51   Roll and Subtract
3: 1–52   Add 'Em Up: Lots of Lines
3: 1–53   Add 'Em Up: Paper Shapes
3: 1–54   Add 'Em Up: Yarn
3: 1–55   Add 'Em Up: Yarn Shapes
3: 1–56   Add 'Em Up: Containers
3: 1–57   Add 'Em Up: Cover It Up
3: 1–58   Add 'Em Up: Measuring Things in the Room
3: 1–59   Solving Story Problems

Comparing Quantities

Also include some of the comparing-quantities activities. Give children opportunities to figure out the differences between numbers. Most children will work with these by determining how many more one number is than another. Some children will be able to express their ideas as written subtraction problems.

Begin with a few activities and then gradually replace some of these with others that have been previously introduced.

3: 1–32   Lots of Lines, Level 3
3: 1–33   Paper Shapes, Level 3
3: 1–34   Yarn, Level 3
3: 1–36   Containers, Level 3
3: 1–37   Cover It Up, Level 3
3: 1–38   Measuring Things in the Room, Level 3

Teacher-Directed, Small-Group Focus Work
(10–20 minutes, 2 to 3 times a week)

Materials: You can do any of the recommended activities if you have individual chalkboards, chalk, and erasers on hand along with connecting cubes, Color Tiles, collections (or other counters), and the following items in the Teacher Tub of Materials available to use as needed.

Teacher Tub of Materials

Number cubes (marked 0–5, 1–6, and 4–9)
Number shapes
Clear-the-Deck game boards (1 per child)

Continue to provide small-group work to better meet individual needs.

Addition and Subtraction of Numbers to 20

2: 3–28 Related Combinations: Tall Stacks
2: 3–29 How Do You See It? Adding Number Shapes
2: 3–31 A Ten-Shape and More: Subtraction

Working with Tens and Ones

3: 1–30 Give-and-Take with Tens and Ones

Addition and Subtraction of Two-Digit Numbers

3: 1–45 Addition and Subtraction of Two-Digit Numbers
3: 1–46 Story Problems
3: 1–47 Figure It Out

Shared Experiences/Mathematical Events
(35–50 minutes, 1 or 2 times about every two weeks)

Provide Additional Math Experiences as Time Allows

- Problem Solving and/or Math and Literature
- Sorting
- Geometry

Second-Grade Planning Chart

Seventh Planning Period: 8–10 Weeks (May, June)

Focus: Addition and Subtraction of Large Numbers,
Number Patterns in the Environment

Whole-Class Work: Mini-Lessons	
Shorter Mini-Lesson (5–10 minutes, 3 to 5 times a week)	**Longer Mini-Lesson** (15–25 minutes, as needed)
Pattern Experiences 1: 2–20 Creating a Number Chart 1: 2–21 Looking for Patterns on the Calendar **Estimation Experiences to 100 and Beyond** **Multiplication Word Problems** 3: 2–2 Acting Out Multiplication Stories: Using Real Objects	**Multiplication Word Problems** 3: 2–3 Acting Out Multiplication Stories: Using Counters **Number Talks: Addition and Subtraction of Two-Digit Numbers** 3: 1–45 Addition and Subtraction of Two-Digit Numbers 3: 1–46 Story Problems 3: 1–47 Figure It Out **Pattern Searches** 3: 1–16 Introducing Pattern Searches

Ongoing Independent-Station Work (35–50 minutes, 3 to 5 times a week)	
Addition and Subtraction Stations (to 100) 3: 1–48 Partner Add-It 3: 1–49 Partner Take-Away 3: 1–50 Roll and Add 3: 1–51 Roll and Subtract 3: 1–52 Add 'Em Up: Lots of Lines 3: 1–53 Add 'Em Up: Paper Shapes 3: 1–54 Add 'Em Up: Yarn 3: 1–55 Add 'Em Up: Yarn Shapes 3: 1–56 Add 'Em Up: Containers 3: 1–57 Add 'Em Up: Cover It Up 3: 1–58 Add 'Em Up: Measuring Things in the Room 3: 1–59 Solving Story Problems **Pattern Searches** 3: 1–23 Searching-for-Patterns Stations	**Number-Pattern Stations** 3: 1–17 Recording Various Number Patterns on Strips 3: 1–18 Grab and Add 3: 1–19 Number Patterns in Growing Patterns 3: 1–20 Margie's Grid Pictures 3: 1–21 Looking for Patterns on the 00–99 Chart 3: 1–22 The 00–99 Chart Puzzles **Introduction to Multiplication** 3: 2–11 How Many Cups? 3: 2–12 How Many Groups? 3: 2–13 How Many Rows? 3: 2–14 How Many Towers?

Teacher-Directed, Small-Group Focus Work (10–20 minutes, 2 to 3 times a week)

Addition and Subtraction of Numbers to 20

2: 3–28 Related Combinations: Tall Stacks
2: 3–29 How Do You See It? Adding Number Shapes
2: 3–31 A Ten-Shape and More: Subtraction

Working with Tens and Ones

3: 1–30 Give-and-Take with Tens and Ones

Addition and Subtraction of Two-Digit Numbers

3: 1–45 Addition and Subtraction of Two-Digit Numbers
3: 1–46 Story Problems
3: 1–47 Figure It Out

OR

Shared Experiences/Mathematical Events (35–50 minutes, 1 or 2 times about every two weeks)

Provide Additional Math Experiences as Time Allows
- Problem Solving and/or Math and Literature

Second-Grade Planning Notes

Seventh Planning Period: 8–10 Weeks (May, June)

Focus: Addition and Subtraction of Large Numbers,
Number Patterns in the Environment

Whole-Class Work: Mini-Lessons

You can present new concepts and review previously taught concepts by spending just a few minutes at the beginning of each math period on either a *Shorter Mini-Lesson* (5–10 minutes) or a *Longer Mini-Lesson* (15–25 minutes).

Shorter Mini-Lesson
(5–10 minutes, 3 to 5 times a week)

Pattern Experiences

Continue adding a number each day to a 10×18 matrix in order to create a number chart. Have the children describe the emerging patterns as they notice them.

> 1: 2–20   Creating a Number Chart

Continue adding numbers to the calendar, encouraging children to look for patterns and make predictions.

> 1: 2–21   Looking for Patterns on the Calendar

Estimation Experiences to 100 and Beyond

Materials: Assorted clear containers and various objects with which to fill them.

Provide opportunities for the class to estimate the number of small objects that will fill given containers. Encourage children to consider how full the container would need to be for them to feel sure they could make good estimates. Ask questions such as, "What if we don't have enough of these objects to fill the whole container? Would you still be able to know if your estimate was close or not?" and "How full is the container when you think you know how many objects it would take to fill it?"

Multiplication Word Problems

Introduce multiplication stories for the children to act out. Intersperse addition and subtraction problems so that the children need to focus on choosing the correct process. If children seem ready, tell division stories as well.

> 3: 2–2   Acting Out Multiplication Stories: Using Real Objects

Longer Mini-Lesson
(15–25 minutes, as needed)

Multiplication Word Problems

       3: 2–3   Acting Out Multiplication Stories: Using Counters

Number Talks: Addition and Subtraction of Two-Digit Numbers

Number Talks become very important at this time of year and should occur almost daily. Give the children a variety of problems to solve, writing some on the board and presenting others in the context of story problems. Make sure you have manipulatives available and follow the procedure outlined in the following activity.

       3: 1–45   Addition and Subtraction of Two-Digit Numbers

Also provide story problems and work with symbols as described in these activities.

       3: 1–46   Story Problems
       3: 1–47   Figure It Out

Pattern Searches

Introduce children to the pattern searches during a whole-class time before giving them several weeks to work independently with them.

       3: 1–16   Introducing Pattern Searches

Ongoing Independent-Station Work
(35–50 minutes, 3 to 5 times a week)

Addition and Subtraction Stations (to 100)

Materials: Concept Development Packets—each set up to accommodate six children.

           Continue providing children with opportunities to practice addition and subtraction.

       3: 1–48   Partner Add-It
       3: 1–49   Partner Take-Away
       3: 1–50   Roll and Add
       3: 1–51   Roll and Subtract
       3: 1–52   Add 'Em Up: Lots of Lines
       3: 1–53   Add 'Em Up: Paper Shapes
       3: 1–54   Add 'Em Up: Yarn
       3: 1–55   Add 'Em Up: Yarn Shapes
       3: 1–56   Add 'Em Up: Containers
       3: 1–57   Add 'Em Up: Cover It Up
       3: 1–58   Add 'Em Up: Measuring Things in the Room
       3: 1–59   Solving Story Problems

Pattern Searches

After introducing pattern searches to the whole class, give children several weeks to work independently with them.

> 3: 1–23 Searching-for-Patterns Stations

Number-Pattern Stations

Materials: Concept Development Packets—each set up to accommodate six children.

Also, bring back any pattern stations children previously worked with that they need to work with again.

> 3: 1–17 Recording Various Number Patterns on Strips
> 3: 1–18 Grab and Add
> 3: 1–19 Number Patterns in Growing Patterns
> 3: 1–20 Margie's Grid Pictures
> 3: 1–21 Looking for Patterns on the 00–99 Chart
> 3: 1–22 The 00–99 Chart Puzzles

Introduction to Multiplication

Add a few multiplication stations for those children who are ready to work with multiplication independently.

> 3: 2–11 How Many Cups?
> 3: 2–12 How Many Groups?
> 3: 2–13 How Many Rows?
> 3: 2–14 How Many Towers?

Teacher-Directed, Small-Group Focus Work
(10–20 minutes, 2 to 3 times a week)

Materials: You can do any of the recommended activities if you have individual chalkboards, chalk, and erasers on hand along with connecting cubes, Color Tiles, collections (or other counters), and the following items in the Teacher Tub of Materials available to use as needed.

Teacher Tub of Materials

> Number cubes (marked 0–5, 1–6, and 4–9)
> Number shapes
> Clear-the-Deck game boards (1 per child)

Continue to provide small-group work to better meet individual needs.

Addition and Subtraction of Numbers to 20

2: 3–28 Related Combinations: Tall Stacks
2: 3–29 How Do You See It? Adding Number Shapes
2: 3–31 A Ten-Shape and More: Subtraction

Working with Tens and Ones

3: 1–30 Give-and-Take with Tens and Ones

Addition and Subtraction of Two-Digit Numbers

3: 1–45 Addition and Subtraction of Two-Digit Numbers
3: 1–46 Story Problems

Shared Experiences/Mathematical Events
(35–50 minutes, 1 or 2 times about every two weeks)

Provide Additional Math Experiences as Time Allows

- Problem Solving and/or Math and Literature

Third Grade

CONCEPT DEVELOPMENT CHARTS

PLANNING CHARTS AND NOTES

	Creating the Environment See *Math Time: The Learning Environment.*	**Number** See *Developing Number Concepts:* Book Two (Ch. 2 & 3) and Book Three (Ch. 1).	**Pattern** See *Developing Number Concepts:* Book Three (Ch. 1).
Beginning of the Year: (Sept., Oct., Nov.)	**Self-Directed Exploration** *This is a very important time as it establishes expectations for the children's work for the whole year.* During this time children will learn to: ■ work hard ■ make responsible choices ■ work independently ■ share and cooperate ■ stay engaged and focused ■ take responsibility for cleaning up	**Strengthening Number Concepts** *and* **Understanding Tens and Ones** Children have the opportunity to solidify previously worked with concepts to ensure that they are able to work with numbers to 100 with flexibility, that they think of a number as being made up of tens and ones, that they are able to take numbers apart in a variety of ways, and that they can compare quantities to 100. **Reviewing Basic Number Combinations** *Make sure that children know the number combinations to 10 with ease and flexibility and that they can use strategies and relationships when working with numbers to 20.* **Developing an Understanding of Three-Digit Numbers** Children work with base-ten blocks to develop a sense of quantity for numbers beyond 100. **Adding and Subtracting Two- and Three-Digit Numbers** Children begin working to develop strategies for determining answers to addition and subtraction problems involving numbers beyond 100.	**Analyzing Growing Patterns** Children work with growing patterns learning to create, describe, and label them with numbers. They find number patterns in the growing patterns and then work with number patterns in a variety of settings.

* Adapted from workshop materials presented by Mathematical Perspectives: Kathy Richardson and Associates.

Measurement	Geometry	Sorting	Data Collection
See *Developing Number Concepts: Book Three* (Ch. 1).	See *Understanding Geometry*.	See *Developing Number Concepts: Book One* (Ch. 1 & 3).	See *Developing Number Concepts: Book One* (Ch. 3).

Exploring Volume and Weight Children explore various containers and scales and make direct comparisons of volume and weight. They also use indirect measures; for example, by finding the number of scoopfuls of sand needed to fill a container or by finding the number of tiles, cubes, or blocks needed to equal the weight of an object. **Exploring Length and Area** Children determine length and area at the addition and subtraction stations using materials such as shape puzzles, line puzzles, and yarn. Children work with the idea of precision. They consider questions such as, "Why do you think that Linda and Paul got different answers when they measured their desks with Color Tiles?"	**Exploring Shapes and Three-Dimensional Objects** During self-directed exploration, children work with geometric shapes and solids using materials such as Pattern Blocks, geoboards, attribute blocks, geoblocks, Discovery Blocks, and building blocks and boxes. If mirrors are provided, children can use them to explore reflections and symmetry. **Creating and Recording Designs and Shapes** Children create designs and shapes using geoboards, lids, and Pattern Blocks. They record and write about their creations. *Help children see the need for using the language of geometry to communicate their ideas precisely.* **Filling in Shapes Using Smaller Shapes** Children discover relationships between shapes and see how small shapes can be used to make larger ones by filling in shape outlines with Pattern Blocks, tangrams, or Discovery Blocks. **Observing and Describing Shapes and Figures** Children use geometric terms to describe various shapes and their attributes. They look for geometric shapes in their environment. **Sorting Shapes** Children become familiar with attributes of various geometric shapes and three-dimensional objects by sorting them in a variety of ways. They use their own language to tell how they sorted. *Model geometric language, as appropriate.*	**Exploring Sorting** During self-directed exploration, children sort collections and other math manipulatives. They identify and label the categories into which they are sorted.	**Organizing and Describing Data** Children participate in class activities during which they organize data into a graph and then describe the information they get from looking at the graph. **Collecting and Organizing Data** Children conduct simple surveys and organize their data into graphs.

	Creating the Environment See *Math Time: The Learning Environment.*	**Number** See *Developing Number Concepts:* Book Three (Ch. 1 & 2).	**Pattern** See *Developing Number Concepts:* Book Three (Ch. 1 & 2).
Middle of the Year: (Dec., Jan., Feb., Mar.)	**Self-Directed Exploration** *Make sure to give children opportunities to explore any new materials you introduce.*	**Multiplying** Children begin their work with multiplication by acting out word problems and by exploring the combining of equal groups. After a few weeks, children begin looking for patterns that emerge when multiplying. Then they learn to write multiplication equations. **Adding and Subtracting** Children continue to work to develop increasingly efficient strategies for adding and subtracting two-digit numbers.	**Searching for Patterns** Children investigate real-world patterns that they record and sort. For example, they work with patterns such as the number of ears for growing numbers of people (2, 4, 6, 8, ...) and the number of sides for growing numbers of squares (4, 8, 12, 16, ...). They also learn to describe the elements of patterns that appear in sequential multiplication equations ($1 \times 4 = 4$, $2 \times 4 = 8$, $3 \times 4 = 12$, ...).

Measurement	Geometry	Sorting	Data Collection
See *Developing Number Concepts:* Book Three (Ch. 1).	See *Understanding Geometry.*	See *Developing Number Concepts:* Book One (Ch. 1 & 3).	See *Developing Number Concepts:* Book One (Ch. 3).

Exploring Volume and Weight

Children work at the science center as they continue to explore the volume of containers and the weight of objects.

Analyzing Shapes

Children see how many different ways they can create a shape with a given number of sides.

Analyzing Solids: Using Boxes and Blocks

Children discover that some geometric solids are composed of faces. They identify these faces as plane geometric shapes.

Exploring Rotation and Symmetry: Using Quilting

Children explore the ideas of rotation and symmetry through their work with quilting.

Sorting Shapes

Children continue to become familiar with attributes of various geometric shapes and three-dimensional objects by sorting them in a variety of ways. They use geometric terms to identify the attributes.

Sorting and Re-sorting

Children find many different ways to sort a particular set of objects.

Using Sorting

Children use sorting to create categories for graphing. They also use sorting to explore the attributes of geometric shapes and solids.

Collecting and Organizing Data

Children continue to collect data in order to answer questions. They conduct surveys and then organize their data into graphs that others can interpret.

	Creating the Environment See *Math Time: The Learning Environment.*	**Number** See *Developing Number Concepts:* Book Three (Ch. 1, 2, & 3).	**Pattern** See *Developing Number Concepts:* Book Three (Ch. 2 & 3).
End of the Year: (Apr., May, June)	**Self-Directed Exploration** *As children work with the materials over time, you will see how their creative work evolves.*	**Dividing** Children begin their work with division by acting out word problems and by exploring the making of equal groups. After a few weeks, children begin looking for patterns that emerge when dividing. Then they learn to write division equations. **Adding, Subtracting, and Multiplying** Children continue to work with addition and subtraction of two- and three-digit numbers and with multiplication.	**Discovering Patterns in Multiplication and Division** Children discover patterns as part of their work with multiplication and division.

Measurement	Geometry See *Understanding Geometry.*	Sorting	Data Collection
Exploring Volume and Weight: Using Standard Measures *Give children tasks that require them to use standard units of measure. Pose such questions as "How many cupfuls?" "How many inches?" and "How many grams (or pounds)?"* **Measuring Area** Children determine the areas of simple geometric shapes on the geoboard in terms of square units and half-square units. They also use the green Pattern-Block triangle as a unit with which to measure various shapes.	*Children should have the opportunity to continue to work with the following tasks, all begun in the middle of the year, in order to deepen their understanding of the concepts being learned.* **Analyzing Shapes** Children see how many different ways they can create a shape with a given number of sides. **Analyzing Solids: Using Boxes and Blocks** Children discover that some geometric solids are composed of faces. They identify these faces as plane geometric shapes. **Exploring Rotation and Symmetry: Using Quilting** Children explore the ideas of rotation and symmetry through their work with quilting. **Sorting Shapes** Children continue to become familiar with attributes of various geometric shapes and three-dimensional objects by sorting them in a variety of ways. They use geometric terms to identify the attributes.	**Using Sorting** Children use sorting to form categories for graphing and to explore the attributes of geometric shapes and solids. **Exploring the Idea of Overlapping Categories (Venn Diagrams)** Children consider how to sort numbers or objects that belong to two categories at the same time.	**Collecting and Organizing Data** Children continue to collect data order to answer questions. They conduct surveys and then organize their data in a variety of ways.

An Overview of the Year's Planning Periods

This overview highlights the concepts of number and pattern that will form the core of the third-grade math program. The school year has been divided into six planning periods. The given time periods are offered simply as a point of reference. Adjust them to fit your own school calendar and the needs of your particular class. During each planning period, spend a day or two on other math experiences such as sorting, measurement, geometry, data collection, and problem solving. Occasionally spend a week or two between planning periods on one of these other areas of mathematics.

First Planning Period: 6–8 weeks (Sept., Oct.)

It is important to establish the work environment at the beginning of the year through children's self-directed exploration of the math manipulatives. Also during this time, you should review basic number concepts to ensure that all children have the opportunity to solidify concepts that were introduced in previous years. Find out whether or not your children:

- know the number combinations to 10 with ease and flexibility.
- can use strategies and relationships when working with numbers to 20.
- can work with numbers to 100 with flexibility.
- are able to take numbers apart in a variety of ways.
- can compare quantities to 100.

The information you gather at this time will help you provide children with appropriate math experiences in the weeks to come.

Second Planning Period: 3–4 Weeks (Oct., Nov.)

The emphasis during this period is on pattern. The children work with growing patterns learning to create, describe, and label them with numbers. Then they work with number patterns in a variety of settings. At the same time, the children continue to solidify their work with word problems and number combinations to 20, and they develop flexibility with numbers to 100.

Third Planning Period: 3–4 Weeks (Nov., Dec.)

The focus for this period is on developing ease and flexibility in adding and subtracting two- and three-digit numbers. The children need ongoing work with this all year long, but at this time they work with a variety of independent activities that support the development of this skill.

Fourth Planning Period: 6–8 Weeks (Jan., Feb., Mar.)

Children spend the next three months working on multiplication. They are introduced to multiplication in ways that help them understand both the process and the idea of equal groups. Children get a lot of practice combining groups and develop more and more efficient strategies for determining *how many.* They learn to write equations to describe the multiplication process. They also work with the multiplication patterns that emerge from their work.

Fifth Planning Period: 4–6 Weeks (Mar., Apr.)

Based on their understanding of multiplication, the children are introduced to division. They have opportunities for continued work in solving addition, subtraction, and multiplication problems.

Sixth Planning Period: 3–4 Weeks (May, June)

Your children's needs will dictate the topics you work with during this last period of the year. You may choose to devote this time to measurement, geometry, fractions, and/or other areas of mathematics. Continue to provide children with practice in addition, subtraction, multiplication, and division through the use of mini-lessons.

A Typical Third-Grade "Math Time"

1. Whole-Class Work: *Shorter Mini-Lesson* (5–10 minutes)*

All the children gather on the rug. Math time begins with a short lesson that provides ongoing practice with concepts previously worked with.

> 3: 1–30 Give-and-Take with Tens and Ones, Ext.
> 3: 2–11 Estimation: "How many scoops of sand will it take to fill this jar?"

2. Preparation for Working with a Small Group

The teacher then asks a small group of children to stay in the rug area. She gives them a short task—to write all the different ways they can to arrange the number 68 as groups of tens and ones—to occupy them while they are waiting for her to make sure that the rest of the children are working appropriately at independent stations.

3. Independent-Station Work (35–50 minutes)

Now the rest of the children are excused to work on their own with the following two- and three-digit addition and subtraction activities, which had been previously introduced over the past three or four days.

> 3: 1–48 Partner Add-It
> 3: 1–49 Partner Take-Away
> 3: 1–50 Roll and Add
> 3: 1–51 Roll and Subtract
> 3: 1–52 Add 'Em Up: Lots of Lines
> 3: 1–53 Add 'Em Up: Paper Shapes
> 3: 1–55 Add 'Em Up: Yarn
> 3: 1–56 Add 'Em Up: Yarn Shapes

4. Teacher-Directed, Small-Group Focus Work (10–20 minutes)

The teacher uses these activities to review facts to 20 with a particular group of children.

> 2: 3–29 How Do You See It? Adding Number Shapes
> 2: 3–31 A Ten-Shape and More: Subtraction

After the small-group lesson is over, the teacher excuses the children to choose an independent activity.

* Each activity number refers to book, chapter, and activity. For example, 2: 1–14 means book 2, chapter 1, activity 14. Notice whether each activity appears in Book One (1:), Book Two (2:), or Book Three (3:).

5. Teacher Observation of Children Working Independently

The teacher moves around the room observing and interacting with individual children.

6. Cleanup Time

After about 50 minutes of working independently, the children clean up their stations and meet back together again on the rug.

7. Whole-Class Work: Brief Discussion of Math Time

The class reviews what went on during math time.

Third-Grade Planning Chart*

First Planning Period: 6–8 Weeks (Sept., Oct.)

Focus: Establishing the Work Environment, Determining Children's Needs,
Numbers to 100: Taking Numbers Apart and Comparing Quantities,
Reviewing Basic Addition and Subtraction Facts

Whole-Class Work: Mini-Lessons	
Shorter Mini-Lesson (5–10 minutes, 3 to 5 times a week)	**Longer Mini-Lesson** (15–25 minutes, as needed)
Pattern Experiences 3: 1–12 Patterns on the 00–99 Chart **Estimation Experiences** **Number Talks: Addition and Subtraction of Numbers to 20** 2: 3–28 Related Combinations: Tall Stacks 2: 3–29 How Do You See It? Adding Number Shapes, Level 1 2: 3–31 A Ten-Shape and More: Subtraction **Addition and Subtraction Stories** 2: 1–11 Working with Complex Addition and Subtraction Stories **Working with Tens and Ones** 3: 1–30 Give-and-Take with Tens and One	**Addition and Subtraction Stories** 2: 1–11 Working with Complex Addition and Subtraction Stories **Number Talks: Addition and Subtraction of Numbers to 20** 2: 3–29 How Do You See It? Adding Number Shapes, Level 2 2: 3–30 Working with Ten-Shapes 2: 3–31 A Ten-Shape and More: Subtraction **Working with Tens and Ones** 3: 1–24 Rearrange It: Arranging Loose Counters into Tens and Ones 3: 1–25 Rearrange It: Breaking Up Trains into Tens and Ones 3: 1–26 Rearrange It: Finding All the Ways 3: 1–27 Rearrange It: How Many Cubes? (10–20) and (20 and beyond) 3: 1–28 Rearrange It: Breaking Up Tens 3: 1–29 Build It Fast 3: 1–31 Think About the Symbols

* Each activity number refers to book, chapter, and activity. For example, 2: 1–14 means book 2, chapter 1, activity 14. Notice whether each activity appears in Book One (**1:**), Book Two (**2:**), or Book Three (**3:**).

Ongoing Independent-Station Work
(35–50 minutes, 3 to 5 times a week)

Introduce math manipulatives and establish expectations for independent work.

Self-Directed Exploration

Connecting cubes
Color Tiles
Wooden cubes
Toothpicks
Collections
Pattern Blocks
Base-ten blocks

Also include any other math materials you plan to use for instruction.

After a few weeks, gradually introduce the following activities.

Working with Tens and Ones:
Comparing Quantities

3: 1–32 Lots of Lines, Level 3
3: 1–33 Paper Shapes, Level 3
3: 1–34 Yarn, Level 3
3: 1–36 Containers, Level 3
3: 1–37 Cover It Up, Level 3
3: 1–38 Measuring Things in the Room, Level 3
3: 1–39 Measuring Myself

Teacher-Directed, Small-Group Focus Work (10–20 minutes, 2 to 3 times a week)

Addition and Subtraction of Numbers to 20

2: 3–29 How Do You See It? Adding Number Shapes, Level 1 or 2
2: 3–30 Working with Ten-Shapes
2: 3–31 A Ten-Shape and More: Subtraction, Level 1 or 2

Number Relationships

2: 3–32 Exploring Number Relationships with the Magic Box

Basic Number Combinations and Relationships

2: 3–5   Related Combinations: Short Stacks
2: 3–6   What Do You Think? Using Counting Boards
2: 3–7   What Do You Think? Using Grab Bags
2: 3–8   What Do You Think? Using Tubs
2: 3–9   Let's Pretend: Grab Bags
2: 3–10 Let's Pretend: Counting Boards
2: 3–11 Let's Pretend: Numbers Trains
2: 3–12 Let's Pretend: Number Shapes

OR

Shared Experiences/Mathematical Events
(35–50 minutes, 1 or 2 times about every two weeks)

Intersperse work at independent stations with whole-class experiences.

Addition and Subtraction

2: 1–10 Writing Stories To Go with Equations

Provide Additional Math Experiences as Time Allows

■ Problem Solving and/or Math and Literature

Self-directed exploration provides informal opportunities for children to work with sorting, measurement, and geometry so additional work in these areas is not necessary at this time.

Third-Grade Planning Notes

First Planning Period: 6–8 Weeks (Sept., Oct.)

Focus: Establishing the Work Environment, Determining Children's Needs,
  Numbers to 100: Taking Numbers Apart and Comparing Quantities,
  Reviewing Basic Addition and Subtraction Facts

Whole-Class Work: Mini-Lessons

You can present new concepts and review previously taught concepts by
spending just a few minutes at the beginning of each math period on
either a *Shorter Mini-Lesson* (5–10 minutes) or a *Longer Mini-Lesson*
(15–25 minutes).

Shorter Mini-Lesson

(5–10 minutes, 3 to 5 times a week)

Choose from the following experiences each day before the children work with
the independent activities. This will allow you to provide a review of basic concepts and at the same time get information about your children's needs.

Pattern Experiences

Occasionally provide opportunities for the children to look for and describe
patterns on a 00–99 chart.

> 3: 1–12 Patterns on the 00–99 Chart

Estimation Experiences

Materials: Assorted clear containers and various objects with which to fill them.

Give the children opportunities to estimate the number of small objects needed
to fill a container. After children have estimated, have them count along with
you as you place objects into the container, one by one. When the container has
been partially filled, allow the children to revise their estimates. Continue
adding objects to the container and counting along until the container is filled.

Vary the estimation experience so that children will begin looking for and discovering number relationships. Do this either by filling the same container with
different objects or by filling another container with the same objects. Notice the
kinds of number relationships that children use. Notice whether their estimates
are reasonable and whether they use number relationships to determine their
estimates.

Number Talks:* Addition and Subtraction of Numbers to 20

Hold up various combinations of two number shapes. These will provide visual models of the various number relationships for numbers to 20 and will help children strengthen their ability to combine numbers and take them apart.

2: 3–28   Related Combinations: Tall Stacks
2: 3–29   How Do You See It? Adding Number Shapes, Level 1
2: 3–31   A Ten-Shape and More: Subtraction

Addition and Subtraction Stories

Children should have opportunities to act out complex addition and subtraction situations. This will give them practice with missing addends, comparative subtraction, and equalizing problems. Use problems with small numbers until the children become able to interpret the language of these problems with ease.

2: 1–11   Working with Complex Addition and Subtraction Stories

Working with Tens and Ones

3: 1–30   Give-and-Take with Tens and Ones

Longer Mini-Lesson
(15–25 minutes, as needed)

These lessons take a little more time than do the shorter mini-lessons because they require the children to use manipulatives.

Addition and Subtraction Stories

In addition to performing themselves and/or using classroom props to act out problems, the children should have opportunities to act out problems using counters to represent the people or objects in the stories.

2: 1–11   Working with Complex Addition and Subtraction Stories

Number Talks: Addition and Subtraction of Numbers to 20

Provide opportunities for the children to work with the number shapes themselves and to record the equations they are working with.

2: 3–29   How Do You See It? Adding Number Shapes, Level 2
2: 3–30   Working with Ten-Shapes
2: 3–31   A-Ten Shape and More: Subtraction

---

* Number Talks are experiences that allow children to solve addition, subtraction, multiplication, and division problems in a variety of ways, generally using number relationships. The children should be given opportunities to describe the ways they solve the problems. Make sure you present a variety of problems for children to solve. See the video series, *Thinking with Numbers*, published by Educational Enrichment, Norman, OK, for more information about Number Talks.

Working with Tens and Ones

The following activities will give the children the opportunity to explore the many ways that numbers can be broken down into groups of tens and ones. This will support children's developing understanding of conservation of number. It will also give them experiences in taking numbers apart in a variety of ways.

3: 1–24   Rearrange It: Arranging Loose Counters into Tens and Ones
3: 1–25   Rearrange It: Breaking Up Trains into Tens and Ones
3: 1–26   Rearrange It: Finding All the Ways
3: 1–27   Rearrange It: How Many Cubes? (10–20) and (20 and beyond)
3: 1–28   Rearrange It: Breaking Up Tens
3: 1–29   Build It Fast
3: 1–31   Think About the Symbols

Ongoing Independent-Station Work
(35–50 minutes, 3 to 5 times a week)

Self-Directed Exploration

Materials: Connecting cubes, Color Tiles, wooden cubes, toothpicks, collections, Pattern Blocks, and base-ten blocks.* Include any additional math materials that you plan to use for instruction.

Establishing routines and expectations is the most important work for the beginning of the school year. If the children are going to accomplish all that they can throughout the year, they need to learn what it means to work hard, how to make choices, and how to get along with the other children in the class. This time is critical to the children as they need to work with manipulatives using their own ideas before they can focus on specific activities. While all the children will be exploring these manipulatives on their own, you will be free to focus on helping to develop the work environment.

Introduce the manipulatives gradually over a period of several days, making sure the children understand how to use them appropriately. Go over the rules for using them and the procedures for cleaning up. (See "Establishing the Learning Environment" on p. xxii.)

After you have introduced the manipulatives, have a few children deliver them to the various stations around the room. Excuse the rest of the children, a few at a time, to choose where they will work. Observe and interact with them while they are at work, commenting on their work and redirecting them, if necessary. At the end of the math period, spend a minute or two discussing the good hard work you observed and/or reminding the children of any behaviors that need to be changed.

---

* Although base-ten blocks are not presented in the *Developing Number Concepts* series, they are appropriate for use by third-graders and can be substituted for connecting cubes or beans and cups in many activities. Base-ten blocks, especially the centimeter cubes and decimeter rods, can also provide an introduction to standard units of measurement.

Working with Tens and Ones: Comparing Quantities

Materials: Concept Development Packets—each set up to accommodate six children.

After several weeks, gradually replace the self-directed exploration stations with the activities that will provide the children with practice in comparing numbers to 100.

    3: 1–32 Lots of Lines, Level 3
    3: 1–33 Paper Shapes, Level 3
    3: 1–34 Yarn, Level 3
    3: 1–36 Containers, Level 3
    3: 1–37 Cover It Up, Level 3
    3: 1–38 Measuring Things in the Room, Level 3
    3: 1–39 Measuring Myself

Teacher-Directed, Small-Group Focus Work
(10–20 minutes, 2 to 3 times a week)

While the whole-class activities can be of value to the children, it is important that you also work with small groups of children so that you can give them the precise help they need. Give children a variety of experiences, choosing from the following activities according to the children's needs and responses. Do two to four activities for a few minutes each during any one lesson.

Addition and Subtraction of Numbers to 20

    2: 3–29 How Do You See It? Adding Number Shapes, Level 1 or 2
    2: 3–30 Working with Ten-Shapes
    2: 3–31 A Ten-Shape and More: Subtraction, Level 1 or 2

Number Relationships

    2: 3–32 Exploring Number Relationships with the Magic Box

Basic Number Combinations and Relationships

Continue to give these experiences to any children who still have not internalized the combinations to 10.

    2: 3–5   Related Combinations: Short Stacks
    2: 3–6   What Do You Think? Using Counting Boards
    2: 3–7   What Do You Think? Using Grab Bags
    2: 3–8   What Do You Think? Using Tubs
    2: 3–9   Let's Pretend: Grab Bags
    2: 3–10 Let's Pretend: Counting Boards
    2: 3–11 Let's Pretend: Numbers Trains
    2: 3–12 Let's Pretend: Number Shapes

OR

Shared Experiences/Mathematical Events
(35–50 minutes, 1 or 2 times about every two weeks)

You can vary the usual routine through occasional whole-class experiences. The shared experiences generally require the entire math period and involve the children in working with manipulatives.

Addition and Subtraction

2: 1–10 Writing Stories To Go with Equations

Provide Additional Math Experiences as Time Allows

■ Problem Solving and/or Math and Literature

This guide focuses on planning for the development of number and pattern concepts. You will also want to provide additional math experiences for your children. Sometimes, instead of having the children work with the independent stations, you may have them spend a day solving a problem presented through literature. Other times, you may have them spend a week or more focusing on another math strand, such as geometry or sorting. During this first planning period, you will not need to present additional math experiences since self-directed exploration provides children with informal opportunities to work with sorting, geometry, and measurement concepts. Later in the year, you will need to integrate these other experiences into your math time.

Third-Grade Planning Chart

Second Planning Period: 3–4 Weeks (Oct., Nov.)

Focus: Growing Patterns, Number Patterns, Solidifying Addition and Subtraction to 20, Numbers to 100: Developing Flexibility with Numbers and Understanding Number Relationships

Whole-Class Work: Mini-Lessons	
Shorter Mini-Lesson (5–10 minutes, 3 to 5 times a week)	**Longer Mini-Lesson** (15–25 minutes, as needed)
Pattern Experiences 3: 1–12 Patterns on the 00–99 Chart **Estimation Experiences** **Number Talks: Addition and Subtraction of Numbers to 20** 2: 3–28 Related Combinations: Tall Stacks 2: 3–29 How Do You See It? Adding Number Shapes, Level 1 2: 3–30 Working with Ten-Shapes 2: 3–31 A Ten-Shape and More: Subtraction, Level 1 **Working with Tens and Ones** 3: 1–30 Give-and-Take with Tens and Ones **Addition and Subtraction Stories** 2: 1–11 Working with Complex Addition and Subtraction Stories	**Addition and Subtraction** 2: 1–11 Working with Complex Addition and Subtraction Stories **Working with Tens and Ones** 3: 1–24 Rearrange It: Arranging Loose Counters into Tens and Ones 3: 1–25 Rearrange It: Breaking Up Trains into Tens and Ones 3: 1–26 Rearrange It: Finding All the Ways 3: 1–27 Rearrange It: How Many Cubes? (10–20) 3: 1–28 Rearrange It: Breaking Up Tens 3: 1–29 Build It Fast 3: 1–31 Think About the Symbols, Ext.

(Chart continues on next page.)

(Continued from previous page.)

Ongoing Independent-Station Work (35–50 minutes, 3 to 5 times a week)

Growing-Pattern Stations

The following Book-One activities are optional.

1: 2–16 Exploring Growing Patterns
1: 2–17 Growing-Patterns Task Cards
1: 2–18 Creating Growing Patterns
3: 1–19 Number Patterns in Growing Patterns

Number-Pattern Stations

3: 1–17 Recording Various Number Patterns on Strips
3: 1–18 Grab and Add
3: 1–19 Number Patterns in Growing Patterns
3: 1–20 Margie's Grid Pictures, Ext.
3: 1–21 Looking for Patterns on the 00–99 Chart
3: 1–22 The 00–99 Chart Puzzles
3: 1–23 Searching-for-Patterns Station

Teacher-Directed, Small-Group Focus Work (10–20 minutes, 2 to 3 times a week)

Choose several activities over time, using two to four of them during any one lesson.

Addition and Subtraction of Numbers to 20

2: 3–28 Related Combinations: Tall Stacks
2: 3–29 How Do You See It? Adding Number Shapes
2: 3–30 Working with Ten-Shapes
2: 3–31 A Ten-Shape and More: Subtraction

Number Relationships

2: 3–32 Exploring Number Relationships with the Magic Box

OR

Shared Experiences/Mathematical Events
(35–50 minutes, 1 or 2 times about every two weeks)

Exploring Growing Patterns

3: 1–14 Analyzing Growing Patterns
3: 1–15 Finding the Number Patterns in Growing Patterns

Exploring Pattern Searches

3: 1–16 Introducing Pattern Searches

Provide Additional Math Experiences as Time Allows

- Problem Solving and/or Math and Literature
- Data Collection and Graphing
- Geometry
- Measurement
- Informal Work with Fractions

Third-Grade Planning Notes

Second Planning Period: 3–4 Weeks (Oct., Nov.)

Focus: Growing Patterns, Number Patterns, Solidifying Addition and Subtraction to 20, Numbers to 100: Developing Flexibility with Numbers and Understanding Number Relationships

---

Whole-Class Work: Mini-Lessons

You can present new concepts and review previously taught concepts by spending just a few minutes at the beginning of each math period on either a *Shorter Mini-Lesson* (5–10 minutes) or a *Longer Mini-Lesson* (15–25 minutes).

As you continue giving the children experiences with the mini-lessons over time, notice how their interactions and responses change.

Shorter Mini-Lesson

(5–10 minutes, 3 to 5 times a week)

Pattern Experiences

Continue to give children opportunities to look for and describe number patterns.

> 3: 1–12 Patterns on the 00–99 Chart

Estimation Experiences

Materials: Assorted clear containers and various objects with which to fill them. Dried beans and/or sand and small scoops of various sizes.

Have the children estimate how many scoopfuls of beans are needed to fill a container. Then fill the container, counting the number of scoops needed. Use containers of different sizes over a period of several days. Then challenge the children to estimate the number of beans a particular container can hold. Ask them to think about a way to figure this out without actually counting all the beans. Have them consider how knowing the number of beans in one scoop can help them.

Number Talks: Addition and Subtraction of Numbers to 20

Continue spending a few minutes working with the number shapes and writing number problems (sums to 20) on the board as long as some children still need this practice.

      2: 3–28   Related Combinations: Tall Stacks
      2: 3–29   How Do You See It? Adding Number Shapes, Level 1
      2: 3–30   Working with Ten-Shapes
      2: 3–31   A Ten-Shape and More: Subtraction, Level 1
      3: 1–30   Give-and-Take with Tens and Ones

Addition and Subtraction Stories

      2: 1–11   Working with Complex Addition and Subtraction Stories

---

Longer Mini-Lesson
(15–25 minutes, as needed)

Addition and Subtraction Stories

Occasionally, give the children complex addition and subtraction stories to act out and record until most of the children can easily interpret the language and record the corresponding equations.

      2: 1–11   Working with Complex Addition and Subtraction Stories

Working with Tens and Ones

Use the recommended activities to be sure that children know how to break up a two-digit number into groups of tens and ones in different ways. Once they can work with tens and ones with ease, extend the activities by having children use base-ten blocks, instead of connecting cubes or Color Tiles, to discover how to break up a three-digit number into groups of hundreds, tens, and ones.

      3: 1–24   Rearrange It: Arranging Loose Counters into Tens and Ones
      3: 1–25   Rearrange It: Breaking Up Trains into Tens and Ones
      3: 1–26   Rearrange It: Finding All the Ways
      3: 1–27   Rearrange It: How Many Cubes? (10–20)
      3: 1–28   Rearrange It: Breaking Up Tens
      3: 1–29   Build It Fast
      3: 1–31   Think About the Symbols, Ext.

Ongoing Independent-Station Work
(35–50 minutes, 3 to 5 times a week)

Growing-Pattern Stations

If the children have not had previous experience working with growing patterns, you may wish to give them time to work with the growing-patterns task cards to create growing patterns. You will also want to provide whole-class experiences with growing patterns. (See "Shared Experiences/Mathematical Events.") Then have children use numbers to label the parts of the patterns. If they have had previous experiences with growing patterns, children can move on more quickly to working with number-pattern stations. The following activities from *Book One* are optional.

1: 2–16   Exploring Growing Patterns
1: 2–17   Growing-Patterns Task Cards
1: 2–18   Creating Growing Patterns

3: 1–19   Number Patterns in Growing Patterns

Number-Pattern Stations

3: 1–17   Recording Various Number Patterns on Strips
3: 1–18   Grab and Add
3: 1–19   Number Patterns in Growing Patterns
3: 1–20   Margie's Grid Pictures, Ext.
3: 1–21   Looking for Patterns on the 00–99 Chart, Ext. (Have children also explore what happens when the grid is extended beyond 99 to 199.)
3: 1–22   The 00–99 Chart Puzzles
3: 1–23   Searching-for-Patterns Station

Teacher-Directed, Small-Group Focus Work
(10–20 minutes, 2 to 3 times a week)

It is important that you work with children having similar needs to help them focus on developing understanding of particular concepts. Give children a variety of experiences, choosing from the following activities. Do two to four of the activities for a few minutes each during any one lesson.

Addition and Subtraction of Numbers to 20

2: 3–28   Related Combinations: Tall Stacks
2: 3–29   How Do You See It? Adding Number Shapes
2: 3–30   Working with Ten-Shapes
2: 3–31   A Ten-Shape and More: Subtraction

Number Relationships

> 2: 3–32   Exploring Number Relationships with the Magic Box

OR

Shared Experiences/Mathematical Events
(35–50 minutes, 1 or 2 times about every two weeks)

You can vary the usual routine through occasional whole-class experiences. You can then continue to work with previously introduced concepts or present new concepts.

Exploring Growing Patterns

Children should have experiences with growing patterns in a teacher-directed setting.

> 3: 1–14   Analyzing Growing Patterns
> 3: 1–15   Finding the Number Patterns in Growing Patterns

Exploring Pattern Searches

Provide opportunities for the children to look for number patterns that emerge from various explorations.

> 3: 1–16   Introducing Pattern Searches

Provide Additional Math Experiences as Time Allows

- Problem Solving and/or Math and Literature
- Data Collection and Graphing
- Geometry
- Measurement
- Informal Work with Fractions

Third-Grade Planning Chart

Third Planning Period: 6–8 Weeks (Nov., Dec.)

Focus: Addition and Subtraction of Two- and Three-Digit Numbers,
Working with Hundreds: Number Relationships

Whole-Class Work: Mini-Lessons	
Shorter Mini-Lesson (5–10 minutes, 3 to 5 times a week)	**Longer Mini-Lesson** (15–25 minutes, as needed)

Pattern Experiences 3: 1–12 *Extend number patterns beyond the 00–99 chart. (See notes.)* **Estimation Experiences** **Number Talks: Addition and Subtraction of Numbers to 20** 2: 3–28 Related Combinations: Tall Stacks 2: 3–29 How Do You See It? Adding Number Shapes, Level 1 2: 3–30 Working with Ten-Shapes 2: 3–31 A Ten-Shape and More: Subtraction, Level 1 **Working with Tens and Ones** 3: 1–30 Give-and-Take with Tens and Ones, Ext. **Addition, Subtraction, and Multiplication Stories** 2: 1–11 Working with Complex Addition and Subtraction Stories 3: 2–1 Looking for Equal Groups in the Real World 3: 2–2 Acting Out Multiplication Stories: Using Real Objects	**Addition, Subtraction, and Multiplication Stories** 2: 1–11 Working with Complex Addition and Subtraction Stories 3: 2–3 Acting Out Multiplication Stories: Using Counters **Number Talks: Addition and Subtraction of Numbers to 20** *If needed.* 2: 3–28 Related Combinations: Tall Stacks 2: 3–29 How Do You See It? Adding Number Shapes 2: 3–30 Working with Ten-Shapes 2: 3–31 A Ten-Shape and More: Subtraction **Number Talks: Addition and Subtraction of Two- and Three-Digit Numbers** *Problems Posed by the Teacher* 3: 1–45 Addition and Subtraction of Two-Digit Numbers 3: 1–46 Story Problems

(Chart continues on next page.)

(Continued from previous page.)

Ongoing Independent-Station Work (35–50 minutes, 3 to 5 times a week)

Addition and Subtraction Stations of Numbers to 100 and Beyond

Adapt the following activities so that they include numbers in the hundreds. Include some Level 3 activities, Comparing Quantities, if children still need work with this.

3: 1–48 Partner Add-It
3: 1–49 Partner Take-Away
3: 1–50 Roll and Add
3: 1–51 Roll and Subtract
3: 1–52 Add 'Em Up: Lots of Lines*
3: 1–53 Add 'Em Up: Paper Shapes*
3: 1–54 Add 'Em Up: Measuring Things in the Room*
3: 1–55 Add 'Em Up: Yarn*

3: 1–56 Add 'Em Up: Yarn Shapes
3: 1–57 Add 'Em Up: Containers
3: 1–58 Add 'Em Up: Cover It Up*
3: 1–59 Solving Story Problems

Use base-ten blocks.

Addition and Subtraction of Numbers to 20

2: 3–21 Grab-Bag Addition Station
2: 3–22 Grab-Bag Subtraction Station
2: 3–33 Number-Shape Pairs
2: 3–34 Two Ten-Shapes: Addition and Subtraction
2: 3–35 A Ten-Shape and More: Subtraction Station

Teacher-Directed, Small-Group Focus Work (10–20 minutes, 2 to 3 times a week)

Choose several activities over time, using two to four of them during any one lesson.

Addition and Subtraction of Two- and Three-Digit Numbers

Extend to include three-digit numbers if the group is ready to work with them.

3: 1–45 Addition and Subtraction of Two-Digit Numbers
3: 1–46 Story Problems
3: 1–47 Figure It Out

Addition and Subtraction of Numbers to 20

Choose from the following activities according to the needs of your children.

2: 3–28 Related Combinations: Tall Stacks
2: 3–29 How Do You See It? Adding Number Shapes
2: 3–30 Working with Ten-Shapes
2: 3–31 A Ten-Shape and More: Subtraction

Working with Hundreds, Tens, and Ones

3: 1–30 Give-and-Take with Tens and Ones, Ext.

OR

Shared Experiences/Mathematical Events (35–50 minutes, 1 or 2 times about every two weeks)

Growing Patterns

Intersperse work at independent stations with whole-class experiences.

3: 1–14 Analyzing Growing Patterns
3: 1–15 Finding the Number Patterns in Growing Patterns

Provide Additional Math Experiences as Time Allows

■ Problem Solving and/or Math and Literature
■ Data Collection and Graphing
■ Measurement
■ Fractions

Third-Grade Planning Notes

Third Planning Period: 6–8 Weeks (Nov., Dec.)

Focus: Addition and Subtraction of Two- and Three-Digit Numbers,
Working with Hundreds: Number Relationships

Whole-Class Work: Mini-Lessons

You can present new concepts and review previously taught concepts by
spending just a few minutes at the beginning of each math period on
either a *Shorter Mini-Lesson* (5–10 minutes) or a *Longer Mini-Lesson*
(15–25 minutes).

Shorter Mini-Lesson

(5–10 minutes, 3 to 5 times a week)

Pattern Experiences

Extend the 00–99 chart at least to 199 so that children can discover additional
number patterns.

Estimation Experiences

Materials: Assorted clear containers and various objects with which to fill them.

Hold up a container. Challenge the children to estimate the number of small
objects it will take to fill it. Count out the objects as you put them into the container to form one or two layers. At this point, allow any children who would
like to change their estimates to do so. Continue the count until the container is
filled. Have children compare their estimates with the actual count. Discuss
which estimate was closer, their first or their second, and why.

Number Talks: Addition and Subtraction of Numbers to 20

Continue to provide ongoing practice with numbers to 20 if some children
need this.

> 2: 3–28   Related Combinations: Tall Stacks
> 2: 3–29   How Do You See It? Adding Number Shapes, Level 1
> 2: 3–30   Working with Ten-Shapes
> 2: 3–31   A Ten-Shape and More: Subtraction, Level 1

Working with Hundreds, Tens, and Ones

> 3: 1–30   Give-and-Take with Tens and Ones, Ext.

Addition, Subtraction, and Multiplication Stories

Continue to work with addition and subtraction and introduce multiplication as well.

2: 1–1   Acting Out Stories: Using Real Things
2: 1–2   Acting Out Stories: Using Fantasies
2: 1–11 Working with Complex Addition and Subtraction Stories
3: 2–1   Looking for Equal Groups in the Real World
3: 2–2   Acting Out Multiplication Stories: Using Real Objects

---

Longer Mini-Lesson
(15–25 minutes, as needed)

Addition, Subtraction, and Multiplication Stories

Give the children occasional opportunities to act out story problems involving equalizing, comparative subtraction, and missing addends. Have the children write equations to record their actions. Begin to present multiplication problems as well.

2: 1–11 Working with Complex Addition and Subtraction Stories
3: 2–3   Acting Out Multiplication Stories: Using Counters

Number Talks: Addition and Subtraction of Numbers to 20

You can continue to meet the needs of any child who requires a review of addition and subtraction to 20. Spend two or three minutes a day on problems that deal with smaller numbers along with the work with two- and three-digit numbers.

2: 3–28 Related Combinations: Tall Stacks
2: 3–29 How Do You See It? Adding Number Shapes
2: 3–30 Working with Ten-Shapes
2: 3–31 A Ten-Shape and More: Subtraction

Number Talks: Addition and Subtraction of Two- and Three-Digit Numbers

Give the children a variety of problems to solve. Write some on the board and present others in the context of story problems. Make manipulatives available and be sure to follow the teaching procedure outlined in activity 3: 1–45.

3: 1–45 Addition and Subtraction of Two-Digit Numbers
3: 1–46 Story Problems

Ongoing Independent-Station Work
(35–50 minutes, 3 to 5 times a week)

Most of the recommended activities provide children with the experiences of adding and subtracting to 100, but the activities can be adapted to include addition of numbers in the hundreds. Children can work with the starred activities using base-ten blocks as measuring tools. For example, the children can fill the paper shapes with base-ten hundreds, tens, and ones blocks; they can measure the lengths of pieces of yarn with tens and ones blocks. To meet the range of needs in your classroom and to help children develop facility with smaller numbers, a few of the experiences provide review of adding to 20.

Make a few addition and subtraction stations available at first. Include some that focus on numbers to 20 as well as those that focus on larger numbers. Then gradually add more stations, replacing some of the previously introduced activities.

Addition and Subtraction Stations of Numbers to 100 and Beyond

3: 1–48 Partner Add-It
3: 1–49 Partner Take-Away
3: 1–50 Roll and Add
3: 1–51 Roll and Subtract
3: 1–52 Add 'Em Up: Lots of Lines*
3: 1–53 Add 'Em Up: Paper Shapes*
3: 1–54 Add 'Em Up: Measuring Things in the Room*
3: 1–55 Add 'Em Up: Yarn*
3: 1–56 Add 'Em Up: Yarn Shapes
3: 1–57 Add 'Em Up: Containers
3: 1–58 Add 'Em Up: Cover It Up*
3: 1–59 Solving Story Problems

Addition and Subtraction of Numbers to 20

2: 3–21 Grab-Bag Addition Station
2: 3–22 Grab-Bag Subtraction Station
2: 3–33 Number-Shape Pairs
2: 3–34 Two Ten-Shapes: Addition and Subtraction
2: 3–35 A Ten-Shape and More: Subtraction Station

Teacher-Directed, Small-Group Focus Work
(10–20 minutes, 2 to 3 times a week)

You will have children with a range of needs that can best be met through small-group work. This allows you to tailor the problems to meet the particular needs of the group. Keep the experiences short but frequent so that the children will get the practice they need to internalize the number combinations and to develop ease in adding and subtracting.

Addition and Subtraction of Two- and Three-Digit Numbers

Extend these activities to include three-digit numbers if the group is ready to work with them.

      3: 1–45 Addition and Subtraction of Two-Digit Numbers
      3: 1–46 Story Problems
      3: 1–47 Figure It Out

Addition and Subtraction of Numbers to 20

      2: 3–28 Related Combinations: Tall Stacks
      2: 3–29 How Do You See It? Adding Number Shapes
      2: 3–30 Working with Ten-Shapes
      2: 3–31 A Ten-Shape and More: Subtraction

Working with Hundreds, Tens, and Ones

      3: 1–30 Give-and-Take with Tens and Ones, Ext.

   OR

Shared Experiences/Mathematical Events
(35–50 minutes, 1 or 2 times about every two weeks)

Growing Patterns

Vary the routine by giving children opportunities to continue their work with growing patterns.

      3: 1–14 Analyzing Growing Patterns
      3: 1–15 Finding the Number Patterns in Growing Patterns

Provide Additional Math Experiences as Time Allows

- Problem Solving and/or Math and Literature
- Data collection and Graphing
- Measurement
- Fractions

Third-Grade Planning Chart
Fourth Planning Period: 6–8 Weeks (Jan., Feb., Mar.)

Focus: Introduction to Multiplication, Multiplication Equations,
  Multiplication Patterns

Whole-Class Work: Mini-Lessons	
Shorter Mini-Lesson (5–10 minutes, 3 to 5 times a week)	**Longer Mini-Lesson** (15–25 minutes, as needed)

Pattern Experiences
3: 1–12 Patterns on the 00-99 Chart
  Extend to numbers beyond 100.
 	
Estimation Experiences
 	
Number Talks: Addition and Subtraction of Two- and Three-Digit Numbers
Teacher poses problems and models them.
 	
Working with Hundreds, Tens, and Ones
3: 1–30 Give-and-Take with Tens and
  Ones, Ext.
	For this planning period, the longer mini-lessons have been replaced with the series of teacher-directed, whole-class lessons that follows.

Teacher-Directed, Whole-Class Lessons (35–50 minutes, as needed)
Multiplication as Counting Groups 3: 2–1 Looking for Equal Groups in the Real World 3: 2–2 Acting Out Multiplication Stories: Using Real Objects 3: 2–3 Acting Out Multiplication Stories: Using Counters 3: 2–4 Building Models of Multiplication Problems 3: 2–5 Building Related Models **Multiplication Equations** 3: 2–6 Modeling the Recording of Multiplication Experiences 3: 2–7 Introducing the Multiplication Sign 3: 2–8 Interpreting Symbols 3: 2–10 Learning To Write the Multiplication Sign, Levels 1 and 2 **Multiplication Patterns** 3: 1–16 Introducing Pattern Searches

(Chart continues on next page.)

(Continued from previous page.)

Ongoing Independent-Station Work (35–50 minutes, 3 to 5 times a week)

Multiplication Stations

3: 2–11 How Many Cups?
3: 2–12 How Many Groups?
3: 2–13 How Many Rows?
3: 2–14 How Many Towers?

Reading Equations

Introduce this activity after you have presented the multiplication sign.

3: 2–15 Counting Boards:
Multiplication, Level 1

Writing Multiplication Equations

Add these activities when the children are able to write equations.

3: 2–15 Counting Boards:
Multiplication, Levels 2 and 3
3: 2–16 Problems for Partners:
Multiplication

3: 2–17 Roll and Multiply
3: 2–18 Discovering Patterns: Cupfuls,
Level 1
3: 2–19 Discovering Patterns: Buildings,
Level 1
3: 2–20 Discovering Patterns: Number
Shapes, Level 1
3: 2–23 Lots of Rectangles
3: 2–24 Shape Puzzles: Multiplication
3: 2–25 Mixing Them Up

Multiplication Patterns

3: 2–18 Discovering Patterns: Cupfuls,
Level 2
3: 2–19 Discovering Patterns: Buildings,
Level 2
3: 2–20 Discovering Patterns: Number
Shapes, Level 2
3: 2–21 Pattern Search: Multiplication

Teacher-Directed, Small-Group Focus Work (10–20 minutes, 2 to 3 times a week)

Multiplication

3: 2–2   Acting Out Multiplication Stories: Using Real Objects
3: 2–3   Acting Out Multiplication Stories: Using Counters
3: 2–4   Building Models of Multiplication Problems
3: 2–5   Building Related Models
3: 2–8   Interpreting Symbols
3: 2–10 Learning To Write the Multiplication Sign, Levels 1 and 2

OR

Shared Experiences/Mathematical Events (35–50 minutes, 1 or 2 times about every two weeks)

Intersperse work at independent stations with whole-class experiences.

Provide Additional Math Experiences as Time Allows

- Problem Solving and/or Math and Literature
- Sorting
- Geometry

Third-Grade Planning Notes

Fourth Planning Period: 6–8 Weeks (Jan., Feb., Mar.)

Focus: Introduction to Multiplication, Multiplication Equations,
        Multiplication Patterns

Whole-Class Work: Mini-Lessons

You can present new concepts and review previously taught concepts by
spending just a few minutes at the beginning of each math period on
either a *Shorter Mini-Lesson* (5–10 minutes) or a *Longer Mini-Lesson*
(15–25 minutes).

Shorter Mini-Lesson
(5–10 minutes, 3 to 5 times a week)

Pattern Experiences

Extend the 00–99 chart at least to 199 so that children can discover additional
number patterns.

Estimation Experiences

Materials: Assorted clear containers and various objects with which to fill them.

Hold up a container. Challenge the children to estimate the number of small
objects it will take to fill it. Count out the objects as you put them into the container to form one or two layers. At this point, allow any children who would
like to change their estimates to do so. Continue the count until the container is
filled. Have children compare their estimates with the actual count. Discuss
which estimate was closer, their first or their second, and why.

Number Talks: Addition and Subtraction of Two- and Three-Digit Numbers

Although your main focus will be on multiplication, occasionally present an
addition or subtraction problem for children to solve as ongoing review.

Working with Hundreds, Tens, and Ones

Use base-ten blocks to extend the activity.

> 3: 1–30 Give-and-Take with Tens and Ones, Ext.

*For this planning period, the longer mini-lessons have been replaced with the
series of teacher-directed, whole-class lessons that follows.*

Teacher-Directed, Whole-Class Lessons
(35–50 minutes, as needed)

Introduce the multiplication activities; then have children repeat them in order, as needed.

Multiplication as Counting Groups

3: 2–1 Looking for Equal Groups in the Real World
3: 2–2 Acting Out Multiplication Stories: Using Real Objects
3: 2–3 Acting Out Multiplication Stories: Using Counters
3: 2–4 Building Models of Multiplication Problems
3: 2–5 Building Related Models

Multiplication Equations

3: 2–6 Modeling the Recording of Multiplication Experiences
3: 2–7 Introducing the Multiplication Sign
3: 2–8 Interpreting Symbols
3: 2–10 Learning To Write the Multiplication Sign, Levels 1 and 2

Multiplication Patterns

3: 1–16 Introducing Pattern Searches

Ongoing Independent-Station Work
(35–50 minutes, 3 to 5 times a week)

Make a few multiplication stations available at first. Then gradually add more stations, replacing some with others that were previously introduced.

Multiplication Stations

These activities focus on counting groups.

3: 2–11 How Many Cups?
3: 2–12 How Many Groups?
3: 2–13 How Many Rows?
3: 2–14 How Many Towers?

Reading Equations

After you have introduced the multiplication sign, add this activity which requires children to read equations.

3: 2–15 Counting Boards: Multiplication, Level 1

Writing Multiplication Equations

Once children are able to write equations, add these stations.

3: 2–15 Counting Boards: Multiplication, Levels 2 and 3
3: 2–16 Problems for Partners: Multiplication
3: 2–17 Roll and Multiply
3: 2–18 Discovering Patterns: Cupfuls, Level 1
3: 2–19 Discovering Patterns: Buildings, Level 1
3: 2–20 Discovering Patterns: Number Shapes, Level 1
3: 2–23 Lots of Rectangles
3: 2–24 Shape Puzzles: Multiplication
3: 2–25 Mixing Them Up

Multiplication Patterns

The children will also look for patterns as they work with the multiplication stations.

3: 2–18 Discovering Patterns: Cupfuls, Level 2
3: 2–19 Discovering Patterns: Buildings, Level 2
3: 2–20 Discovering Patterns: Number Shapes, Level 2
3: 2–21 Pattern Search: Multiplication

Teacher-Directed, Small-Group Focus Work
(10–20 minutes, 2 to 3 times a week)

Multiplication

Some children may need additional work in acting out multiplication stories and/or in writing equations.

3: 2–2 Acting Out Multiplication Stories: Using Real Objects
3: 2–3 Acting Out Multiplication Stories: Using Counters
3: 2–4 Building Models of Multiplication Problems
3: 2–5 Building Related Models
3: 2–8 Interpreting Symbols
3: 2–10 Learning To Write the Multiplication Sign, Levels 1 and 2

OR

Shared Experiences/Mathematical Events
(35–50 minutes, 1 or 2 times about every two weeks)

Provide Additional Math Experiences as Time Allows

- Problem Solving and/or Math and Literature
- Sorting
- Geometry

Third-Grade Planning Chart
Fifth Planning Period: 4–6 Weeks (Mar., Apr.)

Focus: Introduction to Division; Continuation of Work with Addition, Subtraction, and Multiplication Problems

Whole-Class Work: Mini-Lessons	
Shorter Mini-Lesson (5–10 minutes, 3 to 5 times a week)	**Longer Mini-Lesson** (15–25 minutes, as needed)
Pattern Experiences **Number Talks:** **Addition and Subtraction of Two- and Three-Digit Numbers** *Problems Posed by the Teacher* **Solving Multiplication Problems** *Problems Posed by the Teacher* **Solving Division Problems** *Problems Posed by the Teacher*	*For this planning period, the longer mini-lessons have been replaced with the series of teacher-directed, whole-class lessons that follows.*

Teacher-Directed, Whole-Class Lessons
(40–50 minutes, as needed)

Introducing Division

3: 3–1   Acting Out Division Stories: Using Real Objects
3: 3–2   Acting Out Division Stories: Using Counters
3: 3–3   Building Models of Division Problems
3: 3–6   Interpreting Symbols

Writing Division Equations

3: 3–4   Odds and Evens
3: 3–5   Modeling the Recording of Division Experiences
3: 3–7   Learning To Write the Division Sign

Ongoing Independent-Station Work (35–50 minutes, 3 to 5 times a week)

Division Stations

3: 3–9   Counting Boards: Division, Level 1,
          then Levels 2 and 3
3: 3–10   Number Shapes: Division
3: 3–11   Making Rows
3: 3–12   Problems for Partners: Division
3: 3–13   Cups of Cubes
3: 3–14   How Many Buildings?
3: 3–15   Creation Cards for Division

Gradually introduce these stations.

3: 3–5   Modeling the Recording of
          Division Experiences
3: 3–6   Interpreting Symbols, Var.
3: 3–8   Multiplication and Division
          Together: Story Problems

Teacher-Directed, Small-Group Focus Work (10–20 minutes, 2 to 3 times a week)

Division

3: 3–3   Building Models of Division
          Problems
3: 3–7   Learning To Write the Division Sign

Number Talks:

**Addition and Subtraction of Two-
and Three-Digit Numbers**

Solving Multiplication Problems

Solving Division Problems

OR

Shared Experiences/Mathematical Events
(35–50 minutes, 1 or 2 times about every two weeks)

**Provide Additional Math Experiences
as Time Allows**

- Problem Solving and/or Math
  and Literature

- Sorting
- Geometry
- Fractions
- Data Collection

Third-Grade Planning Notes

Fifth Planning Period: 4–6 Weeks (Mar., Apr.)

Focus: Introduction to Division; Continuation of Work with Addition, Subtraction, and Multiplication Problems

---

Whole-Class Work: Mini-Lessons

You can present new concepts and review previously taught concepts by spending just a few minutes at the beginning of each math period on either a *Shorter Mini-Lesson* (5–10 minutes) or a *Longer Mini-Lesson* (15–25 minutes).

Shorter Mini-Lesson
(5–10 minutes, 3 to 5 times a week)

Spend a few minutes reviewing concepts previously worked with.

Pattern Experiences

Extend the 00–99 chart at least to 199 so that children can discover additional number patterns.

Number Talks:

Addition and Subtraction of Two- and Three-Digit Numbers

Solving Multiplication Problems

Solving Division Problems

Continue to provide opportunities for children to solve a variety of problems using all four arithmetical processes.

For this planning period, the longer mini-lessons have been replaced with the series of teacher-directed, whole-class lessons that follows.

Teacher-Directed, Whole-Class Lesson
(40–50 minutes, as needed)

Introducing Division

Begin by introducing division as the sharing, or partitioning, of groups.

3: 3–1   Acting Out Division Stories: Using Real Objects
3: 3–2   Acting Out Division Stories: Using Counters
3: 3–3   Building Models of Division Problems
3: 3–6   Interpreting Symbols

Writing Division Equations

After several days, introduce the writing of division equations. Use these division experiences to have children explore the concept of odd and even numbers.

3: 3–4   Odds and Evens
3: 3–5   Modeling the Recording of Division Experiences
3: 3–7   Learning To Write the Division Sign

Ongoing Independent-Station Work
(35–50 minutes, 3 to 5 times a week)

Make a few division stations available at first. Then gradually add more stations, replacing some of those that were previously introduced.

Division Stations

Begin with these stations that do not require writing.

3: 3–9   Counting Boards: Division, Level 1, then Levels 2 and 3
3: 3–10   Number Shapes: Division
3: 3–11   Making Rows
3: 3–12   Problems for Partners: Division
3: 3–13   Cups of Cubes
3: 3–14   How Many Buildings?
3: 3–15   Creation Cards for Division

Add these stations that require children to write equations.

3: 3–5   Modeling the Recording of Division Experiences
3: 3–6   Interpreting Symbols, Var.
3: 3–8   Multiplication and Division Together: Story Problems

> ## Teacher-Directed, Small-Group Focus Work
> (10–20 minutes, 2 to 3 times a week)

Provide extra help to those children who need it.

Division

3: 3–3	Building Models of Division Problems
3: 3–7	Learning To Write the Division Sign

Number Talks:

Addition and Subtraction of Two- and Three-Digit Numbers

Solving Multiplication Problems

Solving Division Problems

Continue to present problems, adapting them to fit the needs of each particular group of children.

OR

> ## Shared Experiences/Mathematical Events
> (35–50 minutes, 1 or 2 times about every two weeks)

Provide Additional Math Experiences as Time Allows

- Problem Solving and/or Math and Literature
- Sorting
- Geometry
- Fractions
- Data Collection

Third-Grade Planning Chart

Sixth Planning Period: 3–4 Weeks (May, June)

Focus: Provide any previously taught math concepts that the children need to practice.

Whole-Class Work: Mini-Lessons	
Shorter Mini-Lesson (5–10 minutes, 3 to 5 times a week)	**Longer Mini-Lesson** (15–25 minutes, as needed)
Number Talks: **Addition and Subtraction of Two-Digit Numbers** *Problems Posed by the Teacher* **Solving Multiplication and Division Problems** *Problems Posed by the Teacher*	**Multiplication and Division** 3: 2–5 Building Related Models 3: 2–8 Interpreting Symbols 3: 3–6 Interpreting Symbols 3: 3–8 Multiplication and Division Together: Story Problems

Ongoing Independent-Station Work (35–50 minutes, 3 to 5 times a week)

During this time, you can provide an in-depth focus on other areas of mathematics, such as geometry or measurement. Continue to allow children to work at multiplication and division stations two or three days a week.

Multiplication and Division Stations

3: 2–13 How Many Rows?
3: 2–14 How Many Towers?
3: 2–15 Counting Boards: Multiplication
3: 2–16 Problems for Partners: Multiplication
3: 2–17 Roll and Multiply
3: 2–23 Lots of Rectangles
3: 2–24 Shape Puzzles: Multiplication
3: 2–25 Mixing Them Up
3: 3–9   Counting Boards: Division
3: 3–10 Number Shapes: Division
3: 3–11 Making Rows
3: 3–15 Creation Cards for Division

(Chart continues on next page.)

(Continued from previous page.)

Teacher-Directed, Small-Group Focus Work (10–20 minutes, 2 to 3 times a week)
Number Talks: **Addition and Subtraction of Numbers Having Three or More Digits** *Problems Posed by the Teacher* **Solving Multiplication and Division Problems** *Problems Posed by the Teacher*

OR

Shared Experiences/Mathematical Events (35–50 minutes, 1 or 2 times about every two weeks)
Provide Additional Math Experiences as Time Allows ■ Data Collection and Graphing ■ Probability ■ Sorting ■ Geometry ■ Measurement ■ Fractions

Third-Grade Planning Notes

Sixth Planning Period: 3–4 Weeks (May, June)

Focus: Provide any previously taught math concepts that the children
need to practice.

Whole-Class Work: Mini-Lessons

You can present new concepts and review previously taught concepts by
spending just a few minutes at the beginning of each math period on
either a *Shorter Mini-Lesson* (5–10 minutes) or a *Longer Mini-Lesson*
(15–25 minutes).

Number Talks:

> Addition and Subtraction of Two-Digit Numbers
>
> Solving Multiplication and Division Problems

Continue to provide opportunities for children to solve a variety of problems
using all four arithmetical operations.

Ongoing Independent-Station Work

(35–50 minutes, 3 to 5 times a week)

You may be able to provide children with an in-depth focus on other areas of
mathematics, such as geometry or measurement. Continue to give children
opportunities to work at multiplication and division stations two or three days a
week, as needed.

Teacher-Directed, Small-Group Focus Work

(10–20 minutes, 2 to 3 times a week)

Present number talks to small groups of children so that you can gear the problems to their particular needs.

Number Talks:

> Addition and Subtraction of Numbers Having Three or More Digits
>
> Solving Multiplication and Division Problems

OR

Shared Experiences/Mathematical Events
(35–50 minutes, 1 or 2 times about every two weeks)

Provide Additional Math Experiences as Time Allows

- Data Collection and Graphing
- Probability
- Sorting
- Geometry
- Measurements
- Fractions

Notes To Teachers of Multi-Age Classes

Teachers of multi-age classes must take into consideration the wide range of children's needs that have to be met. Even though it is possible for children working at many different levels to do the same set of activities at the same time and benefit from them in different ways, the timing and pacing of the activities is not usually optimal for everyone. Every child should get an appropriate amount of time to work on a concept. For example, most six-year-olds need to spend several months working on number combinations to 10 while most seven-year-olds need several months working on place-value concepts. In order to get an idea of the recommended timing and pacing of activities for the age groups in your class, look through the planning guide for the grade levels represented in your classroom and integrate the activities for each of the grade levels according to the guidelines for the following instructional settings.

Whole-Class Work

Mini-Lessons (*Shorter Mini-Lesson:* 5–10 minutes, 3 to 5 times a week; *Longer Mini-Lesson*: 15–25 minutes, as needed)

Keep the time you work with the whole class relatively short, most often using the shorter mini-lesson format. You will find that any particular activity you present will be a review for some children, at an appropriate instructional level for other children, and a challenge for still others. Present tasks of varying levels of difficulty in order to make sure that you are meeting various children's needs. For example, you might start a lesson by having the children add 1 cube to a train of 11 to find the total number of cubes in the train. You might then have the children determine the total number of cubes in a train made up of 9 green and 8 orange cubes. On one day, you might do an estimation task using a jar containing 15 objects; on another day, you might use a jar containing 40 objects. You will find that what otherwise might be presented as a longer mini-lesson will often be more effectively presented as part of a small-group lesson that allows you to tailor the activities to meet the needs of the specific group.

Ongoing Independent-Station Work

(35–50 minutes, 3 to 5 times a week)

Independent-station time is the instructional setting that can most closely meet the needs of individual children. The tasks are expandable; that is, they are designed to meet a range of needs. The children choose both the task and the amount of time they work with it. You will find that the wide range of needs of a multi-age group cannot generally be met through the use of a single set of activities. For example, at the same time that some children need to work with addition and subtraction to 10, other children may need to work with two- and three-digit addition and subtraction. You can best meet these different needs by providing two sets of independent activities.

Teacher-Directed, Small-Group Focus Work

(10–20 minutes, 2 to 3 times a week)

In a multi-age classroom, it is important to spend more time working with small groups of children than you might in a single-grade classroom because the small-group setting allows you to provide the particular instruction that various children need.

Shared Experiences/Mathematical Events

(35–50 minutes, 1 or 2 times about every two weeks)

Occasionally, you will be able to present a single experience that the whole class can benefit from at once. This is likely to be a problem-solving experience or what I call a "mathematical event" and not part of ongoing concept development.

A Typical Multi-Age "Math Time"

(Grades 1–2)

1. Whole-Class Work: *Shorter Mini-Lesson* (5–10 minutes)

Instant recognition of number combinations. The teacher presents some number combinations to 10 and some to 20.

Estimation Activity (as described in grade-level notes)

2. Independent-Station Work (35–50 minutes)*

Two sets of activities are available.

Addition and Subtraction Stations

2: 3–14	Combination Toss
2: 3–15	Build-a-Floor Race
2: 3–16	Apartment Buildings
2: 3–21	Grab-Bag Addition Station
2: 3–22	Grab-Bag Subtraction Station
2: 3–36	What's Missing?

Place-Value Stations

3: 1–32	Lots of Lines
3: 1–33	Paper Shapes
3: 1–34	Containers
3: 1–35	Yarn Shapes
3: 1–37	Cover It Up
3: 1–39	Measuring Myself
3: 1–42	Building Stacks

3. Teacher-Directed, Small-Group Focus Work (10–20 minutes)

The teacher works with two small groups. She presents the following activities to one small group of children who need to work with number combinations to 10.

2: 2–1	Snap It
2: 2–3	The Wall Game
2: 2–4	The Cave Game
2: 2–6	Grab-Bag Subtraction
2: 2–9	Number Shapes: On and Off

* Each activity number refers to book, chapter, and activity. For example, 2: 1–14 means book 2, chapter 1, activity 14. Notice whether each activity appears in Book One (1:), Book Two (2:), or Book Three (3:).

The teacher then works with a second group of children who are ready to work with challenging problems involving two- and three-digit addition and subtraction.

> 3: 1–45   Addition and Subtraction of Two-Digit Numbers

4. Teacher Observation of Children Working Independently

The teacher moves around the room observing and interacting with individual children.

5. Cleanup Time

After about 50 minutes of working independently, the children clean up their stations and meet back together again on the rug.

6. Whole-Class Work: Brief Discussion of Math Time (no longer than 5 minutes)

The class reviews what went on during math time.

The "Meeting the Needs of Your Children" Charts

The following charts identify mathematics concepts that children need to know and understand. They also list the Book One (1:) activities—teacher-directed and independent—that can be used to support children's learning of the concepts. Some activities meet a variety of needs and so are listed in several places. Refer to the section entitled "Questions to Guide Your Observations," in each Chapter Overview, to help you determine those needs.

Chapter 1: Beginning Number Concepts

If your children need...	Teacher-Directed Activities	Independent Activities
practice with one-to-one counting to ten: These activities help children develop an understanding of one-to-one correspondence. The teacher-directed activities can also be used to help children learn to count out loud in sequence. The independent activities give children simple repetitive practice.	1: 1–1 Slide and Check 1: 1–2 Count and Dump 1: 1–3 Making Towers 1: 1–4 Counting Stories, Level 1 1: 1–5 Creations 1: 1–6 Finger Counting 1: 1–7 Grab-Bag Counting 1: 1–8 Grow and Shrink, Level 1 1: 1–9 Hide It 1: 1–10 Hunt for It, Level 1 1: 1–11 Peek and Count, Level 1 1: 1–12 Find a Match, Level 1	1: 1–21 Counting Boards, Level 1 1: 1–22 Creations Station 1: 1–23 Cover the Dots, Level 1 1: 1–24 Counting with the Number Shapes, Level 1 1: 1–25 Roll-a-Tower Race (1–6), Level 1
practice in counting in order to develop consistency, accuracy, and confidence: These activities are especially helpful for children who can count but who occasionally lose track while counting, are inconsistent, or recount to make sure. Since the emphasis is on counting objects, the children do not have to be able to read numerals. Use dot cubes rather than number cubes when required.	1: 1–3 Making Towers 1: 1–6 Finger Counting 1: 1–7 Grab-Bag Counting 1: 1–8 Grow and Shrink, Level 2 1: 1–9 Hide It 1: 1–10 Hunt for It, Level 2 1: 1–12 Find a Match, Level 2 1: 1–14 Break It Up 1: 1–15 Tall and Short, Level 1 1: 1–17 Give and Take, Level 1	1: 1–21 Counting Boards, Level 1 1: 1–22 Creations Station 1: 1–25 Roll-a-Tower Race (1–6), Level 1 1: 1–25 Roll-a-Tower Race (4–9), Level 1 1: 1–26 Make-a-Train Race, Level 1 1: 1–27 Build a Staircase, Level 1 1: 1–28 Build a City, Level 1
work with numeral recognition: These activities offer children practice in counting and in looking for relationships along with practice in reading numerals. Use number cubes rather than dot cubes when required.	1: 1–8 Grow and Shrink, Level 3 1: 1–4 Counting Stories, Level 2 1: 1–12 Find a Match, Level 3 1: 1–10 Hunt for It, Level 3 1: 1–15 Tall and Short, Level 2	1: 1–21 Counting Boards, Level 2 1: 1–25 Roll-a-Tower Race (1–6), Level 2 1: 1–25 Roll-a-Tower Race (4–9), Level 2 1: 1–26 Make-a-Train Race, Level 2 1: 1–27 Build a Staircase, Level 2 1: 1–28 Build a City, Level 2 1: 1–29 Grab-Bag Counting Station, Level 1 1: 1–30 Shape Puzzles, Level 1 1: 1–31 Line Puzzles, Level 1 1: 1–32 Pick a Number

Chapter 1 (continued)

If your children need...	Teacher-Directed Activities	Independent Activities
practice in writing numerals: These activities help children develop a sense of number while they practice writing numerals. Numerals are used purposefully to communicate or to label *how many.*	1: 1–4 Counting Stories, Level 3 1: 1–11 Peek and Count, Level 2 1: 1–17 Give and Take, Level 2 1: 1–18 Hiding One More 1: 1–19 Hiding One Less	1: 1–21 Counting Boards, Levels 3 and 4 1: 1–29 Grab-Bag Counting Station, Level 2 1: 1–30 Shape Puzzles, Level 2 1: 1–31 Line Puzzles, Level 2 1: 1–33 Grab a Handful 1: 1–34 Hide-It Station 1: 1–35 Give-and-Take Station 1: 1–36 How Long Is It? 1: 1–37 How Many Does It Hold? 1: 1–38 Sorting Colors 1: 1–39 Sorting Collections
work with developing number sense and number relationships: These activities help children move from counting one to one to recognizing groups, noticing relationships, and using what they know to figure out what they do not know. The children work on making reasonable estimates and then consider whether or not to change their estimates as they get new information. The activities can also help children develop an understanding of conservation of number. It is appropriate to work with any level of these activities. One asterisk (*) indicates that the children will need to know how to *read* numerals in order to do the activity. Two asterisks (**) indicate that they must know how to *write* numerals in order to do the task.	1: 1–8 Grow and Shrink 1: 1–6 Finger Counting 1: 1–10 Hunt for It 1: 1–13 Tell Me Fast 1: 1–14 Break It Up 1: 1–15 Tall and Short 1: 1–16 One More/One Less 1: 1–17 Give and Take 1: 1–20 Towers, Towers, Towers	1: 1–27 Build a Staircase 1: 1–28 Build a City 1: 1–29 Grab-Bag Counting Station* 1: 1–30 Shape Puzzles* 1: 1–31 Line Puzzles* 1: 1–35 Give-and-Take Station** 1: 1–36 How Long Is It?** 1: 1–37 How Many Does It Hold?** 1: 1–38 Sorting Colors** 1: 1–39 Sorting Collections* 1: 1–40 Sorting Shape Puzzles* 1: 1–41 Sorting Line Puzzles*
practice in counting up to 20 or 30: These activities can be extended easily, so they are useful to children who need the challenge of counting to higher numbers. At first, children will focus more on the action of counting and less on developing a sense of number or number relationships. The teacher-directed activities can help focus children on relationships.	1: 1–7 Grab-Bag Counting, Ext. 1: 1–14 Break It Up, Ext. 1: 1–16 One More /One Less, Ext. 1: 1–17 Give and Take, Ext.	1: 1–22 Creations Station, Ext. 1: 1–30 Shape Puzzles, Ext. 1: 1–31 Line Puzzles, Ext. 1: 1–33 Grab a Handful, Ext. 1: 1–35 Give-and-Take Station, Ext. 1: 1–36 How Long Is It?, Ext. 1: 1–37 How Many Does It Hold?, Ext. 1: 1–38 Sorting Colors, Ext. 1: 1–39 Sorting Collections, Ext.

Chapter 2: Pattern

REPEATING PATTERNS		
If your children need...	**Teacher-Directed Activities**	**Independent Activities**
to learn to recognize repeating patterns: At first, children will become aware of what a pattern is through a variety of experiences in which they can join in as you lead the group.	1: 2–1 Rhythmic Patterns 1: 2–2 People Patterns 1: 2–3 Patterns in the Environment	
practice in copying and extending patterns: The children begin their independent work with the challenge of extending a pattern on their own.		1: 2–10 Pattern Trains 1: 2–11 Color-Tile Patterns 1: 2–12 Arrangement Patterns 1: 2–13 Collections Patterns
opportunities to create patterns: These activities present a different challenge as children are asked to go beyond copying patterns to creating their own patterns.		1: 2–10 Pattern Trains, Var. 1: 2–11 Color-Tile Patterns, Var. 1: 2–12 Arrangement Patterns, Var. 1: 2–13 Collections Patterns, Var.
practice in describing and analyzing patterns: These activities give the children opportunities to analyze and label patterns.	1: 2–1 Rhythmic Patterns 1: 2–8 How Many Ways?	1: 2–10 Pattern Trains, Ext. 1: 2–11 Color-Tile Patterns, Ext. 1: 2–13 Collections Patterns, Ext.
practice in translating patterns from one form to another: These tasks require the children to identify the underlying structure of a pattern formed with one kind of manipulative and then to replicate that same pattern using a different manipulative.	1: 2–4 Interpreting Rhythmic Patterns with Connecting Cubes or Color Tiles 1: 2–5 Interpreting Rhythmic Patterns with Pattern Blocks 1: 2–6 Interpreting Rhythmic Patterns with Collections 1: 2–7 Interpreting Patterns: Making Arrangements	1: 2–14 Rhythmic-Patterns Task Cards 1: 2–15 ABC-Patterns Task Cards
practice in sorting patterns: Sorting patterns requires the children to look closely for similarities between patterns that, at first glance, appear to be different.	1: 2–8 How Many Ways? 1: 2–9 Creating Patterns	

Chapter 2 (continued)

GROWING PATTERNS		
If your children need...	**Teacher-Directed Activities**	**Independent Activities**
to learn to recognize growing patterns: This teacher-directed activity helps children focus on how some patterns "grow" and how they differ in other ways from repeating pattern	1: 2–16 Exploring Growing Patterns	
practice in copying and extending growing patterns: The children begin their independent work with growing patterns with the challenge of extending a pattern on their own.		1: 2–17 Growing-Patterns Task Cards
opportunities to create growing patterns: This activity presents a different challenge as children are asked to go beyond copying patterns to creating their own patterns.		1: 2–18 Creating Growing Patterns
opportunities to discover the patterns that emerge when breaking apart linear patterns:		1: 2–19 Break-Aparts

NUMBER PATTERNS		
If your children need...	**Teacher-Directed Activities**	**Independent Activities**
opportunities to look for number patterns:	1: 2–20 Creating a Number Chart 1: 2–21 Looking for Patterns on the Calendar	

Chapter 3: The Concepts of More and Less

If your children need...	Teacher-Directed Activities	Independent Activities
practice in determining which of two groups is *more* and which is *less*: The teacher-directed activities help develop the language used to describe the concepts of more and less. When working with the independent activities, the children compare groups and determine which is *more* and which is *less*. Then they label the groups with *More/Less/Same* cards. An asterisk (*) indicates that the activity can be extended for use with numbers to 20.	1: 3–1 Is It More or Is It Less?, Level 1 1: 3–2 Stacks, Level 1 1: 3–3 Two-Color Grab Bag, Level 1* 1: 3–4 Spin and Peek, Level 1 1: 3–5 Graph and See* 1: 3–6 Number Cards, Level 1* 1: 3–7 More-or-Less Spin It, Level 1* 1: 3–8 More-or-Less Counting Stories, Level 1*	1: 3–13 Stack, Tell, Spin, and Win 1: 3–14 Two-Color Grab-Bag Station, Level 1* 1: 3–15 Comparing Lengths, Level 1* 1: 3–16 Comparing Shape Puzzles, Level 1* 1: 3–17 Comparing Line Puzzles, Level 1* 1: 3–18 Comparing Handfuls, Level 1* 1: 3–19 Comparing Containers, Level 1* 1: 3–20 Sort and Compare Colors 1: 3–21 Comparing Numbers* 1: 3–22 Counting Boards: Changing Numbers
practice in adding or subtracting to make two groups the same: Figuring out how to make two groups the same focuses the children's attention on *how many more* or *how many less* one group is than another.	1: 3–1 Is It More or Is It Less?, Level 2 1: 3–2 Stacks, Level 2 1: 3–3 Two-Color Grab Bag, Level 2 1: 3–4 Spin and Peek, Level 2 1: 3–6 Number Cards, Level 2	
practice in determining which group is *more* or *less* than another and in recording the results using either the language of *more* and *less* or the symbols < and >: The children become familiar with recording number relationships through the teacher-directed activities. They then figure out the relationships and record the results. An asterisk (*) indicates that the activity can be extended for use with numbers to 20.	1: 3–11 More or Less 1: 3–12 Roll and Spin	1: 3–14 Two-Color Grab-Bag Station, Level 1* 1: 3–15 Comparing Lengths, Level 1* 1: 3–16 Comparing Shape Puzzles, Level 1* 1: 3–17 Comparing Line Puzzles, Level 1* 1: 3–18 Comparing Handfuls, Level 1* 1: 3–19 Comparing Containers, Level 1* 1: 3–20 Sort and Compare Colors Level 1*

Chapter 3 (continued)

If your children need...	Teacher-Directed Activities	Independent Activities
practice in determining *how many more* or *how many less* one quantity is than another: Understanding these relationships is challenging for young children. Most children are not ready to explore and record these relationships until they reach second grade. An asterisk (*) indicates that the activity can be extended for use with numbers to 20.	1: 3–1 Is It More or Is It Less?, Level 2 1: 3–2 Stacks, Level 2 1: 3–3 Two-Color Grab Bag, Level 2* 1: 3–4 Spin and Peek, Level 2 1: 3–5 Graph and See, Level 2* 1: 3–6 Number Cards, Level 3 1: 3–7 More-or-Less Spin It, Level 2* 1: 3–8 More-or-Less Counting Stories, Level 2* 1: 3–9 Build a Stack* 1: 3–10 Grow, Shrink, and Compare 1: 3–11 More or Less	1: 3–14 Two-Color Grab-Bag Station, Level 2 1: 3–15 Comparing Lengths, Level 2 1: 3–16 Comparing Shape Puzzles, Level 2 1: 3–17 Comparing Line Puzzles, Level 2 1: 3–18 Comparing Handfuls, Level 2 1: 3–19 Comparing Containers, Level 2 1: 3–20 Sort and Compare Colors, Level 2
practice in determining the order of three quantities. You can provide a challenge for those children who are ready by having them order three groups rather than comparing just two groups:		1: 3–16 Comparing Shape Puzzles 1: 3–17 Comparing Line Puzzles 1: 3–18 Comparing Handfuls 1: 3–19 Comparing Containers 1: 3–20 Sort and Compare Colors

The following charts identify mathematics concepts that children need to know and understand. They also list the Book Two (2:) activities—teacher-directed and independent—that can be used to support children's learning of the concepts. Some activities meet a variety of needs and so are listed in several places. Refer to the section entitled "Questions to Guide Your Observations," in each Chapter Overview, to help you determine those needs.

Chapter 1: Interpreting and Symbolizing Addition and Subtraction

If your children need...	Teacher-Directed Activities	Independent Activities
practice interpreting (acting out) addition and subtraction stories: These experiences help children distinguish between the processes of addition and subtraction and help them understand that these processes occur in the real world. This provides a foundation for later work with symbols.	2: 1–1 Acting Out Stories: Using Real Things 2: 1–2 Acting Out Stories: Using Fantasies 2: 1–3 Acting Out Stories: Using Counters	
practice in reading and interpreting addition and subtraction equation cards and in relating each to a corresponding story or action: After acting out addition and subtraction stories, children need to associate these experiences and actions with symbolic representations.	2: 1–4 Modeling Addition and Subtraction Equations 2: 1–5 Acting Out Stories To Go with Equations, Level 1 2: 1–6 Roll and Count 2: 1–7 Listen and Count 2: 1–8 Grow and Shrink: Using the Plus (+) and Minus (−) Signs	2: 1–12 Counting Boards: Reading Equations 2: 1–13 Race to Ten 2: 1–14 Plus-and-Minus Train 2: 1–15 Clear the Deck
practice in writing addition and subtraction equations to describe problems: Children write their own equations to label situations that you have previously modeled.	2: 1–9 Writing Equations To Label Addition and Subtraction Stories, Levels 1 and 2	2: 1–16 Writing Equations with Counting Boards
practice in writing a story problem to go with an equation: Writing stories adds another dimension to interpreting equations. This provides children with a way to permanently record their ideas.	2: 1–10 Writing Stories To Go with Equations	2: 1–17 Writing Stories To Match Equations
practice in interpreting complex addition and subtraction stories: This activity gives children experiences with stories that involve missing addends and comparative subtraction.	2: 1–11 Working with Complex Addition and Subtraction Stories	

Chapter 2: Internalizing Number Combinations to 10

If your children need...	Teacher-Directed Activities	Independent Activities
practice in orally describing the parts of a number: These activities help children think about the different ways in which a number can be broken up into parts.	2: 2–1 Snap It, Level 1 2: 2–2 The Tub Game, Level 1 2: 2–3 The Wall Game 2: 2–4 Bulldozer 2: 2–5 The Cave Game, Level 1 2: 2–7 Finger Combinations 2: 2–8 Working with Number Shapes 2: 2–9 Number Shapes: On and Off 2: 2–10 Working with Number Trains 2: 2–11 Number Trains: On and Off 2: 2–12 Counting Boards: Number-Combination Stories	2: 2–14 Number Arrangements: Using Cubes, Level 1 2: 2–15 Number Arrangements: Using Color Tiles, Level 1 2: 2–16 Number Arrangements: Using Toothpicks, Level 1 2: 2–17 Number Arrangements: Using Collections, Level 1 2: 2–18 Counting Boards: Making Up Number-Combination Stories, Level 1 2: 2–19 Number-Shape Arrangements, Level 1 2: 2–20 Number Shapes: Using Number Cubes, Level 1 2: 2–22 Number-Train Arrangements, Level 1
practice in creating and describing the parts of a number using symbols to label the parts: These activities will help build facility in using symbols and will help bring meaning to the symbolic "number facts."	2: 2–13 Finding and Recording Number Combinations	2: 2–14 Number Arrangements: Using Cubes, Level 2 2: 2–15 Number Arrangements: Using Color Tiles, Level 2 2: 2–16 Number Arrangements: Using Toothpicks, Level 2 2: 2–17 Number Arrangements: Using Collections, Level 2 2: 2–18 Counting Boards: Making Up Number-Combination Stories, Level 2 2: 2–19 Number-Shape Arrangements, Level 2 2: 2–20 Number Shapes: Using Number Cubes, Level 2 2: 2–21 Number Shapes: Using Spinners 2: 2–22 Number-Train Arrangements, Level 2 2: 2–23 Number Trains: Using Number Cubes 2: 2–25 How Many Ways? 2: 2–26 Number-Train Graph 2: 2–27 Building and Rebuilding
practice in determining the missing part of a number: These activities help develop the relationships that children need to know in order to work with basic addition and subtraction facts.	2: 2–1 Snap It, Level 2 2: 2–2 The Tub Game, Level 2 2: 2–5 The Cave Game, Level 2 2: 2–6 Grab-Bag Subtraction	*(The following activities are from Chapter 3.)* 2: 3–13 Counting Boards: How Many Ways? 2: 3–15 Build-a-Floor Race, Levels 1 and 2 2: 3–22 Grab-Bag Subtraction 2: 3–25 The Snap-It Station 2: 3–26 What's Missing?

Chapter 3: Developing Strategies for Adding and Subtracting

WORKING WITH NUMBER COMBINATIONS TO 10		
If your children need...	**Teacher-Directed Activities**	**Independent Activities**
practice in solving addition and subtraction problems using numbers to 10 with increasing efficiency: These activities provide opportunities for children to move from counting to seeing relationships between quantities and developing and applying strategies.	2: 3–1 Combining Stacks: Pick It Up 2: 3–2 Instant Recognition of Number Arrangements 2: 3–3 Instant Recognition of Number Shapes 2: 3–4 Instant Recognition of Number Trains 2: 3–5 Related Combinations: Short Stacks 2: 3–6 What Do You Think? Using Counting Boards 2: 3–7 What Do You Think? Using Grab Bags 2: 3–8 What Do You Think? Using Tubs 2: 3–9 Let's Pretend: Grab Bags 2: 3–10 Let's Pretend: Counting Boards 2: 3–11 Let's Pretend: Number Trains 2: 3–12 Let's Pretend: Number Shapes	2: 3–14 Combination Toss 2: 3–15 Build-a-Floor Race 2: 3–16 Apartment Buildings 2: 3–17 Describing Shape Puzzles 2: 3–18 What Numbers Can You Make? 2: 3–19 Addition-and-Subtraction Spin-It 2: 3–20 Counting Boards: Think and Write 2: 3–21 Grab-Bag Addition 2: 3–22 Grab-Bag Subtraction 2: 3–23 Two-Color Trains 2: 3–24 The Tub-Game Station 2: 3–26 What's Missing? 2: 3–27 Comparing Combinations

Chapter 3 (continued)

WORKING WITH NUMBER COMBINATIONS TO 20		
If your children need...	**Teacher-Directed Activities**	**Independent Activities**
practice in solving addition and subtraction problems using numbers to 20 with increasing efficiency: These activities provide opportunities for children to move from counting to seeing relationships between quantities and developing and applying strategies.	2: 3–5 Related Combinations: Short Stacks 2: 3–28 Related Combinations: Tall Stacks 2: 3–29 How Do You See It? Adding Number Shapes 2: 3–30 Working with Ten-Shapes 2: 3–31 A Ten-Shape and More: Subtraction 2: 3–32 Exploring Number Relationships with the Magic Box	2: 3–33 Number-Shape Pairs 2: 3–34 Two Ten-Shapes: Addition and Subtraction 2: 3–35 A Ten-Shape and More: Subtraction Station 2: 3–36 Roll and Double 2: 3–37 Wipe Out

The following charts identify mathematics concepts that children need to know and understand. They also list the Book Three (**3:**) activities—teacher-directed and independent—that can be used to support children's learning of the concepts. Some activities meet a variety of needs and so are listed in several places. Refer to the section entitled "Questions to Guide Your Observations," in each Chapter Overview, to help you determine those needs.

Chapter 1: Place Value
Section A: Understanding Regrouping—The Process and the Patterns

If your children need...	Teacher-Directed Activities	Independent Activities
practice in forming groups and counting groups: The following activities help children focus on the processes of grouping and regrouping as they work with groups of four, five, and six objects. (Working with groups of less than ten helps children to focus on the grouping process and to make the appropriate generalizations.)	**3:** 1–1 Introducing the Plus-One and Minus-One Games **3:** 1–2 The Grouping Games with Groups of Other Sizes **3:** 1–3 Plus or Minus Any Number **3:** 1–4 Regrouping Beyond Two Places	
to record the patterns that emerge from forming groups: Children discover patterns that emerge as they work with small groups. Later, this will form the basis of their understanding of base-ten number patterns.	**3:** 1–5 Number Patterns in the Plus-One and Minus-One Games **3:** 1–7 Introducing Number Patterns in a Matrix	**3:** 1–6 Recording the Plus-One and Minus-One Patterns, Ext. **3:** 1–8 Recording the Patterns in a Matrix
to form groups of tens and to record the patterns that result: The children will learn how to group numbers by tens, identifying the patterns that result and identifying two-digit numbers as groups of tens and leftovers.	**3:** 1–9 Introducing Grouping by Tens **3:** 1–12 Patterns on the 00–99 Chart	**3:** 1–10 Writing Base-Ten Patterns on a Strip **3:** 1–11 Creating a 00–99 Chart
to connect number patterns to various patterns using manipulatives: Children explore growing patterns using manipulatives. Then they label these growing patterns with numbers.	*(The following activity is from Book One.)* **1:** 2–15 Exploring Growing Patterns **3:** 1–13 Naming Patterns with Colors **3:** 1–14 Analyzing Growing Patterns **3:** 1–15 Finding the Number Patterns in Growing Patterns	*(The following two activities are from Book One.)* **1:** 2–17 Growing-Pattern Task Cards **1:** 2–18 Creating Growing Patterns **3:** 1–19 Number Patterns in Growing Patterns

Chapter 1 (continued)

Section A: Understanding Regrouping—The Process and the Patterns

If your children need...	Teacher-Directed Activities	Independent Activities
to search for patterns in base ten, to understand the patterns formed by numbers to 100, and to become familiar with the 00–99 chart:	3: 1–10 Writing Base-Ten Patterns on a Strip 3: 1–16 Introducing Pattern Searches	3: 1–18 Grab and Add 3: 1–19 Number Patterns in Growing Patterns 3: 1–20 Margie's Grid Pictures 3: 1–21 Looking for Patterns on the 00–99 Chart 3: 1–22 The 00–99 Chart Puzzles 3: 1–23 Searching-for-Patterns Station

Section B: Developing a Sense of Quantities to 100 and Beyond

If your children need...	Teacher-Directed Activities	Independent Activities
to develop a sense of quantities for numbers to 100: The children practice partitioning large numbers in order to develop flexibility in working with numbers as well as to develop an understanding of conservation of large numbers. They make estimates and then determine actual amounts and learn to organize numbers into groups of tens and ones for ease in counting.	3: 1–24 Rearrange It: Arranging Loose Counters into Tens and Ones 3: 1–25 Rearrange It: Breaking Up Trains into Tens and Ones 3: 1–26 Rearrange It: Finding All the Ways 3: 1–27 Rearrange It: How Many Cubes? (10–20) 3: 1–27 Rearrange It: How Many Cubes? (numbers beyond 20) 3: 1–28 Rearrange It: Breaking Up Tens 3: 1–29 Build it Fast 3: 1–30 Give-and-Take with Tens and Ones 3: 1–31 Think About the Symbols	3: 1–32 Lots of Lines, Level 1 3: 1–33 Paper Shapes, Level 1 3: 1–34 Yarn, Level 1 3: 1–35 Yarn Shapes, Level 1 3: 1–36 Containers, Level 1 3: 1–37 Cover It Up, Level 1 3: 1–38 Measuring Things in the Room, Level 1 3: 1–39 Measuring Myself, Level 1 3: 1–41 Making Trails, Level 1 3: 1–43 Race to 100 3: 1–44 Race to Zero
to compare quantities to determine which of two quantities is more and which is less:		3: 1–32 Lots of Lines, Level 2 3: 1–33 Paper Shapes, Level 2 3: 1–34 Yarn, Level 2 3: 1–35 Yarn Shapes, Ext. 3: 1–36 Containers, Level 2 3: 1–38 Measuring Things in the Room, Level 2 3: 1–39 Measuring Myself, Level 2 3: 1–40 Comparing Myself 3: 1–42 Building Stacks

(Chart continues on next page.)

Chapter 1 (continued)
Section B: Developing a Sense of Quantities to 100 and Beyond

If your children need...	Teacher-Directed Activities	Independent Activities
to compare quantities to determine how many more one quantity is than another:		3: 1–32 Lots of Lines, Level 3 3: 1–33 Paper Shapes, Level 3 3: 1–34 Yarn, Level 3 3: 1–36 Containers, Level 3 3: 1–38 Measuring Things in the Room, Level 3 3: 1–39 Measuring Myself, Level 3
to develop a sense of quantities for numbers beyond 100:		3: 1–32 Lots of Lines, Ext. 3: 1–33 Paper Shapes, Ext. 3: 1–34 Yarn, Ext. 3: 1–35 Yarn Shapes, Ext. 3: 1–36 Containers, Ext. 3: 1–41 Making Trails, Ext.

Section C: Addition and Subtraction of Two–Digit Numbers

If your children need...	Teacher-Directed Activities	Independent Activities
to practice solving problems in a variety of ways: The children use manipulatives to learn to interpret addition and subtraction problems and develop their own strategies for determining how many.	3: 1–45 Addition and Subtraction of Two-Digit Numbers 3: 1–46 Story Problems 3: 1–47 Figure It Out	3: 1–48 Partner Add-It 3: 1–49 Partner Take-Away 3: 1–50 Roll and Add 3: 1–51 Roll and Subtract 3: 1–52 Add 'Em Up: Lots of Lines 3: 1–53 Add 'Em Up: Paper Shapes 3: 1–54 Add 'Em Up: Measuring Things in the Room 3: 1–55 Add 'Em Up: Yarn 3: 1–56 Add 'Em Up: Yarn Shapes 3: 1–57 Add 'Em Up: Containers 3: 1–58 Add 'Em Up: Cover It Up 3: 1–59 Solving Story Problems

Chapter 2: Beginning Multiplication

If your children need...	Teacher-Directed Activities	Independent Activities
to develop an understanding of multiplication by searching for and counting groups: The first step in understanding multiplication is to develop the idea of counting equal groups. These activities focus children's attention on multiplication situations as they can occur in the real world. Children are not yet required to write multiplication equations.	3: 2–1 Looking for Equal Groups in the Real World	3: 2–11 How Many Cups? 3: 2–12 How Many Groups? 3: 2–13 How Many Rows? 3: 2–14 How Many Towers?
practice in acting out multiplication stories: These experiences help children build an understanding of the process of multiplication and provide a meaningful basis for later work with symbols.	3: 2–2 Acting Out Multiplication Stories: Using Real Objects 3: 2–3 Acting Out Multiplication Stories: Using Counters	
practice in interpreting the language of multiplication using physical models: Children need to model multiplication in a variety of ways. These include working with cube trains or towers and stacks, rows, piles, and groups of counters.	3: 2–4 Building Models of Multiplication Problems	
to look for relationships when working with related multiplication problems: This should be an ongoing experience for children as they explore what happens when they look for relationships. Repeat this activity on occasion throughout children's work with multiplication.	3: 2–5 Building Related Models	

(Chart continues on next page.)

Chapter 2 (continued)

If your children need...	Teacher-Directed Activities	Independent Activities
practice in reading and interpreting multiplication equations: Children need to connect their multiplication experiences and actions to symbolic representations. These activities should be presented to the children before you ask them to write equations.	3: 2–6 Modeling the Recording of Multiplication Experiences 3: 2–7 Introducing the Multiplication Sign 3: 2–8 Interpreting Symbols	3: 2–15 Counting Boards: Multiplication, Level 1
practice in writing multiplication equations to describe a problem or situation: Children write their own equations to label various situations. These activities provide children with practice in reading, interpreting, and writing multiplication equations.	3: 2–10 Learning To Write the Multiplication Sign	3: 2–15 Counting Boards: Multiplication, Levels 2 and 3 3: 2–16 Problems for Partners: Multiplication 3: 2–17 Roll and Multiply 3: 2–18 Discovering Patterns: Cupfuls, Level 1 3: 2–19 Discovering Patterns: Buildings, Level 1 3: 2–20 Discovering Patterns: Number Shapes, Level 1 3: 2–23 Lots of Rectangles 3: 2–24 Shape Puzzles: Multiplication
to discover the patterns that occur when working with multiplication: Looking for patterns and seeing the same patterns occur over and over again will help children learn multiplication equations.	*(The following activity, from Chapter One, may be used either to introduce pattern searches or to review them.)* 3: 1–16 Introducing Pattern Searches	3: 2–18 Discovering Patterns: Cupfuls, Level 2 3: 2–19 Discovering Patterns: Buildings, Level 2 3: 2–20 Discovering Patterns: Number Shapes, Level 2 3: 2–21 Pattern Search: Multiplication
practice in writing story problems to go with an equation: Writing stories adds another dimension to interpreting equations. This provides children with a way to permanently record their ideas and helps them to connect multiplication with the world outside their classroom.	3: 2–9 Acting Out Stories To Go with Multiplication Problems	3: 2–22 Writing Stories To Go with Multiplication Problems

Chapter 3: Beginning Division

If your children need...	Teacher-Directed Activities	Independent Activities
to develop an understanding of division as the sharing, or partitioning, of equal groups: Children need these kinds of experiences to build an understanding of the process of division and to provide a meaningful basis for later work with symbols.	3: 3–1 Acting Out Division Stories: Using Real Objects 3: 3–2 Acting Out Division Stories: Using Counters	
practice in interpreting the language of division using physical models: Children need to model division in a variety of ways. These include breaking up cube trains or towers into equal stacks, rows, piles, or groups.	3: 3–3 Building Models of Division Problems	
to use division to look for relationships: The activity should be repeated on occasion as the children explore these relationships.	3: 3–4 Odds and Evens	
to learn to read and interpret division equations: Children need to connect their division experiences and actions to corresponding symbolic representations.	3: 3–5 Modeling the Recording of Division Experiences 3: 3–6 Interpreting Symbols	3: 3–9 Counting Boards: Division, Level 1
to learn to write division equations to describe a problem or situation: Children need to connect their division experiences and actions to symbolic representations. This should be presented to the children before they are asked to write equations independently.	3: 3–7 Learning To Write the Division Sign	

(Chart continues on next page.)

Chapter 3   (continued)

If your children need...	Teacher-Directed Activities	Independent Activities
practice in reading, interpreting, and writing division equations:		3: 3–9 Counting Boards: Division, Levels 2 and 3 3: 3–10 Number Shapes: Division 3: 3–11 Making Rows 3: 3–12 Problems for Partners: Division 3: 3–13 Cups of Cubes 3: 3–14 How Many Buildings? 3: 3–15 Creation Cards for Division
practice in writing story problems to go with equations: Writing stories adds another dimension to interpreting equations. This provides children with a way to permanently record their ideas.	3: 3–6 Interpreting Symbols, Ext.	*(The following activity is from Book Two.)* 2: 1–10 Writing Stories To Go with Equations
practice in relating multiplication and division:	3: 3–8 Multiplication and Division Together: Story Problems	

Professional Development Support for *Developing Number Concepts* Teachers

For information on the Mathematical Perspectives Courses and Workshops developed by Kathy Richardson to support the teaching approach in the *Developing Number Concepts* series and Planning Guide, contact:

Mathematical Perspectives
Kathy Richardson and Associates
P.O. Box 29418
Bellingham, WA 98228–9418
Phone: 360–715–2782
Fax: 360–715–2783

Notes

Notes ··

Notes

Notes ....

Notes ···

Notes